PERILOUS TIMES

PERILOUS TIMES
A Study in Eschatological Evil

Kenneth L. Gentry, Jr., Th.D.

VICTORIOUS HOPE
PUBLISHING

Fountain Inn, South Carolina

"Proclaiming the kingdom of God and teaching those things which concern
the Lord Jesus Christ, with all confidence."
(Acts 28:31)

Perilous Times:
A Study in Eschatological Evil
© 1999 by Gentry Family Trust udt April 2, 1999
VICTORIOUS HOPE PUBLISHING publication date: 2012

Published by Victorious Hope Publishing
P.O. Box 1874
Fountain Inn, South Carolina 29644

Website: www.VictoriousHope.com
E-mail: KennethGentry@cs.com

PRINTED IN THE UNITED STATES OF AMERICA

ISBN 978-0-9826206-3-2

VICTORIOUS HOPE PUBLISHING is committed to producing Christian educational materials for promoting the whole Bible for the whole of life. We are conservative, evangelical, and Reformed and are committed to the doctrinal formulation found in the Westminster Standards.

For information on Dr. Gentry's non-profit ministry:
    GoodBirth Ministries
    P.O. Box 1874
    Fountain Inn, SC 29644
    www.GoodBirthMinistries.com

For more books and other materials by Dr. Gentry:
    www.KennethGentry.com

New Printing

In Memory of my Mother
Marjorie L. Barnes
(1930–2006)

CONTENTS

FOREWORD

R. C. Sproul

Albert Schweitzer's watershed work *The Quest For the Historical Jesus* had two far-reaching effects. The first was in his devastating critique of 19th century Liberal Theology of the Religious-Historical School that sought to reduce the teaching of Jesus to mere value judgments in the ethical mode. Schweitzer demonstrated that Jesus's teaching was inescapably tied to an eschatological framework of the motif of the Kingdom of God. Schweitzer exposed Liberalism of the last century for what it was, a crass form of revisionism laced with a dash of Hegelian philosophy and Ritschlian ethics.

The second effect was Schweitzer's sad conclusion that Jesus Himself was wrong about his own eschatological explanations and died in disillusionment when his eschatological hopes failed to materialize, leaving the early church with the need to accommodate Jesus's prophetic failures by creating a framework for "Parousia Delay." It is no overstatement to assert that radical higher criticism down to our day has rested heavily on Schweitzer's skepticism.

There is irony here. Perhaps there is no more astonishing evidence of Jesus's supernatural prophetic power than his amazingly accurate foretelling of the destruction of Jerusalem, the temple, and the dispersion of the Jewish people as described by Christ in his Olivet Discourse. Yet this same discourse is pivotal to Jesus's alleged prophetic failure. Along with his prediction of the judgment that would befall Israel was his prediction of his own return in glory. The discourse sets both the return of Jesus and the destruction of Jerusalem within the time framework of "this generation."

The problem is this: though the destruction of Jerusalem did occur within the time framework of that generation, the "coming" of Jesus seems not to have occurred as predicted. The "delay" of Jesus's Parousia casts a dark shadow on the credibility of Jesus as a prophet and on the New Testament as a trustworthy source. The apologetic problems that flow out of this are enormous. Both the Church's confidence in Christ and the trustworthiness of the Bible are at stake.

All sorts of attempts have been made to solve this dilemma, most notably by C. H. Dodd's "realized eschatology," Oscar Cullmann's "D-Day Analogy," and Herman Ridderbos's conception of the "Already" (and "Not Yet" (*noj neit*) schema of eschatological harmonization.

No conservative or evangelical attempt to solve the problem has been more popular and far-reaching than that espoused by dispensationalism. Dispensationalism has worked out a radical futurism with respect to Jesus's and the Bible's agenda for the redemption of the Jewish nation. From the serious biblical scholarship (particularly that emanating from Dallas Theological Seminary) to the popularizers of this view, such as Hal Lindsey, the evangelical world has been virtually captured by this approach.

Crucial to dispensationalism's solution to the problem is their understanding not only of Revelation and the Olivet Discourse, but especially their interpretation of Daniel's mysterious prophecy of the Seventy Weeks. Daniel's vision forms a critical part of the basis for expecting a "pre-tribulation rapture" and an end-of-the-age salvific agenda for ethnic Israel.

The problem of interpreting the Olivet Discourse involves a reconciliation of the time frame references with the imagery used to refer to Jesus's coming in clouds of glory. It seems that the New Testament interpreter must either interpret the time frame references in a non-literal way or the coming of Jesus in a non-literal way.

Conservative Christians historically are committed to a literal interpretation of Scripture. The Reformation principles of *sensus literalis* has been hopelessly confused. To interpret the Bible "literally," strictly speaking, is to interpret the text according to how it is written. It allows, nay demands that symbols be treated as symbols, images as images, and plain indicative statements as indicative statements. The problem rests in correctly identifying the literary genre of each passage. What is then "literal" and what is "symbolic" or "imaginative" is ultimately a false distinction. Yet in the common language of interpreters there abides the distinction between the "literal" and the "figurative." This is especially relevant to the handling of prophet texts.

Central to Gentry's work is the controlling principle of treating time frame references according to their contextual usage, both in the immediate context and in the wider context of biblical usage. For example, Daniel's seventy weeks are not interpreted as seventy seven-day periods, but rather, following biblical usage, seventy seven-year periods, amounting to 490 years.

On the other hand, Gentry argues as did Schweitzer and Bertrand Russell that the time frame reference of "this generation" in the Olivet Discourse must be interpreted in context as referring to the forty-year period of the immediate hearers of Jesus's prophecy. This is consistent with the use of the term generation throughout the New Testament.

The thrust of this book is to demonstrate that much of the prophecy that many consider not yet fulfilled in history has already been fulfilled in the past. Gentry takes a modified preterist approach to prophecy. He puts much more in the category of the "already" than many conservative scholars are willing to do, but he is by no means a radical preterist. He still sees a "not yet" with respect to the future bodily resurrection and judgment when Christ returns at the end of history. His is an eschatology of optimism.

Gentry's close exegetical study of key prophetic passages is critical of dispensational interpretation. His treatment of Daniel 9 is especially important. He challenges the standard dispensational treatment, charging dispensationalists with faulty exegesis. Combined with his lengthy treatment of Matthew 24 Gentry offers a serious critique of the basic platform of dispensational eschatology.

It will be fascinating to see the response of dispensational scholars to this work. It seems to me that Gentry demolishes dispensational exegesis of Daniel 9 and Matthew 24. If the demolition is as complete as it seems to me, it could be fatal to the whole dispensational system.

Finally, the book gives an in-depth treatment of the redemptive historical significance of the destruction of Jerusalem and the "judgment coming" of Christ at the end of the Jewish age.

I think this work is of vast importance to the task of biblical interpretation. It tackles the problems of the Olivet Discourse head-on and provides a powerful exegetical and apologetical response to the critics of the historical Jesus and the trustworthiness of Scripture. I am grateful for Gentry's insightful work.

R. C. Sproul
Ligonier Ministries

INTRODUCTION

Remember the former things, those of long ago; I am God, and there is no other; I am God, and there is none like me. I make known the end from the beginning, from ancient times, what is still to come. I say: My purpose will stand, and I will do all that I please.

Isaiah 46:9-10

2001: An Eschatological Odyssey

The End is here! Again. With the intriguing year 2000 now upon us we are witnessing an ever-increasing flow of books focusing on the future. *Christianity Today* magazine notes that "on the eve of the third millennium of the Christian era, the church is again beset by apocalyptic speculators."[1] As historian Paul Boyer observes "prophecy remains of absorbing interest to millions of Americans."[2] His historical-sociological research shows that:

> nurtured by the dense network of colleges, seminaries, Bible schools, publication houses, Christian bookstores, radio and television programs, and churches by the tens of thousands that sustain the vast subculture of late-twentieth century. U. S. evangelicalism, the conviction that God's plan for human history lies encrypted in ancient biblical texts remains very much alive as the century draws to its close. From pulpits, cassette tapes, orbiting communications satellites, and the pages of millions of paperbacks, the ancient cry rings out as it has for hundreds of years: "He Is Coming Soon."[3]

Because of this, both secular and religious book stores are awash with a

---

[1] Timothy George, Apocalyptic Fever, *Christianity Today*, 14 December 1992, 12.
[2] Paul Boyer, *When Time Shall Be No More: Prophecy Belief in Modern American Culture* (Cambridge, Mass.: Belknap, 1992), 79.
[3] Ibid., 339.

flood of books on the prospects for the approaching days. During the Persian Gulf War (1991) the prophecy market exploded (no pun intended). Regarding this phenomenon *Christianity Today* published a news article entitled: "Prophecy Books Become Best-sellers."[4] The article noted that John Walvoord's revised and updated *Armageddon, Oil and the Middle East Crisis: What the Bible Says About the Future of the Middle East* sold 1.5 million copies. Charles Dyer's *The Rise of Babylon: Sign of the End Times* sold 500,000 copies. And these were not the only prophetic works published during that political crisis. The interest in the war was not only due to its erupting in the Middle East, a region of undying prophetic interest. But in addition, it broke out in the decade serving as the eve of a new millennium, which will be the seven thousandth year of earth history, according to Usher's biblical chronology. Timothy George bemoans: "we are awash in a sea of apocalypticism. End-times hysteria rules the airwaves."[5]

Interestingly, just two decades ago a whole new secular academic profession arose, known as futurology. Two important recent studies touching on this phenomenon among Christians are: Harvard University's Studies in Cultural History publication by Paul Boyer: *When Time Shall Be No More: Prophecy Belief in Modern American Culture* (1992). And, to a lesser extent, the Fundamentalism Project of The American Academy of Arts and Sciences by Martin E. Marty and R. Scott Appleby: *Fundamentalism's Observed* (1991).[6]

Immensely popular fundamentalist works on prophecy are anticipating momentous events associated with the year 2000 (even though technically the new millennium does not begin until 2001). The number of these books is legion. A quick sampling of currently available titles indicates the apprehension:

+ Hal Lindsey, *Planet Earth — 2000: Will Mankind Survive?*
+ Lester Sumrall, *I Predict 2000*
+ David Allen Lewis, *Prophecy 2000: Rushing to Armageddon*
+ Steve Terrell, *The 90's: Decade of the Apocalypse*
+ Dave Hunt, *How Close Are We?: Compelling Evidence for the Soon Return of Christ*
+ Billy Graham, *Storm Warning*

---

[4] Joe Maxwell, "Prophecy Books Become Best Sellers," *Christianity Today*, 11 March 1991, 60.

[5] Timothy George, "The Lure of the Apocalypse," *Christianity Today*, 19 June 1995, 16.

[6] Boyer, *When Time Shall Be No More*; Martin E. Marty and R. Scott Appleby, eds., *The Fundamentalism Project* (Chicago: University of Chicago, 1991), vol. 1, *Fundamentalism's Observed*, ch. 1.

- Charles C. Ryrie, *The Final Countdown*
- Grant R. Jeffries, *Armageddon: Appointment with Destiny*
- James McKeever, *The Rapture Book: Victory in the End Times*
- Don McAlvanny, *et al., Earth's Final Days*
- Texe Marrs, *Storming Toward Armageddon: Essays in Apocalypse*
- Roberts Liardon, *Final Approach: The Opportunity and Adventure of End-Times Living*
- David Webber and Noah Hutchins, *Is This the Last Century?*
- Peter and Patti LaLonde, *The Edge of Time: The Final Countdown Has Begun*
- W. T. James, ed., *Foreshocks of Antichrist*
- Peter and Paul LaLonde, *2000 A.D.: Are You Ready?*
- Jack Van Impe, *2001: On the Edge of Eternity*
- Ed Dobson, *The End: Why Jesus Could Return by A.D. 2000*
- John Hagee, *Beginning of the End*
- Ed Hindson, *Approaching Armageddon: The World Prepares for War with God*
- William T. James, ed., *Foreshocks of Anti-Christ*
- Grant R. Jeffrey, *Final Warning*
- John Hagee, *Beginning of the End* [7]

---

[7] Hal Lindsey, *Planet Earth — 2000: Will Mankind Survive?* (Palos Verdes, Calif.: Western Front, 1994). Lester Sumrall, *I Predict 2000* (South Bend: LeSea, 1987). David Allen Lewis, *Prophecy 2000: Rushing to Armageddon* (Green Forest, Ark.: Green Leaf, 1990). Steve Terrell, *The 90's: Decade of the Apocalypse* (S. Plainfield, N.J.: Bridge, 1992). Dave Hunt, *How Close Are We?: Compelling Evidence for the Soon Return of Christ* (Eugene, Ore.: Harvest, 1993). Billy Graham, *Storm Warning* (Dallas: Word, 1992). Charles C. Ryrie, *The Final Countdown* (Wheaton, Ill.: Victor, rep. 1991). Ed Hindson, *Approaching Armageddon: The World Prepares for War with God* (Eugene, Ore.: Harvest, 1997). Ed Dobson, *The End: Why Jesus Could Return by A.D. 2000* (Grand Rapids: Zondervan, 1997). William T. James, ed., *Foreshocks of Anti-Christ* (Eugene, Ore.: Harvest, 1997). Grant R. Jeffrey, *Final Warning* (Toronto: Frontier Research, 1995). Grant R. Jeffrey, *Armageddon: Appointment with Destiny* (Toronto: Frontier Research, 1988). Peter and Patti LaLonde, *The Edge of Time: The Final Countdown Has Begun* (Eugene, Ore.: Harvest, 1997). John Hagee, *Beginning of the End* (Nashville: Thomas Nelson, 1997). Peter and Paul LaLonde, *2000 A.D.: Are You Ready?* (Nashville: Thomas Nelson, 1997). James McKeever, *The Rapture Book: Victory in the End Times* (Medford, Ore.: Omega, 1987). Don McAlvanny, *et al., Earth's Final Days* (Green Forest, Ariz.: New Leaf, 1994). Texe Marrs, *et al., Storming Toward Armageddon: Essays in Apocalypse* (Green Forest, Ariz.: New Leaf, 1992). Roberts Liardon, *Final Approach: The Opportunity and Adventure of End-Times Living* (Orlando: Creation House, 1993). David Webber and Noah Hutchins, *Is This the Last Century?* (Nashville: Thomas

Some of the writers are more dogmatic than others. One popular writer effuses: "This is the most exciting time to be alive in all of human history. We are about to witness the climax of God's dealing with man."[8] A recent best-seller set off a furor with its date-setting title: *1994?*[9]

Most apocalypticists, however, guard against charges of date-setting by avoiding overly dogmatic assertions. Generally they qualify their predictions somewhat: "We are not saying that Jesus will come back at the year 2000. We are saying if this parallel continues to hold, it is possible that Jesus will come back around the year 2000, plus or minus thirty years."[10] "When these events are placed in their proper order, the result is a prophetic calendar of what may soon happen in the world. An understanding of biblical prophecy has led many intelligent students of the Bible to believe that the world has already begun the countdown leading to Armageddon."[11] Some writers even title their books thus: *The End: Why Jesus Could Return by A.D. 2000.*

Or their prognostications may merely be suggestions: One writer's prophetic research leads him to "suggest that the year A.D. 2000 is a probable termination date for the 'last days.'"[12] "What does all this mean? It suggests that God's prophetic clock is beginning to move again. . . . Doubtless the closer we get to the year 2000, the more people will begin to expect the Lord's return . . . .We have far more evidence today that Christ could come in our lifetime than there was in the A.D. 992."[13]

Sometimes their predictions are based on feelings: "One cannot know these prophecies and live in the world of the 20th century without feeling

---

Nelson, 1979). Peter and Patti LaLonde, *The Edge of Time: The Final Countdown Has Begun* (Eugene, Ore.: Harvest, 1997). W. T. James, ed., *Foreshocks of Antichrist* (Eugene, Ore.: Harvest, 1997). Peter and Paul LaLonde, *2000 A.D.: Are You Ready?* (Nashville: Nelson, 1997). Jack Van Impe, *2001: On the Edge of Eternity* (Nashville: Word, 1996). John Hagee, *Beginning of the End* (Nashville: Nelson, 1997).

[8] Hal Lindsey, *The Rise of Babylon and the Persian Gulf Crisis* (Palos Verdes, Calif.: Lindsey Ministries, 1991), 51.

[9] Harold Camping, *1994?*. See news items in *Christianity Today*: "Rapture Date Set — Again" (November 23, 1992), 48; "Apocalyptic Fever" (December 14, 1992), 12; "Camping Misses End-time Deadline" (October 24, 1994), 84-85.

[10] McKeever, *The Rapture Book*, 22.

[11] John F. Walvoord, *Armageddon, Oil, and the Middle East Crisis: What the Bible says about the future of the Middle East and the end of Western Civilization* (Grand Rapids: Zondervan, 1990), 13.

[12] Jeffries, *Armageddon*, 193.

[13] Tim LaHaye, *No Fear of the Storm: Why Christians Will Escape All of the Tribulation* (Sisters, Ore.: Multnomah Press, 1992), 20.

keenly that these events will begin to happen shortly."[14]

Contemporary evangelicals should be alerted to two remarkable facts concerning such end-time speculation. One is that this sort of confident crisis speculation has continually recurred throughout church history. Consider the following alarming calls for the end from church fathers over a thousand years ago, calls being made just as enthusiastically and confidently today: Tertullian (160-220) in *De Fuga* 12 asserts: the Antichrist "is now close at hand." Cyprian (A.D. 195-258) exclaims in *De Mort* (25): "The world is failing, passing away, and it witnesses to its ruin, not now by the age, but by the end of things" and "still more terrible things are imminent." Firmicus Maternus (*ca.* A.D. 346) warns with utter alarm in his *De Profanarum Religionum* (25:3): "Already the heavenly fire is giving birth, already the approach of divine punishment is manifest, already the doom of coming disaster is heralded." Evodius of Uzala (*ca.* A.D. 412) begs his readers: "Consider, I beg you, whether the age can bear this for long?" Paulinus of Nola (A.D. 353-431) is certain that "All creation now waits in suspense for his arrival. . . . The world, which must be transformed anew, is already pregnant with the end that is to come on the final day."

Remarkably the popular Christian expectation regarding the future is in an important sense not very different from the secularist view. Both the evangelical Christian community and the larger secular world anticipate a future of chaos and despair. Christopher Lasch observes: "As the twentieth century approaches its end, the conviction grows that many other things are ending too. The 'sense of ending,' which has given shape to so much of the twentieth century literature, now pervades the popular imagination."[15] Indeed, "the present period is witnessing an especially acute epidemic of future consciousness."[16] In fact, while documenting the inevitability of a gloomy future, most popular Christian prophecy writers employ the data derived from secular analyses. Historical despair is rampant.

"This present world is rapidly coming to an end. It is on an irreversible collision course with destiny."[17]

---

[14] Ryrie, *The Final Countdown*, 120.

[15] Christopher Lasch, *The Culture of Narcissism: American Life in an Age of Diminishing Expectations* (New York: Norton, 1978), 3.

[16] Ted Peters, *Futures: Human and Divine* (Atlanta: John Knox, 1978), 11.

[17] Jack Van Impe, "There Is Hope!" (Troy, Mich.: Jack Van Impe Ministries International, December, 1991), 1.

"The world will progressively harden its heart against the Gospel and plunge itself into destruction."[18] Regarding celebrations of the year 2000, this popular prophecy writer comments: "Just for the record: I'm not planning to attend. In fact, looking at the state of the world today, I wouldn't make any long-term earthly plans."[19]

"One thing is crystal clear in Jesus' answer: This world is not going to get any easier to live in. Almost unbelievably hard times lie ahead."[20]

"The biblical point of view is pessimistic, that is, the world as it is now constituted will not be revived and improved, but instead, will be destroyed and replaced."[21]

"In all his or her 'sorrows and persecutions,' the child of God living in January, A.D. 1990 longs for one thing, and one thing only: the coming of Christ to judge the living and the dead. . . . All other hopes are miserable delusions and pipe dreams."[22]

"We do urgently warn our own people and all who will hear us that the kingdom of the beast will come. Indeed, it is coming now. . . . Be prepared for the Antichrist!"[23]

Gone with the Wind?

The times we live in are truly fraught with moral and social concern. Witness the level of national debt, the exploding crime rate, the unabating use of drugs and abuse of alcohol, the persistent educational crises, increasing family dissolution including spousal and child abuse, the consistently high rate of abortions-on-demand, the increasing tolerance of partial birth abortions, growing legal and public acceptance of euthanasia, the controlling secularistic mind set, widespread hedonistic amorality, the rampant spread of AIDS, the proliferation of pornography, and such. No thinking Christian would deny that we

---

[18] Hal Lindsey, *The Road to Holocaust* (New York: Bantam Books, 1989), 36.

[19] Lindsey, *Planet Earth — 2000 A.D.*, 305.

[20] Charles C. Ryrie, *The Living End* (Old Tappan, N.J.: Revell, 1976), 21.

[21] John F. Walvoord, Review of Donald Guthrie, *The Relevance of John's Apocalypse* in *Bibliotheca Sacra* 147:586 (April-June, 1990): 251.

[22] David J. Engelsma, "The Reformed Faith — Theology of Hope," *Standard Bearer*, 66:7 (Jan. 1, 1990): 149.

[23] David J. Engelsma, "Jewish Dreams," *The Standard Bearer* (January 15, 1995): 175.

live in dismal times, times defined by "profound social and cultural transition."[24]

* But is this *all* we may expect in the historical *long-run*?
* Does biblical prophecy presage relentlessly dismal
  cultural decline?
* Must the present world, in fact, "be destroyed and replaced"
  because apart from the Second Advent of Christ "all other hopes
  are miserable delusions and dreams"?
* Are our children doomed to *Perilous Times*?
* In short, *must* we be pessimistic regarding the future
  development of world history?

For most Christians today these queries are merely rhetorical questions with foregone conclusions:[25] "We know that our efforts to make society Christianized are futile because the Bible doesn't teach it. . . . [Paul and Peter] assumed that civilization as a whole is hopeless and subject to God's judgment."[26] "[W]e *do* know that in the last days men shall become worse and worse. That's plainly set forth. . . ."[27]

Certainly the Bible contains prophecies of great misery and horror, warning of "perilous times" (1 Tim. 3:1). And what evangelical Christian committed to Scripture's inspiration would dispute their credibility? Yet I am firmly convinced — along with an increasing number of like-minded Christians — that these terrifying prophecies speak of calamities *impending during biblical days long ago*, not our own. In this work I will provide in-depth studies of several of the principle passages leading many evangelicals to historical pessimism: Daniel 9, Matthew 24, 2 Thessalonians 2, Revelation 13, and Revelation 17.

These are crucial passages for eschatological pessimists, as is apparent in

---

[24] Rodney Clapp interview of Alister McGrath, "Why Christianity Has a Future," in *Academic Alert* 4:1 (Winter, 1995): 1.

[25] A Christianity Today Institute Survey indicates that 60% of Christians are premillennial. *Christianity Today*, 6 February 1987, 9-I. Premillennialism teaches the inevitable decline of history as we approach more closely to the return of Christ. Of the 9% who reported a belief that Christ would return after the millennium, many of these would be amillennialists, which is an equally pessimistic eschatology. See: Kenneth L. Gentry, Jr., *The Greatness of the Great Commission: The Christian Enterprise in a Fallen World* (Tyler, Tex.: Institute for Christian Economics, 1991).

[26] John F. Walvoord, in "Our Future Hope: Eschatology and Its Role in the Church," *Christianity Today*, 6 February 1987, 5-I, 6-I.

[27] Gleason Archer, in ibid., 6-I. Emphasis mine.

their studies. In chapter five of *The Future Explored* Timothy Weber points to four apocalyptic sections necessary for understanding the Antichrist and the Great Tribulation. His headings parallel our study: "Daniel's Prophecy," "The Olivet Discourse" (i.e., Matthew 24); "The Second Letter to the Thessalonians"; and "The Book of Revelation." LaHaye lays down a rule of discrimination that employs these same passages: "As a general rule, those who believe the pre-Trib Rapture accept Tribulation teachings in Revelation, 2 Thessalonians, Matthew 24, and Daniel 9 literally." In several of his works Walvoord draws on our five passages, as does Ryrie.[28]

I firmly believe we hopelessly misinterpret these prophecies when we apply them to *our own* future. My chapter titles derive from the biblical passages I will analyze — passages that portray fearsome biblical images of evil, chaos, and despair.

Does not the prophecy of the seventy weeks in Daniel 9 mark off with foreboding an era of historical development in which "desolations are determined" (Chapter 1)? Ryrie informs us: "The Tribulation actually begins with the signing of a covenant between the leader of the 'Federated States of Europe' and the Jewish people. This will set in motion the events of the seventieth week (or seven years) of Daniel's prophecy."[29]

Who does not sense the dread in the prophecy of "wars and rumors of wars" (Chapter 2), which are but harbingers of the "great tribulation" (Chapter 3)? Weber correctly observes that "when Christians speak about the 'signs of the times' — one of the first passages they turn to is the Olivet Discourse."[30]

And what of those evil eschatological figures casting their dark shadows over the prophetic scenery of Scripture: "the man of lawlessness" in 2 Thessalonians 2 (Chapter 4), the "scarlet beast full of blasphemous names" in Revelation 13 (Chapter 5), and "Babylon the Great, Mother of Harlots" in Revelation 17 (Chapter 6)? Surely these images strike terrible chords in fearful hearts. Ryrie warns that the Antichrist is "also called 'the man of lawlessness' (2 Thes. 2:3), and is referred to as the beast (Rev. 11:7; 13:1; 17:11; 19:20). At the beginning of the Tribulation he will make a covenant, or enter a league, with Israel."[31]

As an evangelical Christian I am convinced that the prophetic record of

---

[28] Timothy P. Weber, *The Future Explored* (Wheaton, Ill.: Victor, 1978), ch. 5. LaHaye, *No Fear of the Storm*, 50-51. Walvoord, *Armageddon, Oil, and the Middle East Crisis*, chs. 6-8, 10, and 12 and Walvoord, *The Rapture Question* (Grand Rapids: Zondervan, 1957), ch. 3. Ryrie, *The Final Countdown*, ch. 8.

[29] Ryrie, *The Final Countdown*, 91.

[30] Weber, *The Future Explored*, 37.

[31] Charles C. Ryrie, *Basic Theology* (Wheaton, Ill.: Victor, 1986), 465.

Scripture is infallibly certain — when properly interpreted. But what of these eras, characters, and events forming the basis of our study? Are they looming in our future? Without a doubt these lay off in the future *when originally written.* But so did the birth of Christ, which was prophesied in Isaiah 7:14. And the crucifixion of the Lord, recorded in Psalm 22. Though Isaiah 7:14 and Psalm 22 are biblical prophecies, they are not future to *our* own times. Despite popular opinion, neither are the terrifying prophecies we will study.

Conclusion

If the reader will lay aside his prophetic preconceptions, I will attempt to show by sound exegesis that the leading judgment passages commonly applied to our future have already been fulfilled. To avoid any misapprehension on the reader's part, I must note that I do hold to a future orientation for many other prophecies of Scripture. I am convinced beyond doubt, for instance, that the Bible teaches the future bodily resurrection and a great judgment. These will occur when the Lord Jesus Christ returns visibly and bodily in great power and glory to end history and to establish the eternal state. Due to the nature of the inquiry in the following pages, however, my focus will not be on the Second Advent of our Lord and its eschatological sequelae.[32]

I urge the reader to take his Bible in hand and carefully follow my presentation — to "search the Scriptures to find out whether these things are so" (Acts 17:11). Our study is significant in that the Christian's outlook for the future is terribly important for a soundly biblical worldview — for "where there is no vision, the people perish" (Prov. 29:18). An erroneous future orientation is detrimental to a fully biblical Christian endeavor. As the prophet laments: "My people are destroyed for lack of knowledge" (Hos. 4:6). I hope this study will wash away the pessimistic foundations that support a false understanding of these leading judgment prophecies.

Unfortunately, the ominous features of certain eschatological passages are more interesting to Christians than the uplifting prospects of others. Among premillennialists, for instance, studies of "last days" evil far outnumber those of millennial glory. The runaway Hal Lindsey best-sellers, such as *The Late Great Planet Earth* and *The 1980s: Countdown to Armageddon,* are cases in point.

My ultimate goal in writing this book is a positive one. Through biblical research and careful argumentation I hope to encourage a more optimistic orientation for the future. If Christians would extricate themselves from the morass of pessimism and adopt an optimistic vision of the future, we could "turn the world upside down" (Acts 17:6), as did our forefathers.

---

[32] For a study of these and other eschatological phenomena, see my *He Shall Have Dominion: A Postmillennial Eschatology* (2d ed.: Tyler, Tex.: Institute for Christian Economics, 1997).

CHAPTER ONE

DESOLATIONS ARE DETERMINED
Daniel 9:24-27

Seventy weeks are determined for your people and for your holy city. . . . After sixty-two weeks Messiah shall be cut off, but not for Himself; and the people of the prince who is to come shall destroy the city and the sanctuary. The end of it shall be with a flood, And till the end of the war desolations are determined.

Daniel 9:24a, 27

Introduction

The seventy weeks prophecy in Daniel 9:24-27 is probably one of the more familiar Old Testament passages for evangelical students of prophecy. Yet at the same time it is also one of the most misunderstood. Nevertheless, this difficult prophecy receives special prominence in the dispensational system so widely prevalent today.

We must begin our analysis with caution, recognizing that the Book of Daniel is subject to great mishandling by expositors. Charles H. H. Wright laments: "The commentaries on Daniel are innumerable. On no other book, save the Book of Revelation in the New Testament, has so much worthless matter been written in the shape of exegesis."[1] This problem only intensifies in the treatment of the four verses composing the prophecy before us. Nevertheless, the debate is engaged; let us cautiously enter the fray.

The chronology in Daniel's famous prophecy is a linchpin in the highly popular dispensational argument, although it is not crucial to any of the other

---

[1] Charles H. H. Wright, *An Introduction to the Old Testament* (London: Williams and Norgate, 1906), 197.

major millennial systems. Walvoord comments that the "interpretation of Daniel 9:24-27 is of major importance to premillennialism as well as pretribulationism."Being such, it is the "key" to prophecy and, consequently, "one of the most important prophecies of the Bible." McClain suggests "no single prophetic utterance is more crucial." Pentecost agrees with McClain that Daniel 9 gives us "the indispensable chronological key to all New Testament prophecy." English calls it an "extremely important prophecy."[2] Surely Allis is correct when he observes that "the importance of the prophecy of the Seventy Weeks in Dispensational teaching can hardly be exaggerated."[3]

This dispensational dependence upon Daniel 9, however, is unfortunate for two reasons: Historically, great difficulties are associated with the interpretation of this passage. J. A. Montgomery calls the prophecy "the Dismal Swamp of Old Testament criticism."[4] Young comments that "this passage... is one of the most difficult in all the OT, and the interpretations which have been offered are almost legion."[5] Baldwin warns that "the last four verses present the most difficult text in the book, as commentators agree."[6] The daunting nature of the challenge of the passage is evident in Hengstenberg's classic *Christology of the Old Testament*. He devotes more pages analyzing these four verses than any other Old Testament prophecy: a total of 127 pages.[7]

Even dispensationalists recognize this problem. Kenneth L. Barker writes: "It is admitted that these verses are among the most difficult to interpret in Daniel." Gleason L. Archer, Jr. mentions the long-standing nature of the problem: "It is not to be wondered at that Bible scholars down through the centuries had difficulty dealing with the chronological factors involved in the prophecy of the seventy weeks." L. S. Chafer agrees: "scholars have differed greatly in their interpretation of this passage." Even dispensational enthusiast

---

[2] John F. Walvoord, *The Rapture Question* (Grand Rapids: Zondervan, 1957), 24. John F. Walvoord, *Daniel: The Key to Prophetic Revelation* (Chicago: Moody, 1971), 201, 216. J. Dwight Pentecost, *Things to Come: A Study in Biblical Eschatology* (Grand Rapids: Zondervan, 1958), 240. Alva J. McClain, *Daniel's Prophecy of the 70 Weeks* (Grand Rapids: Zondervan, 1940), 9. E. Schuyler English, "The Gentiles in Revelation," in Charles Lee Feinberg, ed., *Prophecy and the Seventies* (Chicago: Moody, 1971), 242.

[3] O. T. Allis, *Prophecy and the Church* (Philadelphia: Presbyterian and Reformed, 1945), 111.

[4] J. A. Montgomery, *A Critical and Exegetical Commentary on the Book of Daniel (International Critical Commentary)* (New York: Scribner's, 1927), 400.

[5] E. J. Young, *The Prophecy of Daniel* (Grand Rapids: Eerdmans, 1949, 1977), 191.

[6] Joyce G. Baldwin, *Daniel: An Introduction and Commentary (Tyndale Old Testament Commentary)* (Downers Grove, Ill.: InterVarsity, 1978), 163.

[7] E. W. Hengstenberg, *The Christology of the Old Testament* (McLean, Vir.: McDonald, rep. n.d. [trans. 1854]), 2:803-930.

J. Randall Price admits Daniel 9 chronology is "much contested."[8]

In addition to the historical problem, theological problems arise. This "extremely important prophecy" is the most difficult for dispensationalists to make credible to those outside their camp. Dispensationalist Robert Culver admits: "The difficulty of the verses that now lie before us is evident.... Premillennial writers of two or three generations ago were very far apart on the details. Much of the same diversity appears in premillennial contemporary writers."[9] Due to this inherent difficulty and because of certain system requirements of dispensationalism, Daniel's seventy weeks prophecy leads dispensationalists into one of their most strained peculiarities: the doctrine of the gap theory of the Church Age. Allis comments that this teaching flowing out of the dispensational approach to Daniel 9:24-27 is "one of the clearest proofs of the novelty of that doctrine as well as of its revolutionary nature."[10]

Covenantal Structure

As I begin, we must recognize the crucial structure of this unique prophecy. Meredith Kline provides a thorough presentation of the strongly *covenantal* cast of the prophecy. He meticulously demonstrates that Daniel's prayer (Dan. 9:3-19) leading up to the prophecy is "saturated with formulaic expressions drawn from the Mosaic treaties, particularly from the Deuteronomic treaty."[11]

The covenant looms large both in Daniel's prayer and the Lord's answer to it: God is a covenant-keeping God (9:4), even while Israel violates God's covenantal statutes (9:5) to the point of repudiating the prophetic covenant-lawyers (9:6, 10) and enduring covenantal curse (9:11-15). Daniel 9 is the only

---

[8] Lewis Sperry Chafer, *Major Bible Themes*, rev. by John F. Walvoord (Grand Rapids: Zondervan, 1974), 305. Gleason L. Archer, Jr., "Daniel," in Frank E. Gaebelein, ed., *Expositor's Bible Commentary*, vol. 7 (Grand Rapids: Zondervan, 1985), 120. Kenneth L. Barker, "Evidence from Daniel," in Donald K. Clement and Jeffrey L. Townsend, eds., *A Case for Premillennialism: A New Consensus* (Chicago: Moody, 1992), 143n. J. Randall Price, "Prophetic Postponement in Daniel 9 and Other Texts," in Wesley R. Willis and John R. Master, eds., *Issues in Dispensationalism* (Chicago: Moody, 1994), 132.

[9] Robert Duncan Culver, *Daniel and the Latter Days* (2nd ed.: Chicago: Moody, 1977), 144.

[10] Allis, *Prophecy and the Church*, 109. In Kline's analysis of Daniel 9 he is led to call dispensationalism an "evangelical heresy." Meredith Kline, "Covenant of the Seventieth Week," in John H. Skilton, ed., *The Law and the Prophets: Old Testament Studies in Honor of Oswald T. Allis* (n.p.: Presbyterian and Reformed, 1974), 452.

[11] Kline, "The Covenant of the Seventieth Week," 456.

chapter in Daniel to use God's special covenant name *Jehovah* (יהוה "LORD," vv. 2, 4, 10, 13, 14, 20; cf. Exo. 6:2-4). This prayer about covenant loyalty (9:4) receives an answer structured by the covenantal sabbath pattern of seventy weeks (9:24-27), which results in the confirmation of the covenant (9:27).

Recognizing the covenantal framework of the seventy weeks is essential to analyzing the prophecy. As I will show, it virtually demands a focus on Christ's *fulfillment of redemption* during His ministry. Let us see how this is so.

The number *seven* is familiar to students of Old Testament sabbatic law. The prophecy of the seventy weeks follows sabbatic chronology (cf. Lev. 25): The Hebrew word שָׁבֻעִים (*shabuim*), which is translated "week" (Dan. 9:24), literally means "sevened." Daniel receives this prophecy in the first year of Babylon's fall to Persia (Dan. 9:1), while he contemplates the approaching conclusion of the seventy years' captivity (9:2). Israel's failure to observe levitical sabbath-rests for the land (Lev. 26:43; 2 Chron. 36:21) originally causes the Babylonian Captivity. Interestingly, Leviticus 26 emphasizes the number seven in it's threatening punishment of Israel: "I will chastise you again sevenfold for your sins" (Lev. 26:18, 21, 24, 28). In his ninth chapter, Daniel wonders what the future holds for Israel, now that *Jeremiah's* seventy years prophecy is nearing completion. God's answer to Daniel's prayer is to present a *new* period of seventy that issues forth in six primary results (Dan. 9:24). In this prophecy God gives Israel a renewed time period framed by the number seventy: a period of "seventy weeks."

The first phase of the seventy weeks is "seven weeks," or literally "seven sevens" (Dan. 9:25), which results in a value of forty-nine. In Old Testament ceremonial law, forty-nine years leads up to the Year of Jubilee, which is the fiftieth year (Lev. 25:8ff). This is a time of great celebration involving the release of slaves and the return to its owners of all land sold due to indebtedness. This is strongly covenantal in significance and directly relates to the redemptive meaning of the passage.

The total period of "*seventy* sevens" is also covenantal: seventy covers *ten* of these *seven* week periods, thereby standing for a ten-fold Jubilee. The number ten symbolizes *completion*, in that it represents the full number of digits on a man's hands.[12] Thus, the seventy sevens (weeks) would appear to point to a *complete* redemptive Jubilee. This must point to Christ, who brings in the ultimate Jubilee of full and complete redemption (cf. Luke 4:17-21; Isa. 61:1-3; Matt. 24:31[13]) and who is the leading *point* of Daniel's prophecy (Dan. 9:25, 26, 27). Consequently, the seventy weeks demarcates the period in which "the Messianic redemption was to be accomplished."

---

[12] William Taylor Smith, "Number," in James Orr, ed., *International Standard Bible Encyclopedia* (2nd ed.: Grand Rapids: Eerdmans, 1956), 3:2162.

[13] See commentary on Matt. 24:31 in Chapter 3 below.

Chronological Value

But what is the *chronological* value of this period of seventy weeks? The seventy weeks seem to represent a period of seventy times seven *years*, that is, a total period of 490 years. Though framed in sabbatic symbolism, it represents an historical period of time, contrary to some who see it as expressive of an indefinite period.[14] Even upon a cursory reading, this is because the prophecy "bears all the marks of chronological precision."[15] Daniel presents a careful measuring and dividing of this number. This also fits well with Daniel's chronological concern in the Maccabean prophecies in Daniel 8 and 12. Furthermore, ample justification exists in the context and elsewhere in Scripture for days standing for years:

First, a period of a literal seventy weeks would be too short to accomplish all that is expected. Thus, we should look beyond the literal for the proper measure.

Second, in the preceding context the original seventy *years* of Jeremiah's prophecy are clearly on Daniel's mind (Dan. 9:2). Those seventy years even imply the framework of Daniel's prophecy. Thus, the context itself suggests years.

Third, only two verses later, Daniel expressly *redefines* his use of "weeks." Daniel 10:2 reads: "In those days I, Daniel, was mourning three weeks *of days*" (יוֹם, *yom*). He does this, it seems, to distinguish the preceding symbolic weeks-of-*years* from the following *literal* weeks-of-*days*.

Fourth, the Old Testament frequently refers to the sabbath *year* (the seventh year of the sabbath period) as simply "the sabbath." Such passages, then, call a year by a term clearly associated with a day, the *sabbath day*.

Fifth, Scriptural precedent exists for speaking of years in terms of days. In Genesis 29:27-28 Jacob labors a "week" for Rachel: "'Complete the *week* of this one, and we will give you the other also for the service which you shall serve with me for another *seven years*.' And Jacob did so and completed her *week*, and he gave him his daughter Rachel as his wife." This seven-day period clearly stands for seven *years*: "So Jacob served seven years for Rachel and they seemed to him but a few days because of his love for her" (Gen. 29:20). In Numbers 14:34 the *forty years* of wandering result from the *forty days* of

---

[14] Kline, "The Covenant of the Seventieth Week," 452. Young, *Prophecy of Daniel*, 196. C. F. Keil, "Biblical Commentary on the Book of Daniel," in C. F. Keil and Franz Delitzsch, *Commentary on the Old Testament* (Grand Rapids: Eerdmans, rep. 1975), 338-339. Milton S. Terry, *Biblical Apocalyptics: A Study of the Most Notable Revelations of God and of Christ* (Grand Rapids: Baker, rep. 1988 [1898]), 201. Montgomery, *Critical and Exegetical Commentary on the Book of Daniel*, 220-221.

[15] Hengstenberg, *Christology of the Old Testament*, 2:880.

spying the land: "According to the number of days which you spied out the land, forty days, for every day you shall bear your guilt a year, even forty years, and you shall know My opposition." Ezekiel 4:6 employs the same standard of prophetic measure as Daniel: "I have laid on you a day for each year."

The Beginning Point

Undoubtedly an initial problem confronting the interpreter is determining the identity of the "command" in Daniel 9:25: "Know therefore and understand, that from the going forth of the command to restore and build Jerusalem. . . ."

At first we might suspect Cyrus's decree in 538 B.C., which is mentioned in 2 Chronicles 36:22-23 and in Ezra 1:1-4; 5:13, 17, 6:3. Certainly Cyrus gives a command to rebuild the city (Isa. 44:28): yet the bulk of the references to his decree deal with the Temple's rebuilding. Daniel, however, specifically speaks of the command to "*restore* and build *Jerusalem*," which is an important qualification as Hengstenberg so capably shows.[16] Though the Jews make half-hearted efforts to rebuild Jerusalem after Cyrus's decree, the city long remains little more than a sparsely populated, unwalled village.

Yet Daniel speaks of the command to "restore" (לְהָשִׁיב, root: *shub*, "return") Jerusalem (Dan. 9:25). This requires a return to its original integrity and grandeur as per Jeremiah's prophecy: "I will cause the captives of Judah and the captives of Israel to return, and will rebuild those places *as at the first*" (Jer. 33:7). This must involve the restoring of the city complete with its streets and protective wall: "the street shall be built again, and the wall, even in troublesome times" (Dan. 9:25).[17] The Jews did not seriously undertake this until the middle of the fifth century B.C. Hengstenberg points to the decree of Artaxerxes I in Nehemiah 2:1 (cf. v. 18)[18] as the beginning point, which he argues is in 455 B.C.[19] Payne and Boutflower direct our attention to the spiritually charged endeavor under Ezra in Ezra 7:11-26 as the starting point. This date would be in 458 or 457 B.C.[20] Julius Africanus, Vitringa, Ideler, and

---

[16] Hengstenberg, *Christology of the Old Testament*, 2:884ff.

[17] The presence of streets seems to portray a stable, prosperous city open to trade and intercourse; whereas the destruction of streets are gloomy emblems of devastation and judgment. See: 1 Kgs. 20:34; Jer. 7:34; 33:10; 44:6, 17; Zeph. 3:6.

[18] Apparently, Psalm 147:13-14 praises the Lord for Nehemiah's rebuilding of Jerusalem. See: J. A. Alexander, *Psalms Translated and Explained* (Grand Rapids: Baker, rep. 1873), 557.

[19] Hengstenberg, *Christology of the Old Testament*, 2:884-911. See also: "Artaxerxes," in Herbert S. Lockyer, Sr., *Nelson's Illustrated Bible Dictionary* (Nashville: Thomas Nelson, 1986), 106.

[20] J. Barton Payne, *Encyclopedia of Biblical Prophecy* (New York: Harper and Row,

most dispensationalists compute the years by Jewish 360-day years.[21] Adopting any of these closely related scenarios, we discover a possible reason the Jews expect the Messiah in the first century.[22] And he does appear at that time.

In the final analysis, the decree of Ezra in 457 B.C. during the seventh year of Artaxerxes I (454-424 B.C.), seems the best possibility. Ezra certainly understands this as permitting the rebuilding of Jerusalem's walls. This would carry the first sixty nine years up to A.D. 26 (omitting a year in the calculation, because no year 0 exists between 1 B.C. and A.D. 1), which is the year Christ's ministry opens. The Romans then crucify him three and one-half years later in A.D. 30 — a date accepted by most evangelicals scholars.[23]

References decades after Cyrus's decree, make abundantly clear that little was done toward rebuilding Jerusalem. Nehemiah laments that Jerusalem's walls are "broken down" (Neh. 1:3; 2:3-5, 17; 7:4). Zechariah speaks of Jerusalem as "destroyed" in his day (Zech. 14:11), even mentioning its *soon-coming* rebuilding (Zech. 1:16).[24] The enemies of the Jews warn Artaxerxes that the Jews will become a problem *if* they rebuild the city (Ezra 4:12-23). This explains why Ezra mentions Jerusalem's utter affliction "even to this day" (Ezra 9:7-9, 15).

The process of diligent rebuilding climaxes in Jerusalem's restoration. This process probably begins either in *seed* during the spiritual revival under Ezra (Ezra 7) or in *actuality* under the administration of Nehemiah (Neh. 2:1, 17-18; 6:15-16; 12:43).[25] Several political commands prepare for the restoring

---

1973), 388ff. C. Boutflower, *In and Around the Book of Daniel* (London: SPCK, 1923), 195ff.

[21] Julius Africanus, in Eusebius, *Demonstration of the Gospel* 8:2. This may be found in Alexander Roberts and James Donaldson, eds., *The Ante-Nicene Fathers* (Grand Rapids: Eerdmans, rep. 1885), 6:134. For Vitringa and Ideler, see: Hengstenberg, *Christology of the Old Testament*, 2:891 n2. Harold Hoehner, *Chronological Aspects of the Life of Christ* (Grand Rapids: Zondervan, 1977). J. Dwight Pentecost, "Daniel," in John F. Walvoord and Roy B. Zuck, *Bible Knowledge Commentary: Old Testament* (Chicago: Moody, 1985), 1363-1365.

[22] Matt. 11:3; Mark 15:43; Luke 1:76-79; 2:25, 26, 38; 3:15.

[23] "The choices that seem most viable in dating the life of Jesus are a three-and-a-half year ministry, with A.D. 30 as the date of Jesus' crucifixion and resurrection and sometime before April, 4 B.C. for his birth." L. A. Foster, "The Canon of the New Testament" in Gaebelein, *Expositor's Bible Commentary*, 1:598-599. See also: Richard L. Niswonger, *New Testament History* (Grand Rapids: Zondervan, 1988),168.

[24] See also: Zech. 1:12; 2:1; 7:7; 8:5-6.

[25] Julius Africanus held the second view long ago. See his comments cited in Eusebius, *Demonstration of the Gospel* 8:2.

of Jerusalem, as well as one divine command: "So the elders of the Jews built, and they prospered through the prophesying of Haggai the prophet and Zechariah the son of Iddo. And they built and finished it, according to the commandment of the God of Israel, and according to the command of Cyrus, Darius, and Artaxerxes king of Persia" (Ezra 6:14).

Now let us consider the constituent elements of the time-frame of the prophecy. The first period of seven weeks must mark off some event, in that Daniel distinguishes it from the two other periods. If it were not significant, he would speak of "sixty-nine weeks," rather than "seven weeks and sixty-two weeks" (Dan. 9:25). Although we cannot be certain, this seven weeks (or forty-nine years) apparently covers the period of Jerusalem's actual rebuilding.[26] The Jews rebuild the city during this era, despite the opposition in "troublesome times" that God ordains (cp. Neh. 4:18; Dan. 9:25). Daniel does not clearly enunciate the time-frame, thus it has no bearing upon the prophetic debate.

As I will show, the second period of sixty-two weeks extends from the conclusion of Jerusalem's rebuilding to Messiah's formal introduction to Israel at his baptism (Dan. 9:25). This is sometime around A.D. 26. Conservative scholars widely agree on such an interpretation, which is virtually "universal among Christian exegetes"[27] — excluding dispensationalists.

The third period of one week is the subject of intense scholarly controversy between dispensationalism and other conservative traditions. Much of my discussion below will deal with that final week.

In that our inquiry into the seventy weeks is eschatological and not apologetical, we need not finally determine the exact starting point for the time of the command. We do take comfort in the several closely related possibilities open to us, however. Yet the Messianic events to which Daniel alludes are more crucial to our eschatological concerns than the determination of the date of the command. We turn now to consider significant differences separating dispensationalism from the other evangelical viewpoints.

Daniel 9:24

Daniel 9:24 provides the overriding, glorious expectation of the prophecy: "Seventy weeks are determined for your people and for your holy city, to finish the transgression, to make an end of sins, to make reconciliation for iniquity, to bring in everlasting righteousness, to seal up vision and prophecy, and to anoint the Most Holy." Let me briefly sketch the events in verse 24 within the context of the whole prophecy.

---

[26] Hengstenberg, *Christology of the Old Testament*, 894ff.
[27] Montgomery, *Daniel*, 332.

The Importance of Verse 24

The six infinitival phrases of verse 24 form three *couplets*, which serve as the main point of the prophecy and as the heading to the explication that follows. "Know therefore and understand" (9:25) introduces that explication. Correspondences should exist, then, between the events of verse 24 and the prophecy of verses 25-27.

Among non-dispensational evangelicals the general view of Daniel 9:24 holds that "the six items presented . . . settle the *terminus ad quem* of the prophecy,"[28] meaning that these items occur during the first advent 2000 years ago. Contrary to this view, Culver puts the matter into bold dispensational relief: these events are "not to be found in any event near the earthly lifetime of our Lord."[29] Ryrie points to this verse and applies it to *our* future: "God will once again turn His attention in a special way to His people the Jews and to His holy city Jerusalem, as outlined in Daniel 9:24."[30] The dispensationalist adopts a decidedly futurist approach to the prophecy — *when he gets past the first sixty-nine weeks.*

The seventy weeks prophecy definitely focuses on Israel (v. 24), as we may surmise from Daniel's contemplating Israel's captivity (Dan. 9:2) and his prayer of confession in her behalf (Dan. 9:4-22). But, of course, Israel's Messiah is the only Savior of men, so the accomplishments of His work reach beyond the Jewish people — as the Old Testament makes abundantly clear (e.g., Psa. 72:8; Isa. 2:2-4; 11:9-10).[31] We see this universal saving work in other prophecies; we see it again here. Still, a significant emphasis on Israel appears here. Daniel ends with the "anointing of the Most Holy" (v. 24), not because it is chronologically final, but so that he may lead directly to the presentation of the "Messiah" (וְלִמְשֹׁחַ, from: *messhua*, "anointed one," v. 25).[32] As I shall show, these six elements involve a mixture of blessing and curse, a common phenomenon in covenantal promises.

The Interpretation of Verse 24

Let us notice, first, that the seventy weeks will result in the *finishing of the transgression*. Remember that Daniel's prayer of confession regards *Israel's* sins (Dan. 9:4ff) and the prophecy's *focus* is on Israel (Dan. 9:24a). Consequently, this *finishing* (לְכַלֵּא, from: *kala*) *the transgression* refers to Israel's completing her transgression against God. This occurs when Israel culminates her resistance

---

[28] Ibid., 201.

[29] Culver, *Daniel and the Latter Days*, 155.

[30] Ryrie, *Basic Theology*, 465.

[31] See: Gentry, *He Shall Have Dominion: A Postmillennial Eschatology*, chs. 10, 12.

[32] See Payne's argument in Payne, "Goal of Daniel's Seventy Weeks," 97-115. (I do not follow all of Payne's argument.)

to God by rejecting his Son and having Him crucified, as Christ Himself prophesies in parabolic form: "*Last* of all he sent his son to them, saying, 'They will respect my son.' But when the vinedressers saw the son, they said among themselves, 'This is the heir. Come, let us kill him and seize his inheritance'" (Matt. 21:37-38).[33]

The second part of the couplet directly relates to the first: upon finishing the transgression against God by rejecting the Messiah, Israel's *sins are sealed up* (NASB and ASV marg.; וְלַחְתֹּם, from: *chatham*).[34] As Payne observes, the idea here is to seal or to "reserve sins for punishment."[35] Because of Israel's rejecting her Messiah, God reserves punishment for her. God will execute her punishment by finally and conclusively destroying her Temple. God *reserves* this punishment from the time of Jesus's crucifixion in A.D. 30 until A.D. 70 (Matt. 24:2, 34). The sealing or reserving of the sins indicates that *within* the "seventy weeks" Israel will complete her transgression and God will act to reserve her sins for judgment — and that judgment will fall upon her *after* the expiration of the seventy weeks time-frame. This is a major point in the Lord's Olivet Discourse: though just before his crucifixion Christ says, "Your house is left to you desolate" (Matt. 23:38),[36] He then reserves his judgment for one generation (Matt. 24:2, 34).

The third result (beginning the second couplet) provides "*reconciliation for iniquity.*"[37] The Hebrew word for "reconciliation" is כָּפַר, *kaphar*, which we may also translate "atonement." It clearly speaks of Christ's atoning death, which is the ultimate atonement to which all Temple rituals point (Heb. 9:26).[38] This also occurs during his earthly ministry — at his death. The dispensationalist, however, prefers to interpret this result as *application* rather than *effecting*, as subjective appropriation instead of objective accomplishment. Walvoord admits that this result "seems to be a rather clear picture of the

---

[33] The Bible frequently emphasizes the Jewish betrayal of Christ: Matt. 20:18-19; 21:33-45; 23:37-38; 27:11-25; Mark 10:33; 15:1; Luke 18:32; 23:1-2; John 18:28-31; 19:12, 15; Acts 2:22-23; 3:13-15a; 4:26-27; 5:30; 7:51-52.

[34] See also: Robert Young, *Young's Literal Translation of the Holy Bible* (3rd.: n.p.: Edinburgh, 1898; reprint, Grand Rapids: Baker, n.d.), 552. B. Otzen, חתם (*hatam*), vol. 5, in G. J. Botterweck and Helmer Ringgren, *Theological Dictionary of the Old Testament* (Grand Rapids: Eerdmans, 1986), 263-269.

[35] Payne, "Goal of Daniel's Seventy Weeks," 111.

[36] This happens at his death, in the rending of the veil (Matt. 27:51).

[37] The definite article, which occurs before "transgression" and "sins," is lacking here. There it refers to the particular situation of Israel. Here it considers the more general predicament of mankind.

[38] Heb. 1:3; 7:27; 9:7-12, 26, 28; 10:9-10. See also: John 1:29; Rom. 3:25; 2 Cor. 5:19; 1 Pet. 2:24; 1 John 2:2.

cross of Christ," but then he asserts that "the actual application of it is again associated with the second advent as far as Israel is concerned."[39] On the basis of the Hebrew verb, however, the passage surely speaks of actually *making reconciliation* (or *atonement*).

This atonement for sin secures the fourth result, *everlasting righteousness*, which speaks of the objective accomplishment of righteousness, not its subjective appropriation. Christ secures this within the seventy week period, while in his redemptive activity on earth. Speaking of Christ's work, Paul writes: "But *now* the righteousness of God apart from the law is revealed, being witnessed by the Law and the Prophets, even the righteousness of God even the righteousness of God which is through faith in Jesus Christ to all and on all who believe. For there is no difference; for all have sinned and fall short of the glory of God, being justified freely by his grace through the redemption that is in Christ Jesus, whom God set forth to be a propitiation by his blood, through faith, to demonstrate his righteousness, because in his forbearance God had passed over the sins that were previously committed" (Rom. 3:21-25).

The fifth result (the first portion of the third couplet) also reflects Christ's ministry on earth, which his baptism introduces: He comes "*to seal up vision and prophecy.*" This speaks of Christ's fulfilling — and thereby confirming — prophecy. Committed dispensationalists resist this idea, arguing that Christ does not fulfill *all* prophecy at that time.[40] But neither does He in the seventieth week at the supposed future Tribulation. Nor in the dispensationalist's millennium. For following these are the final apostasy, the resurrection, and the New Heavens and New Earth.

Actually, the "sealing of prophecy" is limited by the express statement of purpose in Daniel 9: the full accomplishing of redemption from sin through blood atonement. And Christ does effect this: "Behold, we are going up to Jerusalem, and *all* things that are written by the prophets concerning the Son of Man will be accomplished" (Luke 18:31; cp. Luke 24:44; Acts 3:18).[41]

Finally, the seventy weeks of years will witness the following goal: "*to*

---

[39] Walvoord, *Daniel*, 221, 222.

[40] Leon Wood, *A Commentary on Daniel* (Grand Rapids: Zondervan, 1973), 250.

[41] Walvoord slips by letting this prophecy cover "the cessation of the New Testament prophetic gift seen both in oral prophecy and in the writing of the Scriptures" (Walvoord, *Daniel*, 222). On his own basis this does not occur in either the first sixty-nine weeks (up to "just before the time of Christ's crucifixion") or in the seventieth week (the future Great Tribulation), the periods which he claims involve the 490 years. John F. Walvoord, *Prophecy Knowledge Handbook* (Wheaton, Ill.: Victor, 1990), 258. Yet he specifically says that the "six major events characterize the 490 years" (Ibid., 251).

anoint the Most Holy." This anointing (וְלִמְשֹׁחַ, from: *mashach*) speaks of the formal introduction of Christ by means of his baptism, rather than the anointing of the Temple. This seems clear from the following:

(1) The overriding concern of Daniel 9:24-27 is Messianic. The Temple built after the Babylonian Captivity will be destroyed after the seventy weeks (v. 27). Daniel makes no further mention of it; nor does his prophecy allow for its re-building for the millennium.

(2) In the verses following the anointing, Daniel mentions the Messiah (מָשִׁיחַ, *mashiyach*, "anointed one") twice (vv. 25, 26).

(3) Contrary to the interpretation of some dispensationalists, no Temple is *anointed* in Scripture — whether Solomon's original Temple, Zerubbabel's re-built Temple, Ezekiel's visionary Temple, or Herod's expanded Temple. Thus, even some dispensationalists will allow that Christ Himself is in view.[41]

(4) The phrase "most holy" speaks of the Messiah who is "that Holy One who is to be born" (Luke 1:35).[42] Isaiah prophesies of Christ in the ultimate redemptive Jubilee: "The Spirit of the Lord GOD is upon Me, because the LORD has *anointed* Me to preach good tidings to the poor; He has sent Me to heal the brokenhearted, to proclaim liberty to the captives, and the opening of the prison to those who are bound; to proclaim the acceptable year of the LORD" (Isa. 61:1-2a; cp. Luke 4:17-21). At his baptismal anointing the Spirit comes upon Him (Mark 1:9-11) to prepare Him for his ministry, of which we read three verses later: "Jesus came to Galilee, preaching the gospel of the kingdom of God, and saying, '*The time* is *fulfilled* [the sixty-ninth week?], and the kingdom of God is at hand. Repent, and believe in the gospel'" (Mark 1:14-15). Christ is preeminently *the* Anointed One.[43]

The Seventieth Week

The prophecy now points to something Israel will experience "after the sixty-two weeks" (Dan. 9:26) that follow the "seven weeks" (v. 25). This is to occur, then, *after* the sixty-ninth week. A natural reading of the text demands that this be during the seventieth week, for that is the only time remaining to accomplish the stated goals of the prophecy (Dan. 9:24).

At that time "Messiah shall be *cut off.*" The English rendering "cut off" translates the Hebrew כָּרַת, *karath*, which "is used of the death penalty, Lev. 7:20; and refers to a violent death."[45] Thus, it refers to the death of Christ on the cross.

---

[42] Pentecost, "Daniel," *Bible Knowledge Commentary,* 1361.
[43] Cf. Luke 4:34, 41. See also: Mark 1:24; Acts 3:14; 4:27, 30; 1 John 2:20; Rev. 3:7.
[44] Psa. 2:2; 132:10; Isa. 11:2; 42:1; Hab. 3:13; Acts 4:27; 10:38; Heb. 1:9.
[45] Young, *Daniel,* 206.

Given the Hebraic pattern of repetition, we may easily discern a parallel between verses 26 and 27: verse 27 expands on verse 26. Negatively, Messiah's *cutting off* in verse 26 results from Israel's completing her transgression culminating (v. 24) in her crucifying the Messiah.[46] Verse 27 states: "He shall *confirm a covenant* with many for one week; but in the middle of the week He shall bring an end to sacrifice and offering." Positively, then, confirming the covenant with "many" effects reconciliation and brings in everlasting righteousness (v. 24). Thus, these parallels refer to the same event when viewed from the two angles of blessing and curse (cp. Deut. 11:26; 30:1). Both occur *within* the seventy weeks.

The Confirming of the Covenant

What are we to make of the "*confirming of the covenant*" in verse 27? This surely refers to the prophesied covenantal actions of verse 24. These actions result from the perfect covenantal Jubilee (seventy weeks) and are a result of Daniel's covenantal prayer (cf. v. 4). This covenant must be the *divine* covenant of God's redemptive grace.[47] Messiah comes to *confirm* the covenantal promises: "to perform the mercy promised to our fathers and to remember his holy covenant" (Luke 1:72).[48] He confirms the covenant by his death on the cross: "by so much more Jesus has become a surety of a better covenant" (Heb. 7:22b).[49]

Furthermore, the word translated "confirm" (הִגְבִּיר, *higbir*) is related to the name of the angel Gabriel who brings Daniel the revelation of the seventy weeks (he also later brings the revelation of Christ's birth [Luke 1:19, 26]). "Gabriel" (גַּבְרִיאֵל, *gabriel*) is based on the Hebrew גִּבּוֹר, *gibbor*, "strong one," a concept frequently associated with the covenant God.[50] The related word found in Daniel 9:27 means to "make strong, confirm."[51] This certainly is a

---

[46] Matt. 20:18-19; 27:11-25; Mark 10:33; 15:1; Luke 18:32; 23:1-2; John 18:28-31; 19:12, 15; Acts 2:22-23; 3:13-15a; 4:26-27; 5:30; 7:52.

[47] When "covenant" is mentioned in Daniel, it always refers to God's covenant, see: Daniel 9:4; 11:22, 28, 30, 32. This includes even Dan. 11:22; see: Pentecost, "Daniel," *Bible Knowledge Commentary*, 1:1369.

[48] His covenants are "the covenants of the promise" (Eph. 2:12). See: Luke 1:72; Acts 3:25-26; 13:32; 26:6-7; Rom. 1:2; 4:16; 9:4; 15:8; 2 Cor. 1:20; Gal. 3:16-22; Eph. 3:6; Heb. 7:22; 13:20.

[49] Matt. 26:28; Mark 14:24; Luke 22:20; 1 Cor. 11:25; 2 Cor. 3:6; Heb. 8:8, 13; 9:15; 12:24.

[50] Deut. 7:9, 21; 10:17; Neh. 1:5; 9:32; Isa. 9:6; Dan. 9:4. Hengstenberg argues convincingly that the source of Daniel 9 is Isaiah 10:21-23, where God is the "Mighty God" who blesses the faithful remnant.

[51] Young, *Daniel*, 209; Allis, *Prophecy and the Church*, 122; Hengstenberg, *Christology of the Old Testament*, 856.

"firm covenant" for it brings about "*everlasting* righteousness" (Dan. 9:24).

Daniel's prayer is particularly for Israel (Dan. 9:3ff) and it recognizes that God promises mercy to those who love Him (v. 4). Therefore, the prophecy holds that the covenant will be confirmed with *many* for *one week*. The reference to the "many" speaks of the faithful in Israel. "Thus a contrast is introduced between *He* and the *Many*, a contrast which appears to reflect upon the great Messianic passage, Isa. 52:13-53:12 and particularly 53:11. Although the entire nation will not receive salvation, the many will receive."[52]

This confirming of God's covenant with the "many" of Israel will occur in the middle of the *seventieth week* (v. 27). This timing parallels "after the sixty-two [and seven] weeks" (v. 26), while providing more detail. We know Christ's three and one-half year ministry in the first half of the seventieth week decidedly focuses on the Jews, for he commands his disciples: "Do not go into the way of the Gentiles, and do not enter a city of the Samaritans" (Matt. 10:5b; cp. Matt. 15:24). Then for three and one-half years after the crucifixion, the apostles focus almost exclusively on the Jews.[53] They begin first "in Judea" (Acts 1:8; Acts 2:14) because "the gospel of Christ" is "for the Jew first" (Rom. 1:16; cf. 2:10; John 4:22).

Although Daniel clearly specifies the event that serves as the terminus of the sixty-ninth week, he does not specify the terminus of the seventieth week. Apparently, an exact event ending the seventieth is not as significant to know. Interestingly though, at the stoning of Stephen, the first recorded martyr of Christianity, the covenantal proclamation begins turning to the Gentiles. The apostle to the Gentiles appears on the scene at Stephen's death as the Jewish persecution against Christianity breaks out: "Now Saul was consenting to his death. At that time a great persecution arose against the church that was at Jerusalem; and they were all scattered throughout the regions of Judea and Samaria, except the apostles" (Acts 8:1). Acts informs us that Paul's mission is to take the growing faith beyond a narrow Jewish focus: "he is a chosen vessel of Mine *to bear My name before Gentiles*, kings, and the children of Israel" (Acts 9:15). Paul's conversion shortly after Stephen's stoning occurs in about A.D. 34 or 35.[54]

This confirming of the covenant occurs "in the middle of the week" (v. 27). I show above that the seventieth week begins with the baptismal anoint-

---

[52] Young, *Daniel*, 213.

[53] Payne, "The Goal of Daniel's Seventy Weeks," 109n. Boutflower, *In and Around the Book of Daniel*, 195ff. Hengstenberg, *Christology of the Old Testament*, 2:898. Young, *Daniel*, 213.

[54] D. A. Carson, Douglas J. Moo, and Leon Morris, *An Introduction to the New Testament* (Grand Rapids: Zondervan, 1992), 230-231.

ing of Christ. Then after three and one-half years of ministry — the middle of the seventieth week — Christ is crucified.[55] The prophecy states that by his conclusive confirming of the covenant, Messiah will "bring an end to sacrifice and offering" (v. 27). He does this by offering up Himself as a sacrifice for sin: "Now, once at the end of the ages, He has appeared to put away sin by the sacrifice of Himself" (Heb. 9:25-26; cp. Heb. 7:11-12, 18-22). Consequently, at his death the Temple veil rips from top to bottom (Matt. 27:51). This is miraculous evidence God is *legally disestablishing* the sacrificial system (cf. Matt. 23:38). Christ is the Lamb of God (John 1:29; 1 Pet. 1:19) who opens the Holy of holies to his people (Heb. 4:14; 9:12, 24-26; 10:19-22).

The Destruction of Jerusalem

But how are we to understand the latter portions of verses 26 and 27? What are we to make of the destruction of "the city and sanctuary" (v. 26)? What does Daniel mean by "the abomination that causes desolation" (v. 27)? Do not most evangelical commentators agree that this speaks of A.D. 70, which occurs *forty years after* the crucifixion? And in this, do they not follow Josephus? Josephus applies Daniel 9:27 to the A.D. 70 events: "In the very same manner Daniel also wrote concerning the Roman government, and that our country should be made desolate by them" (*Ant.* 10:11:7).

In verse 26 we learn there are *two* events to occur *after* the sixty-ninth week: (1) Messiah is to be "cut off" and (2) the city and sanctuary are to be destroyed. Verse 27a informs us that Messiah's cutting off (v. 26a) confirms the covenant and occurs at the half-way point of the seventieth week. So Messiah's death is clearly within the time-frame of the seventy weeks (as we expect, since he is the major figure of the prophecy).

The events involving the destruction of the city and the sanctuary with war and desolation (vv. 26b, 27b) are the *consequences* of the cutting off of the Messiah. They do not necessarily occur in the seventy weeks time-frame — they are an *addendum* to the point of the prophecy stated in verse 24.

This prophecy *anticipates*, however, the destructive acts occurring in A.D. 70: in the divine act of *sealing up* (or reserving) Israel's sin for punishment. Israel's climactic sin is completing her transgression (v. 24) in "cutting off" Messiah (v. 26a). In response to this, God reserves her judgment for later.

---

[55] Luke alludes to the length of his ministry in Luke 13:6-9. Scholars widely agree that he dies after three and one-half years of ministry. A. T. Robertson, *A Harmony of the Gospels* (New York: Harper and Row, 1922, 1950), 270. Eusebius comments: "since he began his work during the high priesthood of Annas and taught until Caiaphas held the office, the entire time does not comprise quite four years" (*Eccl. Hist.* 1:10:3).

God *will* judge Israel's sin — after the seventy weeks expire. He will neither forget her sin nor delay her punishment forever. This explains the "very indefinite" phrase "till the end of the war": the "end" will not occur in the seventy weeks. We today know the end occurs in A.D. 70, as Christ makes abundantly clear in Matthew 24:15.[56]

The Dispensational Interpretation

There are three fundamental errors in the dispensational approach to Daniel's seventy weeks. These involve: (1) The proper understanding of the terminus; (2) the unity of the seventy weeks; and (3) the identity of the covenant of verse 27.

The Terminus of the Seventy Weeks

Dispensationalists are pressed by their system to radically re-interpret Daniel 9:24. They place these events in our future, deferring them until Israel's return to the Lord during a seven year Great Tribulation.[57] Pentecost observes that "this future period is the unfulfilled seven years of Daniel's prophecy of the seventy weeks (Dan. 9:24-27)."[58] Price agrees, admitting this is a peculiar dispensational approach: "A distinctive tenet of dispensational interpretation is the recognition of prophetic postponement. . . . Daniel 9:26-27 [is] a much contested model for demonstrating time intervals in eschatological passages."[59]

The following quotations are from dispensationalist scholar J. Dwight Pentecost, as taken from his commentary on Daniel found in Dallas Seminary's *Bible Knowledge Commentary*.[60] I will use this as representative of classic dispensationalism, which is "one of the most widespread and influential traditions in evangelical theology today."[61]

Pentecost asserts that "to finish the transgression" refers to the removal of Israel's tendency to apostasy. This occurs at the Second Advent when she is "restored to the land and blessed." The making "an end to sins" means that

---

[56] See pages 58-59 below.

[57] Walvoord, *Prophecy Knowledge Handbook*, 251 ff. Charles L. Feinberg, *Millennialism: The Two Major Views* (Chicago: Moody, 1980), 150.

[58] J. Dwight Pentecost, *Thy Kingdom Come* (Wheaton, Ill.: Victor, 1990), 122.

[59] Price, "Prophetic Postponement," 132.

[60] Walvoord and Zuck, *Bible Knowledge Commentary*. All quotes are taken from pages 1361-1362.

[61] Craig A. Blaising and Darrell L. Bock, *Progressive Dispensationalism: An Up-to-Date Handbook of Contemporary Dispensational Thought* (Wheaton, Ill.: BridgePoint, 1993), 9. Grenz writes that dispensationalism is "the most widely held viewpoint among fundamentalists and evangelical Christians in America." Stanley J. Grenz, *The Millennial Maze: Sorting Out Evangelical Options* (Downers Grove, Ill.: InterVarsity, 1992), 91

"at Christ's second coming He will remove Israel's sin." To "make reconciliation" for sins "relates to God's final atonement of Israel when she repents at Christ's second coming." The bringing in of "everlasting righteousness" indicates "that God will establish an age characterized by righteousness. This is a reference to the millennial kingdom."

According to Pentecost, "to seal up vision and prophecy" means that "all that God through the prophets said He would do in fulfilling his covenant with Israel will be fully realized in the millennial kingdom." To "anoint the Most Holy," according to Pentecost, "may refer to the dedication of the most holy place in the millennial temple" or "it may refer not to a holy place, but to the Holy One, Christ. If so, this speaks of the enthronement of Christ" as "King of kings and Lord of lords in the Millennium." In summary, "these six accomplishments, then, anticipate the establishment of Israel's covenanted millennial kingdom under the authority of her promised King."

Earlier I argue for an interpretation of the terminus in Christ's ministry, a view that is more widely held by evangelical scholars. The dispensational view is surely erroneous, as will become even more evident in the next paragraphs where I consider the gap theory of dispensationalism. At this point the reader should consider how incredible it is that on the dispensationalist interpretation *Daniel totally overlooks the point of the First Advent*: the time during which Christ dies for sin in fulfillment of the Temple symbolism, Old Testament typology, and prophetic anticipation. As Mauro complains, the fundamental idea of verse 24 "happened in an unmentioned gap."[62] In the dispensational view the first two periods of the seventy weeks lead right up to Christ's crucifixion — but then suddenly skip over it.

The Gap in the Seventy Weeks

Dispensationalism interposes this gap or parenthesis between the sixty-ninth and the seventieth weeks; it spans the entire Church Age from the Triumphal Entry to the Rapture.[63] The dispensational arguments for a gap of undetermined length between the sixty-ninth and seventieth weeks are not

---

[62] Philip Mauro, *The Seventy Weeks and the Great Tribulation* (Boston: Hamilton, 1923), 101. See discussion on his pages 91-101.

[63] Walvoord, *Prophecy Knowledge Handbook*, 256-257. Ryrie, *Basic Theology*, 465. Pentecost, "Daniel," *Bible Knowledge Commentary*, 1:161. Walvoord, *Daniel*, 230-231. It is interesting to note that the early Fathers held to a non-eschatological interpretation of the Seventieth Week, applying it either to the ministry of Christ or to A.D. 70. See: Barnabas 16:6; Clement of Alexandria, *Miscellanies* 1:125-26; Tertullian, *An Answer to the Jews* 8; Julius Africanus, *Chronology* 50. See: L. E. Knowles, "The Interpretation of the Seventy Weeks of Daniel in the Early Fathers," *Westminster Theological Journal* 7 (1945): 136-160.

convincing. Let us consider the leading arguments for this gap. I will state the argument briefly with some documentation and then respond.

First, *the peculiar phraseology in Daniel:* Daniel places the cutting off of the Messiah "*after* the 62 'sevens,' not in the 70th 'seven.'"[64] This allows for a gap between the sixty-ninth and seventieth weeks. If the cutting off does not occur *in* the sixty-ninth *or* the seventieth weeks, there must be a gap wherein it does occur.

In response, it is obvious that seventy occurs *after* sixty-nine and thus fits the requirements of the statement. Consequently, such an argument does not prove that "after" *requires* a gap. Besides, Daniel only mentions seventy weeks, and he most certainly does *not* say "after sixty-nine weeks, but not in the seventieth."[65] The dispensational gap is a gratuitous assumption.

Daniel has yet to deal with the seventieth week, though he does deal with the preceding sixty-nine weeks (v. 25). Thus, it is quite natural to assume this cutting off of the Messiah must be within the seven year period covered by the remaining week, the seventieth. The seventy weeks prophecy is the major, over-arching time-frame of the prophecy. The cutting off of the Messiah is an event of unsurpassing prophetic and redemptive significance in general, and is fundamental to explaining the goal of the seventy weeks stated in verse 24 in particular.

Second, *the burden of Daniel's prophecy:* The "six actions [of verse 24] pertain to Daniel's 'people' (Israel) and his 'Holy City' (Jerusalem), not the church."[66] McClain says "the fulfillment of the tremendous events in verse 24 cannot be found anywhere in known history."[67] These have yet to occur for Israel; the events must be future.

As I show above, the leading idea of the seventy weeks prophecy is Messianic redemption. The Messiah is "the Most Holy" who brings in "reconciliation" and effects "eternal redemption" (v. 24). He does this for Israel *and everyone else.* He actually effects this eternal redemption by his death (v. 24), which seems clear enough in his being "cut off" (v. 26). As a matter of historical record, his death occurs within seven years of his baptismal anointing — three-and-one-half years, to be exact. What is to force us outside this unified seventy weeks time-frame?

---

[64] Pentecost, "Daniel," *Bible Knowledge Commentary,* 1364. See Walvoord, *The Rapture Question,* 25.

[65] Hans K. LaRondelle, *The Israel of God in Prophecy* (Berrien Springs, Mich.: Andrews University, 1983), 173.

[66] Pentecost, "Daniel," *BKC,* 1364.

[67] McClain, *Daniel's Prophecy of the Seventy Weeks,* 35.

Third, *a fatal admission*: "Historically the destruction of Jerusalem occurred in A.D. 70 almost forty years after the death of Christ."[68] Since this is given in Daniel's prophecy and is to occur within the seventy weeks, "the continuous fulfillment theory [is] left without any explanation adequate for interposing an event as occurring after the sixty-ninth seven by some thirty-eight years."[69]

Above I explain the relation of the seventy weeks to the Temple's A.D. 70 destruction. It is important to remember that the goal of the seventy weeks is *not* the A.D. 70 destruction of the Temple — verse 24 does not even mention it. That destruction is a later *consequence* of certain events brought to fulfillment within the seventy weeks. The actual act of God's *sealing* or *reserving judgment* (v. 24) occurs within the seventy weeks; the later fulfillment of that reserved judgment does not. There is no necessity at all for a gap.

Fourth, *the general tendency in prophecy*: "Nothing should be plainer to one reading the Old Testament than that the foreview therein provided did not describe the period of time between the two advents. This very fact confused even the prophets (cf. 1 Pet. 1:10-12)."[70] The dispensationalist argues that Old Testament prophecy often merges the First and Second Advents into one scene, though separated by thousands of years. Consequently, we have biblical warrant for understanding the sixty-ninth and seventieth weeks as merged into one scene, although separated by a gap of thousands of years.

This argument is wholly without merit. Clearly the seventy weeks compose a unit, though sub-divided into three unequal parts: (1) It is *one* period of seventy weeks anticipating the events mentioned; the parts make up a unified whole. Three *separate* periods of weeks are not the major chronology in the revelation; these three periods (7+62+1) make up the over-arching time-frame of seventy weeks of years. The plural "seventy weeks" is followed by a *singular* verb "is decreed" which indicates the unity of the time period. Dispensationalists even argue vigorously against allowing a gap in the midst of the seventieth week because "the week is one."[71] Why do they not allow that the seventy weeks "is" one?

(2) An overriding concern of the prophecy, in distinction to all other Messianic prophecies, is that it is specifically designed to be a measuring time-frame. The very first words in the prophecy emphatically point to this fact: "seventy weeks." If there were gaps between the units, the whole idea of measurement in the "seventy weeks" would vanish. An elastic yardstick is a worthless measure. None of the other prophecies brought forward as illustra-

---

[68] Walvoord, *Daniel*, 230.
[69] Ibid., 230.
[70] Walvoord, *Rapture Question*, 25.
[71] Pentecost, *Things to Come*, 198.

tions of a gap claim to be a *measure of time.*[72]

(3) All agree that the first two units in the period (seven weeks and sixty-two weeks) follow consecutively. Why should not the final period of seven weeks? Strangely, Walvoord — a gap theorist[73] — criticizes Mauro for allowing the last week to be an indefinite period of time: "In view of the precision of the seventy years of the captivity, however, mentioned in the same chapter, the context indicates the probability of a more literal intention in the revelation."[74] Mauro allows the seventieth week to last forty years as an extension of God's gracious longsuffering to Israel. Walvoord allows a gap almost 2000 years long, wholly destroying the possibility of temporal measurement. How is Walvoord "more literal"? Mauro's view measures more closely than does Walvoord's — at least the events of this precisely measured time-frame are in the same century. Walvoord's are separated by millennia — so far.

(4) If the dispensational gap theory is true, then the gap separating the seventieth from the sixty-ninth week is almost 2000 years long. *This is four times the whole period of the seventy weeks or 490 years.* How can the dispensationalist credibly argue for the exact fulfillment of the first seventy weeks *to the day,*[75] when they allow an interruption of *millennia* between two of the weeks? Thomas Ice even computes Daniel's time-frame in exacting fractions of a day to come up with the proper dispensational conclusions: "476 years x 365.2421989 days = 173,855 days."[76] Ryrie even chides amillennialists for dating the decree of Daniel 9:24 in 538 B.C., because "this has the effect of allowing the seventy sevens to be imprecise in duration." Ryrie's later argument totally voids this complaint: "there is an interval of undetermined length between the first sixty-nine weeks of seven years each and the last or seventieth week of seven years."[77]

---

[72] Besides this, dispensationalists put asunder what God has joined together. That is, passages such as Isaiah 9:6-7 merge the earthly ministry of Christ with his kingship because they both begin their fulfillment in the first century.

[73] Walvoord, *Daniel,* 230-231.

[74] Ibid., 218.

[75] Robert Anderson, *The Coming Prince* (London: Hodder and Stoughton, 1909). Feinberg, *Millennialism,* 150. H. Wayne House and Thomas D. Ice, *Dominion Theology: Blessing or Curse?* (Portland, Ore.: Multnomah, 1988), 321: "Daniel predicted precisely the year in which Messiah would be cut off." Hoehner, *Chronological Aspects of the Life of Christ,* 139: "The *terminus ad quem* of the sixty-ninth week was on the day of Christ's triumphal entry on March 30, A.D. 33."

[76] Thomas D. Ice and Timothy Demy, *The Truth About the Tribulation* (Eugene, Ore.: Harvest, 1996), 19. The .2421989 of a day computes to 5.8 hours. See our debate over this matter in Thomas D. Ice and Kenneth L. Gentry, Jr., *The Great Tribulation: Past or Future,* (Grand Rapids, Kregel, 1999), chs. 2, 6.

[77] Ryrie, *Basic Theology,* 448, 465.

Fifth, *the order within the prophecy*: "In the record of the prophecy, the destruction of the city [v. 26b] is placed *before* the last week [v. 27a]."[78] Since this occurs in A.D. 70, we must allow a gap to account for it.

This argument overlooks the peculiarities of Hebrew poetic style. Oriental expression often confounds the Occidental concern for chronological succession; the Western framework may not be foisted upon the passage. This "revelational pattern"[79] allows a *parallel rehearsal and expansion of the topic* without requiring actual succession in time. Even classic dispensationalists understand that some prophetic passages do not flow chronologically.[80] A better understanding of the relation between verses 26 and 27 is given above.

Sixth, *the interpretation by Christ*: "The testimony of our Lord Himself [in Matt. 24:15] shows that the Seventieth Week is still future."[81]

This problem is already answered in the exposition of the passage above and in the response given to argument Five. The Lord cites from the portion of Daniel's passage that lies outside the concern of the seventy weeks themselves.[82] There is no need for a gap in Daniel 9 to explain Christ's use of it in Matthew 24.

The Covenant of Verse 27

Dispensationalists woefully misunderstand the confirming of the covenant in verse 27. They apply it to a still future, malevolent ruler who makes, then breaks a political covenant with Israel. According to Walvoord "this refers to the coming world ruler at the beginning of the last seven years who is able to gain control over ten countries in the Middle East. He will make a covenant with Israel for a seven-year period. As Daniel 9:27 indicates, in the middle of the seven years he will break the covenant, stop the sacrifices being offered in the temple rebuilt in that period, and become their persecutor instead of their protector, fulfilling the promises of Israel's day of trouble (Jer. 30:5-7)."[83]

Pentecost states: "This covenant will be made *with many*, that is, with Daniel's people, the nation Israel. 'The ruler who will come' (Dan. 9:26) will be this covenant-maker, for that person is the antecedent of the word *he* in verse 27.

---

[78] McClain, *Daniel's Prophecy of the Seventy Weeks*, 35.

[79] J. B. Payne, "Goal of Daniel's Seventy Weeks," 109.

[80] Regarding certain verses in 2 Thessalonians 2, Constable writes: "These are not necessarily given in strict chronological order." Thomas L. Constable, "2 Thessalonians," in John F. Walvoord and Roy B. Zuck, eds., *Bible Knowledge Commentary: New Testament* (Wheaton, Ill.: Victor, 1983), 718.

[81] McClain, *Daniel's Prophecy of the Seventy Weeks*, 39.

[82] See the following two chapters for a detailed study of Matthew 24.

[83] Walvoord, *Prophecy Knowledge Handbook*, 257.

As a yet-future ruler he will be the final head of the fourth empire (the little horn of the fourth beast, 7:8)."[84]

Many problems plague this interpretation, several of which I deal with above in other connections: (1) The covenant here is not *made*, it is *confirmed*. The usual word for the initial establishment of a covenant is כָּרַתּ (*karat*), "to cut"[85] — here the word is הגביר (*higbar*), "to confirm." This, then, is a confirming of a covenant already extant, i.e., the covenant of God's redemptive grace that Christ confirms (Rom. 15:8).

(2) The word "confirmed" (הגביר, *higbar*) is the emphatic form of גָּבַר (*gabar*). Not only does the root term itself indicate a *confirming* of covenant,[86] but in its present form it is an expression too strong to apply to a covenant made, then broken by the Antichrist.

(3) As I note above, the term is related to the name of the angel of God who delivers the message to Daniel: "Gabriel" means "God is *strong*." The lexical correspondence between the name of God's strong angel (צבריאל, *gabriel*) and the making strong (הגביר, *higbar*) of the covenant suggests the covenant's divine nature. In addition, covenantal passages frequently employ related terms when speaking of the strong God of the covenant.[87]

(4) The parallelism with verse 26 indicates the death of the Messiah directly relates to the confirming of the covenant. He is "cut off" but "not for himself" (v. 26a), for he "confirms the covenant" for the "many" of Israel (v. 27a). His "cutting off" confirms the covenant, for "without shedding of blood there is no remission" (Heb. 9:22). As Christ puts it: "this is My blood of the new covenant, which is shed for many for the remission of sins" (Matt. 26:28).

(5) The indefinite pronoun "he" does not refer back to "the prince who is to come" of verse 26. The word "prince" is a subordinate noun; "the people" is the dominant noun. Thus, the "he" refers to the last dominant individual mentioned: the "Messiah" (v. 26a). The Messiah is the leading figure in the whole prophecy, so that even the destruction of the Temple results from His death. In fact, the people who destroy the Temple are providentially "His armies," according to Christ (Matt. 22:2-7).

(6) It is in the death of Christ that Judaism is legally (covenantally) disestablished, bringing "an end to sacrifice and offering" (Heb. 7:12, 18). The sacri-

---

[84] Pentecost, "Daniel," *Bible Knowledge Commentary*, 1364.

[85] Francis Brown, S. R. Driver, and Charles A. Briggs, eds., *A Hebrew and English Lexicon of the Old Testament* (Rev. ed.: Oxford: Clarendon, 1972), 503.

[86] Ibid., 149.

[87] Gen. 49:24; Deut. 7:21; 10:17; Neh. 1:5; 9:32; Isa. 9:6; Dan. 9:4. See earlier discussion above on pages 23-24 above.

fices are a legal confirmation of the divine covenant with the covenant people Israel: "Gather My saints together to Me, Those who have made a covenant with Me by sacrifice" (Psa. 50:5).[88] An unbreakable connection exists between the death of Christ and the ultimate destruction of the Temple (Luke 20:14-18; 23:28-31) — a connection between legal cause and judicial effect.

Conclusion

A careful study of Daniel's seventy weeks removes from our future the judgmental devastation in its latter verses. Only hermeneutical gymnastics, a suspension of sound reason, and an a priori commitment to the dispensational system allows the importing of a massive gap into Daniel's prophecy. Such ideas interrupt the otherwise chronologically exact time-frame. Yet this gap is necessary if we project Daniel's seventieth week into our future. But as I show above, not only is this difficult to do, but it is wholly unnecessary.

Daniel's famous prophecy finds fulfillment in the first century of our era. Consequently, the pessimistic expectation of many evangelical Christians rooted in this passage is without warrant.

---

[88] Psa. 50:5. Cf.: Exo. 24:8; Lev. 2:13; Num. 18:19; Zech. 9:11. Contra.: Exo. 34:15; 2 Kgs. 17:35; Eze. 44:7.

CHAPTER TWO

WARS AND RUMORS OF WARS
Matthew 24:1-20

And you will hear of wars and rumors of wars. See that you are not troubled; for all these things must come to pass, but the end is not yet. For nation will rise against nation, and kingdom against kingdom. And there will be famines, pestilences, and earthquakes in various places. All these are the beginning of sorrows.

Matthew 24:6-8

Introduction

Matthew 24 is a well-known text that speaks of great prophetic judgments. Who has not heard of "wars and rumours of wars" (v. 6)? "False prophets" (v. 11)? "Enduring to the end" (v. 13)? "The abomination of desolation" (v. 15)? "Great tribulation" (v. 21)? "The powers of the heavens shaken" (v. 29)?

For the most part, futurism controls the popular approach to Matthew 24. Futurists place all the events of Matthew 24:4ff thousands of years off from Jesus's day and into our own approaching future. This is categorically wrong for various reasons that flow readily from the text itself.

The fundamental problem with the futurist dispensational approach to this passage is, once again, its own peculiar theological requirements. Dispensationalists come to this passage with a theological predisposition that hinders contextual exegesis. For instance, while establishing the setting for understanding the disciples's questions in Matthew 24:3, Pentecost comments: "Remember, as mentioned earlier, Jewish eschatology recognized two ages: The first was this present age. . . ; and the second was the age to come. . . . We must note that *Jesus was revealing the prophetic program for Jerusalem, the nation Israel, and the people of Israel.* He made *no* reference to the church or the prophetic program for the church. . . . Because of its Jewish context, therefore, this portion of Scripture *must* be interpreted with reference to Israel and not to the church."[1]

Pentecost is correct in noting that the passage must refer to Israel — that is inescapable. But only a compartmentalization of institutions (Israel/Church) and ages (Church Age/Tribulation) requires a prophetic delay for some Jewish remnant living thousands of years after the ones asking the question. In an important sense Matthew's entire Gospel portrays in great detail the failure of first century Israel. Despite Pentecost, the prevailing drift of Matthew prepares the reader for the Olivet Discourse, which outlines God's holy reflex against the generation that crucifies his Son. Let us consider how this is so.

The Contextual Setting

After giving the account of the birth of Jesus, Matthew's historical record omits the positive Jewish response to his birth found in Luke. He chooses rather to mention the Gentile Magi's coming to Jesus and Israel's governmental resistance to Him (2:1ff). Then his attention turns to John the Baptist and his message of Israel's pending judgment (3:8-12). After Christ's Temptation (4:1-11) the story continues with Jesus's ministry in "Galilee of the *Gentiles*" (4:12-17). A strong undercurrent of antipathy toward Israel flows here.

Matthew's first full record of a discourse by Christ deals with Israel's corruption of the Law (5:17-48), the hypocrisy of Israel's leadership (6:1-18), and the contrast of his religious teaching to that of the Jewish scribes and Pharisees (7:13-29). Then he sets before his reader the healing request by the *Gentile* centurion (8:5-13), to whom Jesus responds: "I have not found such great faith with anyone in Israel" (8:10). In that context he threatens the "sons of the kingdom" (the Jews) with casting out (8:11-12). He registers a warning of great judgment upon Israel (11:20-24) that eventually leads to the religious rulers's assertion that Christ is a minion of Satan (12:24). Skipping ahead, Matthew notes that Christ warns of the "kingdom of God being taken" from Israel and given to the Gentiles (21:33-45).

Ultimately, we read of Christ calling down woes upon Israel's spiritual leaders (23:1ff), noting that they must "fill up then the measure of the guilt" of their fathers (23:32) for "all these things shall come upon this generation" (23:36). Matthew pictures Christ weeping over Jerusalem, warning that her Temple will be left "desolate" (23:37-38).

---

[1] J. Dwight Pentecost, *Thy Kingdom Come* (Wheaton, Ill.: Victory, 1990), 248-249. Emphases his.

Thus, as one purpose in presenting his Gospel, Matthew sketches the dismal spiritual condition of Israel *and provides a revelation of approaching punishment.* These data fit well with an A.D. 70 judgment and seem to anticipate some sort of account of it. Who could deny that Matthew 23, which introduces Matthew 24, relates to a soon coming judgment upon first century Israel? Even Pentecost correctly notes of Matthew 23: "Christ was vividly predicting the coming destruction of Jerusalem by Titus . . . in A.D. 70"[2]

The Near Context

Having traversed through Matthew in large strides we now cautiously enter chapter 24. Regarding Matthew 24 when set in the context of Matthew 23, even Pentecost admits "the discourse is set against the background of the rejection of the Messiah and the imposition of judicial blindness upon that nation."[3] Now the problems begin.

After Jesus leaves the Temple we read that "His disciples came to him for to shew him the buildings of the Temple. And Jesus said unto them, See ye not all these things? Verily I say unto you, There shall not be left here one stone upon another, that shall not be thrown down." Then his disciples ask: "When shall these things be? and what shall be the sign of thy coming, and of the end of the age?" (Matt. 24:1b-3).

At this point Pentecost asserts there is an omission in Matthew's record: "The answer to the first question is not recorded by Matthew, but is given in Luke 21:20-24." He contends that it is in Luke 21:20-24 where we read the "portion of the discourse [that] had to do with the destruction of Jerusalem under Titus in 70 A.D." The next two questions (which are really one) are Matthew's concern, he claims: "The entire passage in Matthew 24 and 25 was written to answer this question concerning the signs of Messiah's coming [i.e., the rapture], which would terminate the age."[4]

As in Daniel 9, this gap theory functions as a *deus ex machina* to save the dispensational system; and it brings confusion into a harmonious context. Despite its surface oddity this is standard dispensational fare: Pentecost repeats this in his more recent book, as do Wiersbe, Walvoord, Barbieri, and others.[5] A few dispensationalists, however, recognize the difficulty of this

---

[2] Ibid.

[3] J. Dwight Pentecost, *Things to Come: A Study in Biblical Eschatology* (Grand Rapids: Zondervan, 1958), 276.

[4] Ibid.

[5] Pentecost, *Thy Kingdom Come*, 249. Warren W. Wiersbe, *Bible Exposition Commentary*, 2 vols. (Wheaton, Ill.: Victor, 1989), 2:86. John F. Walvoord, *Prophecy Knowledge Handbook* (Wheaton, Ill.: Victor, 1990), 381. Louis A. Barbieri, Jr., "Matthew," in John F. Walvoord and Roy B. Zuck, eds., *The Bible Knowledge Commentary: New Testa-*

view and are edging toward a more preterist (past fulfillment) understanding. David L. Turner writes: "The manner in which dispensationalism has traditionally handled this section is thus weak on several fronts. . . . Contemporary dispensationalists should rethink this area of NT exegesis."[6] "It must be concluded that the futurist view, held by traditional dispensationalists, is unconvincing. It does not satisfactorily handle the contextual emphasis on the fall of Jerusalem. . . ."[7] Turner is precisely on target: the problem for the dispensational view is *contextual exegesis*, which its strained theological requirements override.

With all the preparation for Israel's coming judgment in his long record, why would Matthew skip over the leading question of the disciples? Especially since Matthew records their witnessing Christ's weeping over Jerusalem (23:37), hearing him declare the Temple desolate (23:38), and joining together in pointing out the beautiful Temple buildings (24:1). This is especially problematic in that their questions arise from Christ's own statement in 24:2, and since they would need to prepare believers to live through the A.D. 70 holocaust, which literally occurs.[8]

The proposed gap in Matthew's record cannot credibly stand in such a context. Matthew 24 *must* deal with the destruction of the Temple. The proper understanding is, I believe, that *all* of Matthew 24:4-34 refers to A.D. 70.

The Parallel Context

Paralleling Luke 21:20-24 with Matthew 24:15-21 provides reasonably clear evidence against futurism. The two are *not* distinct episodes separated by centuries; they refer to the same era, as even a cursory glance will demonstrate:

Luke 21:20-24:	**Matthew 24:15-20:**
When ye shall see Jerusalem compassed with armies, then know that the desolation thereof is nigh. Then let them which are in Judaea flee to the mountains; and	When ye therefore shall see the abomination of desolation, spoken of by Daniel the prophet, stand in the holy place, (whoso readeth, let him understand)

---

ment (Wheaton, Ill.: Victor, 1983), 76. See also: James F. Rand, "A Survey of the Eschatology of the Olivet Discourse," *Bibliotheca Sacra* 113 (1956): 166. H. Wayne House and Thomas D. Ice, *Dominion Theology: Blessing or Curse?* (Portland, Ore.: Multnomah, 1989), 293.

[6] David L. Turner, "The Structure and Sequence of Matthew 24:1-41: Interaction with Evangelical Treatments," *Grace Theological Journal* 10:1 (Spring, 1989): 7. Turner calls his position a "preterist-futurist" view, 26.

[7] Ibid., 10.

[8] Josephus, *Wars of the Jews* 7:1:1, 7.

let them which are in the midst of it depart out; and let not them that are in the countries enter thereunto. For these be the days of vengeance, that all things which are written may be fulfilled. But woe unto them that are with child, and to them that give suck, in those days, for there shall be great distress in the land, and wrath upon this people. And they shall fall by the edge of the sword, and shall be led away captive into all nations: and Jerusalem shall be trodden down of the Gentiles, until the times of the Gentiles be fulfilled.

Then let them which be in Judaea flee into the mountains: Let him which is on the housetop not come down to take any thing out of his house: Neither let him which is in the field return back to take his clothes. And woe unto them that are with child, and to them that give suck in those days! But pray ye that your flight be not in the winter, neither on the sabbath day.

Besides, we must ask of the dispensationalist: Where is the *contextual cue* in the Lucan passage that distinguishes the events of A.D. 70 (21:20-24) from those of the future rapture era (21:25ff)? Arbitrary assertion will not suffice. As we shall see, the prophecies easily fit the A.D. 70 era, according to careful contextual exegesis.

The Interpretive Key

More significant even than Matthew's contextual flow is the Lord's statement in Matthew 24:34: "Verily I say unto you, This generation shall not pass, till all these things be fulfilled." Here we have an authoritative, clear, and compelling pronouncement of the *time* of the events recorded in 24:4-31.

The matter before us is "solemnly introduced and emphatically affirmed" by Christ.[9] We should note first, that Christ is dogmatic when he begins a statement with ἀμήν (*amen*, "verily"). Hendriksen notes of the word: "In every case . . . in which this word occurs in the New Testament it introduces a statement which not only expresses a truth or fact . . . but an *important*, a *solemn* fact, one that in many cases is at variance with popular opinion or expectation or at least causes some surprise."[10] Thus, Christ emphatically draws the disciples's attention to what he is about to say — just as he does in 24:2, where he makes the statement about the destruction of the Temple that leads to the whole discourse.

Second, Christ further underscores his dogmatism. He does not simply tell them; he emphatically introduces what he is about to say with the declara-

---

[9] William Lane, *The Gospel of Mark* (NICNT) (Grand Rapids: Eerdmans, 1974), 479.

[10] William Hendriksen, *Matthew* (NTC) (Grand Rapids: Baker, 1973), 289-290.

tive "I tell you." The Lord does not leave the temporal expectation as a casual remark, hoping they will catch it. He alerts them to what he is about to say.

Third, the literal rendering of the Greek reads: "Truly I tell you that *by no means* passes away generation this until all these things happen."[11] The "by no means" is a strong, double negative (οὐ μή, *ou me*); *and* it is put early in his statement for added emphasis. He is staking his credibility, as it were, on the absolute certainty of this prophetic pronouncement.[12]

But what does he so dogmatically and carefully declare? Whatever the difficult apocalyptic imagery in some of the preceding verses (e.g., vv. 29-31) may indicate (we will get to that later), Jesus clearly asserts that "*all* these things" will occur *before* "this generation" passes away.

Suggested Interpretations

Basically there are three leading interpretations of the verse before us. Let us consider them carefully.

"This Generation" is "This Race"

What is the time frame so dogmatically set before us by our Lord? What does He mean by "this generation" (γενεά αὕτη, *genea haute*)? Here beats the heart of the futurist/preterist debate. To read Pentecost's latest book, however, the unsuspecting reader would never know there was an issue here demanding resolution. Pentecost just *assumes* his position.[13]

According to an earlier publication of Pentecost "the word generation is to be taken in its basic usage of 'race, kindred, family, stock, breed,' so that the Lord is here promising that the nation Israel shall be preserved until the consummation of her program at the second advent. . . . This seems to be the best explanation."[14]

This interpretation is without basis for a variety of reasons. (1) Such a view ends up as a mere truism if "this generation" simply means "Israel as a nation."[15] For then Christ simply says Israel will not pass away until all these

---

[11] Alfred Marshall, *The Interlinear Greek-English New Testament* (Grand Rapids: Zondervan, 1959), 108

[12] He contrasts the durability and integrity of his prophetic word here with that of the material universe (24:35).

[13] Pentecost, *Thy Kingdom Come*, 255-256.

[14] Pentecost, *Things to Come*, 281 (earlier printing; not later). Cp. L. S. Chafer, *Systematic Theology*, 7 vols., (Dallas, Tex.: Dallas Theological Seminary, 1948), 4:316. C. I. Scofield, *Scofield Reference Bible* (New York: Oxford, 1945), 1034. E. Schuyler English, *Studies in the Gospel According to Matthew* (New York, Revell, 1935), 179. William Kelly, *Lectures on the Gospel of Matthew* (New York: Loizeaux, 1911), 451-453.

[15] H. N. Ridderbos, *Commentary on Matthew* (Grand Rapids: Zondervan, 1987), 450.

things happen to Israel. Besides, in the dispensational view Israel will never pass away anyway, so the statement would be meaningless on its own interpretive presuppositions.

(2) Though the Greek γενέα (*genea*, "generation") is common in Matthew, *he never* employs it in the sense dispensationalists call for here. We find it in Matthew 1:17; 11:16; 12:39-45; 16:4; 17:17; and 23:36. Only with great difficulty may the interpreter contort any of these references to mean "Israel as a nation."

(3) Five other instances in Matthew couple the word γενέα (*genea*) with the near demonstrative αὕτη (*haute*) to read "this generation." In each of these it clearly refers to the generation *then living*. These passages are Matthew 11:16; 12:41, 42, 45; and 23:36. In Scripture the idea of a "generation" of people involves roughly twenty-five to forty years.[16]

"This Generation" is "That Generation"

In more recent writings Pentecost forsakes his earlier view. He now holds the following position: "Since these signs will all occur in the seven years of Daniel's seventieth week, the generation that sees the beginning of these signs will "not pass away until all these things happened" (v. 34), for they all will fall within a brief span of time. Notice that these will *not* be signs given to a generation preceding the Rapture. Instead, these signs will be given to a generation that cannot begin until after the church has been translated."[17]

Fellow dispensationalist John F. Walvoord concurs: "The most natural meaning, however, is to take it as normally used as a reference to a period of twenty-five to forty years. But instead of referring this to the time in which Christ lived, it refers back to the preceding period that is described as the Great Tribulation. As the Great Tribulation is only three-and-a-half years long, obviously, those who see the Great Tribulation will also see the coming of the Lord."[18] Walvoord also refuses to consider the most obvious and legitimate interpretation: that it refers to the generation that actually hears Jesus say this and who witness the destruction of the Temple.

Pentecost's new view involves him in question-begging circularity. He considers it obvious that "these signs will be given to a generation that cannot begin until after the church has been translated." Where is the "translation of the church" (i.e., the rapture) in this passage? He must *assume* his dispensa-

---

[16] A. T. Robertson, *Word Pictures in the New Testament*, 6 vols., (Nashville: Broadman, 1930), 1:194. See: Num. 32:13; Psa. 95:10.

[17] Pentecost, *Thy Kingdom Come*, 256. See also: Wiersbe, *The Bible Exposition Commentary*, 1:89. House and Ice, *Dominion Theology*, 286-287

[18] Walvoord, *Prophecy Knowledge Handbook*, 391 ff.

tional system in order to reinterpret the passage to uphold the system. In fact, Walvoord notes of Matthew 24: "An important notation should be made at this point that the Rapture of the church and the close of the Church Age is [*sic*] nowhere mentioned in this prophecy."[19]

And what of Walvoord's statement that "this generation" actually "refers back to the preceding period that is described as the Great Tribulation"? This also assumes the Great Tribulation does not occur in the first century — simply because of dispensational requirements. I agree that "this generation" refers to "the preceding period that is described as the Great Tribulation." But then I believe Jesus is clearly speaking to his disciples almost 2000 years ago, when he expressly declares its fulfillment in "this generation." The Great Tribulation is tied in with the subject of his discourse: the destruction of the Temple (24:2).

"This Generation" is "This Generation"

Actually a simple reading of 24:34 leaves the inescapable impression that these things are to occur in the generation of the original disciples. Contextual exegesis helps us resolve the "problem" of the meaning of Matthew 24:34. The phrase "this generation" appears in the very context intimately related to and ultimately introducing Matthew 24 (cp. 23:36-38 with 24:1-2).

In Matthew 23:36 "this generation" unquestionably speaks of Jesus's contemporaries, as even most dispensationalists admit.[20] Here Jesus is condemning his adversaries, the scribes and Pharisees (23:2, 13, 14, 14, 16, 23, 25, 26, 27, 29). He specifically observes that his opponents will "fill up the measure of the guilt" of their predecessors (23:32). They will do this by persecuting his followers (23:34), so that "upon you [scribes and Pharisees] may fall the guilt of all the righteous blood shed" (23:35). He concludes: "Verily I say unto you, All these things shall come upon this generation." This employs some of the identical terms as Matthew 24:34, even functioning as its semantic equivalent:

Matthew 23:36
ἀμὴν λέγω ὑμῖν, ἥξει ταῦτα πάντα ἐπὶ τὴν γενεὰν ταύτην
(*amen lego humin, hexei tauta panta epi ten genean tauten*)

---

[19] Walvoord, *Prophecy Knowledge Handbook*, 381.

[20] Barbieri, "Matthew," 75. John F. Walvoord, *The Nations, Israel, and the Church in Prophecy*, 3 vols. in 1 (Grand Rapids: Zondervan, 1988), 2:106. Edward E. Hindson, "Matthew" in Edward E. Hindson and Woodrow Michael Kroll, *Liberty Commentary on the New Testament* (Lynchburg, Vir.: Liberty Commentary, 1978), 77. Pentecost, *Thy Kingdom Come*, 249.

Matthew 24:34

ἀμὴν λέγω ὑμῖν ὅτι οὐ μὴ παρέλθῃ ἡ γενεὰ αὕτη ἕως ἂν πάντα ταῦτα γένηται (*amen lego humin hoti ou me parelthe he genea aute heos an panta tauta genetai*)

As I indicate above, I agree with Walvoord that those who see the beginning of the prophetic signs will see the Great Tribulation (23:33). But Christ expressly tells *who* will see those signs: "this generation" (24:34), i.e., the people to whom he is speaking.

We must notice that preceding the destruction of the Temple are certain signs — signs Jesus urges them not to confuse (24:4ff). The first few he mentions are pre-indicators of the looming judgment (24:8). This point is quite significant because later he turns to consider his distant Second Advent (24:36ff). At that juncture he specifically says of "that"[21] remote event there will be no such signs (24:36-44). This seems evidence enough to divide the passage into separate eras at that point — *but not before.*

Because of such observations, D. A. Carson speaks of the "highly artificial" attempts by dispensationalists to reinterpret the word. He argues that it is obvious the word "can only with the greatest difficulty be made to mean anything other than the generation living when Jesus spoke."[22] Dispensationalist David Turner agrees.[23]

Jesus expressly teaches that the prophetic events of verses 4-31 — "all these things" (24:34) — will occur in "this generation." And just forty years later the Jewish War with Rome brings the total and final destruction of the Temple (24:2). I agree with John Gill: "This is a full and clear proof, that not any thing that is said before [v. 34], relates to the second coming of Christ, the day of judgment, and the end of the world; but that all belong to the coming of the son of man, in the destruction of Jerusalem, and to the end of the Jewish state."[24]

Signs of the Times

Our study to this point shows that Christ expects the events of Matthew 24:4-31 to occur *in the first century.* Let us now engage the passage verse-by-

---

[21] A far demonstrative, in contrast to the near demonstrative "this" in v. 34. See discussion below.

[22] D. A. Carson, "Matthew" in *The Expositor's Bible Commentary* (Grand Rapids: Zondervan, 1984), 8:507.

[23] Turner, "The Structure and Sequence of Matthew 24:1-41," *GTJ*, 7.

[24] John Gill, *An Exposition of the New Testament*, 9 vols., (Streamwood, Ill.: Primitive Baptist Library, rep. 1976), 7:296.

verse. Commentators obscure the clear evidences from contextual flow and express time indicators due to a few interpretively difficult statements in these verses. I believe these are best understood according to context, rather than theological predispositions.

Before I begin the commentary, I will introduce the ancient writer Flavius Josephus to the reader. His historical works are extremely helpful for my interpretation of the passage.

Introducing Josephus

Flavius Josephus is a non-Christian, Palestinian Jew, who is a historian of priestly descent. He lives from A.D. 37 to 101, overlapping virtually the entire apostolic era. When the Jewish War against Rome breaks out in earnest in A.D. 67,[25] he initially serves as a general in the Jewish forces. During the War he suffers defeat by the Romans at Jotapata, surrendering to the Roman general Flavius Vespasian. He befriends Vespasian by interpreting a prophetic oracle to mean that Vespasian would one day be emperor of Rome.[26] He then works with Vespasian attempting to get the Jews to surrender, ceasing their hopeless cause.

After becoming emperor of Rome in A.D. 69, Vespasian sponsors Josephus's writing of his famous book *The Wars of the Jews*. Josephus produces this work about A.D. 75, just five years after the fall of Jerusalem. He changes his name from the very Jewish Joseph Ben Matthias to a more Roman Flavius Josephus, taking on his benefactor's name.

In this work Josephus writes as an eyewitness historian who happens to be in the action on both sides of the conflict. His work is extremely valuable, providing indispensable insights into the events of the War.

Now to the task at hand.

Theological Blinders

Generally, liberal commentators, such as W. G. Kümmel and J. Schniewind, take Jesus's express declaration that the events would occur in his "generation" (Matt. 24:34) at face value. But then they hold that Jesus makes a mistake in prophesying the nearness of these events. This is consistent with humanistic rationalism, as noted in the Foreword to *Perilous Times* by R. C. Sproul.

On the other hand, dispensationalists are prone to reinterpret the plain words of 24:34 *under the pressure of their theological system.* House and Ice write: "Since the phrase 'all these things' governs the timing of 'this generation'... ,

---

[25] See my *Before Jerusalem Fell: Dating the Book of Revelation* (2d ed.: Bethesda, Mary.: Christian Universities Press, 1997), ch. 14.

[26] Suetonius, *Vespasian* 6.

one has to determine what 'all these things' are and when they will be fulfilled. Then we will know whether 'this generation' referred to those in Christ's day or to a future generation."[27]

This is incredible. By every objective measure the unambiguous statement "this generation" should govern the timing of the phrase "all these things," rather than the other way around. But according to dispensationalists, *something other than* the clear statement of Matthew 24:34, which Christ gives for the express purpose of providing chronological information, must inform us when the time will be.

In fact, according to House, Ice, Walvoord, Pentecost and others, Matthew 24:15 — which speaks of "the abomination of desolation" and which says *nothing* about timing — is determinative of the meaning of 24:34. But the meaning of this ambiguous and controversial apocalyptic phrase in 24:15 is predetermined by the dispensational system.[28] In the dispensational system "'the abomination of desolation' could not have been fulfilled in A.D. 70."[29]

The careful interpreter steadfastly resists such a conclusion. He responds that the question of the interpretation and fulfillment of the difficult "abomination of desolation" must be determined by sound exegesis performed in the light of the clear statement of 24:34. So let us see how the prophecies occur in Jesus's generation.

"Take Heed That No Man Deceive You"

Jesus begins his answer with a warning to his disciples: "Take heed that no man deceive you. For many shall come in my name, saying, I am Christ; and

---

[27] House and Ice, *Dominion Theology*, 286.

[28] Strangely, House and Ice state of this alleged future event, that it "will occur three and a half years before the second coming of Christ" (*ibid.*, 288). This is strange because two verses later in 24:36 Jesus conclusively says, "No man knows the day nor the hour" of His Second Coming. A predestined three and a half year period, however, would precisely quantify the amount of time that would elapse between that of the abomination of desolation and the moment of the Second Coming. Unless they import one of their famous gaps, that is, such as the gap that can make a prophetic time frame of 490 years (from Dan. 9:24-27) stretch out for over 2000 years. Even more strangely, House and Ice favorably cite Nathaniel West's deriding interpreters who have "numbers that don't count" (*ibid.*, 325). This is despite Daniel's 490 years not counting properly, though Daniel's prophecy is used by House and Ice as an illustration of "literal" prophecy of great "precision" (*ibid.*, 321).

[29] Ibid., 287. For a detailed debate over the great tribulation, see Thomas Ice and Kenneth L. Gentry, Jr., *The Great Tribulation: Past or Future?* (Grand Rapids: Kregel, 1999).

shall deceive many" (Matt. 24:4-5). Many dispensationalists make these verses refer to the first half of a future tribulation week (e.g., Pentecost, Barbieri, English, and Wiersbe). This is the view I will be countering, though Pentecost outlines *four* distinct dispensational views on the passage.[30]

The word "mislead"[31] (πλανάω, *planao*) indicates Christ's concern that some false Messiah might seduce his disciples. In the first century era the Jews fervently anticipate a conquering Messiah.[32] Jesus warns his disciples not to be caught up in such a Zionistic frenzy.

There are many examples of great pretenders who almost certainly make Messianic claims. In Acts 5:36 we read: "Some time ago Theudas rose up, claiming to be somebody. A number of men, about four hundred, joined him. He was slain, and all who obeyed him were scattered and came to nothing." In Acts 8:9, 10 Simon may be an example of such, for he "bewitched the people of Samaria, giving out that himself was some great one: To whom they all gave heed, from the least to the greatest, saying, This man is the great power of God."

John mentions such false Christs in his first epistle, where he calls them "antichrists." "Little children, it is the last hour; and as you have heard that the Antichrist is coming, even now many antichrists have come, by which we know that it is the last hour" (1 John 2:18). As Robertson notes of 1 John 2:18: "So Jesus taught (Mark 13:6, 22; Matt. 24:5, 15, 24) and so Paul taught (Acts 20:30; 2 Thess. 2:3). These false Christs . . . are necessarily antichrists, for there can be only one. *Anti* can mean substitution or opposition, but both ideas are identical in the word *antichristos*."[33] These are the many (πολλοί, *polloi*) false Christs mentioned in Matthew 24:5, which indicate "it is the last hour" (1 John 2:18).

Justin Martyr speaks of Simon, and others: "after Christ's ascension into heaven the devils put forward certain men who said that they themselves were

---

[30] Pentecost, *Things to Come*, 278.

[31] The Greek word is πλανάω (*planao*), from whence we derive "planet," i.e. "wanderer." That is, planets appear to be stars that have no set place in the sky, because of their movement relative to the backdrop of true stars.

[32] Matt. 2:1-18; Luke 24:21; John 1:20, 41; 4:29; 6:15; 7:27, 31; 11:47-48; 12:34. See also the Jewish apocalyptic literature surrounding the New Testament era: The Psalms of Solomon; 4 Ezra; Apocalypse of Baruch; the Dead Sea Scrolls (1QSb 5:20; 4Q Patriarchal Blessings). Cf. Josephus, *Antiquities* 20:5:1; 20:8:5-6; *Wars* 2:13:5; 2:17:8-10; 6:5:2.

[33] Robertson, *Word Pictures in the New Testament*, 6:215. Dispensationalists agree: Paul N. Benware, *Understanding End Times Prophecy: A Comprehensive Approach* (Chicago: Moody, 1995), 249.

gods."[34] Hippolytus records that "there arose some, saying I am Christ, as Simon Magus, and the rest whose names I have not time to reckon up."[35] Another whose name is associated with Simon Magus in church tradition is Dositheus, who even claims to be the Messiah of Deuteronomy 18:18.[36]

Interestingly, such characters play an important role in the religious and cultural foment that leads to the A.D. 67-70 Jewish War with Rome. Schaff comments that Israel of that era "rose to the most insolent political and religious fanaticism, and was continually inflamed by false prophets and Messiahs, one of whom, for example, according to Josephus, drew after him thirty thousand men."[37]

Josephus mentions the "deceivers and imposters, under the pretense of divine inspiration fostering revolutionary changes" in the A.D. 50s. He also speaks of "the Egyptian false prophet" who even operates at the Mount of Olives (*Wars* 2:13:5; cp. Acts 21:38). Poetic justice allows those who reject the true Christ to be frequently and devastatingly duped by false Christs.

Wars and Rumors of Wars

The familiar sign that serves as the title to this chapter is found in Matthew 24:6-7: "And you will hear of wars and rumors of wars. See that you are not troubled; for all these things must come to pass, but the end is not yet. For nation will rise against nation, and kingdom against kingdom. And there will be famines, pestilences, and earthquakes in various places."

Dispensationalist Wiersbe comments: "Note that wars are not a sign of the end. There have always been wars in the world, and will be until the very end. Wars of themselves do not announce the end of the age nor the coming of the Lord."[38] It is true, of course, that "wars of themselves" do not announce the end. But because of dispensationalism's large investment in futurism, contextual exegesis, allowing wars to be some sort of sign is wholly lost.

The preterist approach to this passage, however, is quite relevant to the situation of Jesus's hearers, his disciples (24:2,3) of "this generation" (24:34). Not only so, but it exposes the error of Walvoord when he states of Matthew 24: "Postmillenarians have a different problem in that they want to support their view that the world is going to get better and better as the Gospel gradu-

---

[34] Martyr, *First Apology* 26.

[35] *The Consummation of the World.*

[36] Origen, *Against Celsus* 6:11. We are not certain when he actually lives, though. *Clementine Recognitions* 2:8 speaks of him as first a disciple, then afterwards the teacher of Simon Magus. He may, however, have been an early second century figure.

[37] Philip Schaff, *A History of the Christian Church*, 3 vols., (3rd. ed.: Grand Rapids: Eerdmans, 1910), 1:394.

[38] Wiersbe, *Bible Exposition Commentary*, 2:87.

ally triumphs; but this passage of Scripture does not support this and, in fact, predicts increasing evil with the climax at the Second Coming."[39] He says this despite admitting in the preceding sentence that there are some evangelicals who "attempt to relate most of the prophecies to the time when Jerusalem was destroyed." In that case the prophecies pose absolutely zero problem for postmillennialists.

As usual, a little familiarity with the cultural and political situation existing in that era is most helpful. "Wars and rumors of wars" do serve as *sign*-ificant harbingers of the end of the Temple (which is the major issue being discussed, Matt. 23:38-24:3). This is because of the dramatically successful *Pax Romana*, the "peace of Rome."

The *Pax Romana* begins with Augustus's establishment of the "Age of Peace" in 17 B.C. The prominent church father Origen (A.D. 185-254) speaks of the "abundance of peace that began at the birth of Christ."[40] It is, indeed, a time of an "abundance of peace" that gives stability to the Mediterranean basin and, by the providence of God, allows for the rapid dissemination of the Christian faith.

Interestingly, scholars observe that "in the Roman Empire proper, this period of peace remained comparatively undisturbed *until the time of Nero*."[41] And Nero engages the Jewish War that results in the destruction of the Temple stone by stone. This is also the time of the Roman Civil Wars, including the infamous "Year of Four Emperors" (A.D. 68-69). In fact, the turmoil of this period is so severe that it almost leads to the collapse of the Roman Empire.[42] Consequently, as the events begin unfolding up to the Jewish War, the Christians remember Christ's prophecy of the coming devastation of Jerusalem, which will be the Great Tribulation (as we shall see). Thus, the "wars and rumors of wars" are truly signs for that "generation." The outbreak of wars in such an era would serve as impressive signs in an era of such remarkable peace.

The engagement of the Jewish War (A.D. 67-70) with the Roman Imperial army includes contributions of troops and horsemen from Rome's client kings

---

[39] Walvoord, *Prophecy Knowledge Handbook*, 381.

[40] Origen, *Romans* 1:3.

[41] Bo Reicke, *The New Testament Era: The World of the Bible from 500 B.C. to A.D. 100* (Philadelphia: Fortress, 1968), 110.

[42] Josephus notes of the Roman Civil Wars of this era: "I have omitted to give an exact account of them, because they are well known by all, and they are described by a great number of Greek and Roman authors" (*Wars* 4:9:2). For more information see my *Before Jerusalem Fell*, 311-314.

and allies.[43] Significantly, Josephus entitles his most famous work of the era "The Wars of the Jews." During the Roman Civil Wars (A.D. 68-69) several nations revolt in an attempt to leave the Empire.[44] It literally is a time of "nation against nation."

Thus, Jesus's day is a time of great peace, known as the *Pax Romana.* He warns that wars and rumors of wars will disrupt it. The disruptions occur in Nero Caesar's latter days and lead to the destruction of Jerusalem and the Temple.

Famines and Pestilences

Christ continues his discourse, warning of famines and pestilences: "there will be famines, pestilences, and earthquakes in various places" (Matt. 24:7b). We may easily apply this also to the first century scene.

Acts 11:28 mentions a devastating, empire-wide famine in the days preceding Nero's reign: "There stood up one of them named Agabus,[45] and signified by the Spirit that there should be great famine throughout all the world: which came to pass in the days of Claudius Caesar." This is probably the famine Josephus mentions as striking Jerusalem: "A famine did oppress them at that time, and many people died for want of what was necessary to procure food withal" (*Ant.* 20:2:5).

There is also the well-known famine that rages in Jerusalem during the Roman siege. In that dearth men cut open the bellies of neighbors, and mothers even eat their own children (*Wars* 5:10:2-5), which is a sign of covenant curse (Deut. 28:55-57; Lam. 2:20). Thus, these prophecies are particularly relevant to the disciples (24:2-3) who will be headquartered in Jerusalem (Acts 8:1; 11:1-2).

Classical writers testify to the widespread, recurring famines of the era of the A.D. 50s through the 60s, as we discover in the works of Suetonius, Dio Cassius, Eusebius, and Orosius.[46] For instance, of A.D. 51 Tacitus (*ca.* A.D. 55-117) writes: "This year witnessed many prodigies . . . . Further portents were seen in a shortage of corn, resulting in famine. . . . It was established that there was no more than fifteen days' supply of food in the city [Rome]"

---

[43] Josephus mentions soldiers from Caesarea, Syria, Arabia, and other cities and nations. Josephus, *Wars* 3:1:3; 3:4:4.

[44] Tacitus, *Histories* 1:2-3. He mentions the Gallic provinces, Britain, Sarmatae, and Suebi.

[45] For a discussion of the important office of prophet and the inspired nature of Agabus, see my: *The Charismatic Gift of Prophecy: A Reformed Response to Wayne Grudem* (2d, ed.: Eugene, OR: Wipf and Stock, 1999).

[46] See: Suetonius, *Life of Claudius* 18:2; Dio Cassius, *History* 60:11; Eusebius, *Chronicle*, Year of Abraham 2065; Orosius, *History* 7:6:17.

(*Annals* 12:43).

Pestilence, of course, follows especially fast in famine's train; and Jerusalem's pestilential woes during its siege are well-known.[47] According to Suetonius (*ca.* A.D. 70-160) a most severe pestilence occurred in that era in Rome, as well: "In a single autumn 30,000 deaths from plague were registered at the Temple of Libitina" (*Nero* 39). Tacitus writes: "At Rome, a plague devastated the entire population . . . . The houses were full of corpses, and the streets of funerals" (*Annals* 16:13).

Earthquakes

The Lord also mentions earthquakes along with the famines and pestilence in Matthew 24:7b: "And there will be famines, pestilences, and earthquakes in various places."

A particularly dreadful quake shakes Jerusalem in A.D. 67. Josephus records this frightful catastrophe: "There broke out a prodigious storm in the night, with the utmost violence, and very strong winds, with the largest showers of rain, and continual lightnings, terrible thunderings, and amazing concussions and bellowings of the earth, that was in an earthquake" (*Wars* 4:4:5).

Tacitus mentions earthquakes in Crete, Rome, Apamea, Phrygia, Campania, Laodicea (of Revelation fame) and Pompeii during the time just before Jerusalem's destruction.[48] Severe earthquakes plague the reigns of the Emperors Caligula (A.D. 37-41) and Claudius (A.D. 41-54).[49] According to Seneca (*ca.* 4 B.C.—A.D. 65), others occur in Asia, Achaia, Syria, and Macedonia.[50] Of this era, Ellicott's commentary observes: "Perhaps no period in the world's history has ever been so marked by these convulsions as that which intervenes between the Crucifixion and the destruction of Jerusalem."[51]

The Beginning of Sorrows

As these portents appear on the historical scene, the disciples must be aware that these are but "the beginning of sorrows." The word "sorrows"

---

[47] See Josephus's *Wars of the Jews.*

[48] See Roman historians: Tacitus, *Annals* 2:47; 12:58 14:27; 15:22; Pliny, *Natural History* 2:86; and Suetonius, *Nero* 48; *Galba* 18. See also: Philostratus, *Life of Apollion* 4:11 and Orosius 7:7.

[49] W. J. Coneybeare and J. S. Howson, *The Life and Epistles of St. Paul,* 2 vols., (New York: Charles Scribner's, 1894), 1:126. Caligula's emperorship is dated A.D. 37-41; Claudius's, A.D. 41-54.

[50] Seneca, *Epistles* 91.

[51] Charles John Ellicott, ed., *Ellicott's Commentary on the Whole Bible,* 8 vols., (Grand Rapids: Zondervan, n.d.), 6:146.

here is ὀδίνων, *(odinon)*, a term that speaks of birth pangs.[52] This is quite suggestive. The rabbis frequently use this word as a technical Messianic term in the phrase "birth pangs of the Messiah."[53] The rabbinic phrase refers to the distress that will precede the Messianic era. Yet, though birth pangs are grievous, they presage joy in the morning.

Jesus employs the term "birth pangs," then, to point to a new *beginning* even as the Temple era approaches a dismal end. For the disciples these troubles are the birth pangs of the kingdom. *Because of these birth pangs, the future is bright with hope, even if initially sore with the pain of labor.* As Jerusalem goes up in smoke, Christ's kingdom enters into its own life, separating from its "mother" (Israel).

As he tells them earlier: "Verily I say unto you that there be some of them that stand here, which shall not taste of death, till they have seen the kingdom of God come with power" (Mark 9:1). This event lay sufficiently far off in the future that some hearing him would die before it becomes evident "with power." Yet it was close enough that others would live to witness it. This cannot be a reference to the Transfiguration which occurs only six days later (Mark 9:2). How many of them will die before that event? It must be the A.D. 70 destruction of the Temple, occurring forty years later.

The salvation Christ secures will make victorious headway in the world, expanding the spiritual principle of the New Creation (2 Cor. 5:17; Eph. 2:10; 6:17). As the old Jerusalem and Temple era end, the New Jerusalem and new Temple begin in earnest (Gal. 4:23-31; Rev. 21:1-2; cp. Rev. 22:6, 10)[54]. The Epistle to the Hebrews clearly speaks of the approaching demise of the priestly old covenant order and the firm establishment of the new in its place (Heb. 8:13; 12:18-28).

In fact, the New Testament looks with holy anticipation to the final change from the old order to the new order, as the Temple system approaches its dramatic disestablishment in A.D. 70. A major redemptive transformation takes place in the apostolic era between A.D. 30 and A.D. 70. This transition leads to "the restoration of all things" (Matt. 17:11), "the regeneration" (Matt. 19:28), the "times of refreshing" (Acts 3:19), the "times of the restitution of all things" (Acts 3:21), the "time of reformation" (Heb. 9:10), a "new heavens and a new earth" (Rev. 21:1; cp. Isa. 65:17-20; 2 Cor. 5:17; Gal. 6:17), "all things new" (Rev. 21:5; cp. 2 Cor. 5:17; Gal. 6:15). Thus, the era that Christ

---

[52] See: Gal. 4:19, 27; Rev. 12:2. Compare the Septuagint at Isa. 66:7; Mic. 4:10.

[53] See: b *Ketuboth* 111a; b *Shabbath* 118a; b *Sanhedrin* 98b; Targum on Psa. 18:4; Targum on 2 Sam. 22:5

[54] See my: "The Preterist View," in C. Marvin Pate, ed., *Four Views on the Book of Revelation* (Grand Rapids: Zondervan, 1998).

legally inaugurates, the Temple's destruction temporally evidences. Since Christ's coming, the era in which we live is the "last days" (Acts 2:17; 1 Cor. 10:11; Heb. 1:2; 9:26; 1 Pet. 1:20; 1 John 2:18). The last days begin in earnest in the transitional era between Christ's death and the Temple's destruction; they stretch from the first coming to his second coming. There are no other days to follow, no 365,000 days (i.e., 1000 years) of Christ's reign upon the earth will succeed these "last days." The former days — old covenant Israel's times — have expired. These are now the *last* days.

Persecution, Apostasy, and False Prophecy

In verse 9 the Lord warns his disciples that they must expect *persecution*: "Then they will deliver you up to tribulation and kill you, and you will be hated by all nations for My name's sake." We may easily show the fulfillment of this prophecy by Jewish opposition to the gospel in Acts.[55] This continues and expands Matthew 23:34-36, and clearly applies to the first century. After the initial *Jewish* persecution of Christians comes the first Roman onslaught just preceding the Temple's destruction (A.D. 64-68).[56] The pagan Roman historian Tacitus speaks of Christians in the era of Nero as universally "hated for their crimes."[57]

In verses 10 and 12 we discover a consequence of the persecution: "And then many will be offended, will betray one another, and will hate one another. . . . And because lawlessness [ἀνομία, *anomia*] will abound, the love of many will grow cold." We may document this, too, in the apostolic era. Paul laments "that all those in Asia have turned away from me" (2 Tim. 1:15) and "Demas has forsaken me, having loved this present world" (2 Tim. 4:10). He comments that "at my first defense no one stood with me, but all forsook me" (2 Tim. 4:16; cp. Gal. 3:1-4; 2 Thess. 3:1).

"Lawlessness" (ἀνομία, *anomia*) well describes Jewish conditions around the era of the destruction of the Temple. Josephus says that the Jewish Zealots act "as though they had covenanted to annul the laws of nature along with those of their country" and that "every human ordinance was trampled under foot" (*Wars* 4:6:3). He notes that "in the first place, all the people of every place betook themselves to rapine; after which they got together in bodies, in

---

[55] See for example: Acts 4:3; 5:18-33; 6:12; 7:54-60; 8:1ff; 9:1-4, 13, 23; 11:19; 12:1-3; 13:45-50; 14:2-5, 19; 16:23; 17:5-13; 18:12; 20:3, 19; 21:11, 27; 22:30; 23:12, 20, 27, 30; 24:5-9; 25:2-15; 25:24; 26:21. See also: 2 Cor. 11:24; 2 Thess. 2:14-15; Heb. 10:32-34; Rev. 2:9; 3:9.

[56] The Neronic persecution is the first and most grievous Roman persecution. It stretches from around November, A.D. 64 to the death of Nero, June 8, A.D. 68. See discussion in chapter 5 below.

[57] Tacitus, *Annals* 15:44.

order to rob the people of the country, insomuch that for the barbarity and iniquity [παρανομια, *paranomia*, from *para* + *anomia*] those of the same nation did no way differ from the Romans; nay, it seemed to be a much lighter thing to be ruined by the Romans than by themselves" (*Wars* 4:3:2).

Josephus again writes: "It is therefore impossible to go distinctly over every instance of these men's iniquity [παρανομία, *paranomia*]. I shall therefore speak my mind here at once briefly: — That neither did any other city ever suffer such miseries, nor did any age ever breed a generation more fruitful in wickedness that this was, from the beginning of the world" (*Wars* 5:10:5).

Elsewhere he continues: "The Idumeans also strove with these men who should be guilty of the greatest madness! for they [all], vile wretches as they were, cut the throats of the high priests, that so no part of a religious regard to God might be preserved; they thence proceeded to destroy utterly the least remains of a political government, and introduced the most complete scene of iniquity [ἀνομία, *anomia*] in all instances that were practicable; under which scene that sort of people that were called Zealots grew up, and who indeed corresponded to the name, for they imitated every wicked work; nor, if their memory suggested any evil thing that had formerly been done, did they avoid zealously to pursue the same; and although they gave themselves that name from their zeal for what was good, yet did it agree to them only by way of irony, on account of those they had unjustly treated by their wild and brutish disposition, or as thinking the greatest mischiefs to be the greatest good" (*Wars* 7:8:1).

John writes of apostasy in the first century: "They *went out from us*, but they were not of us; for if they had been of us, they would have continued with us; but they went out that they might be made manifest, that none of them were of us" (1 John 2:19; cp. 2 and 3 John). The Epistle to the Hebrews indicates a sizeable apostasy from among Jewish converts to Christianity (cf. Heb. 2:1-4; 6:1-6; 10:26-31). Tacitus even alludes to apostasy during the Neronic persecution: "First, Nero had self-acknowledged Christians arrested. Then, *on their information,* large numbers of others were condemned."[58]

False prophets are also a problem during that era, as well as false Christs (cp. Matt. 24:5). "Now when they had gone through the island to Paphos, they found a certain sorcerer, a false prophet, a Jew whose name was Bar-Jesus" (Acts 13:6). Peter, Paul, and John all warn about this danger.[59] Even Josephus records false prophets arising among the Jews (*Wars* 6:5:2-3). In fact, the false prophets in Jerusalem help aggravate the destruction of the city by buoying up the hopes of the zealots. Because of this, Jesus urges his disciples to

---

[58] Tacitus, *Annals* 15.

[59] See also: Acts 20:29; Rom. 16:17,18; 2 Cor. 11:13, 26; 1 Tim. 4:1; 2 Pet. 2:1; 1 John 4:1. Cp. Gal. 2:4; 2 Pet. 2:1.

endure these troublesome times (Matt. 24:12). The chaos surrounding the Temple's destruction will eventually end and peace will return.

The Gospel in the Whole World

Many will write off the evidence for the fulfillment of the general precursory signs as adaptable to any era of history since the inception of Christianity. It is with verse 14 that some argue the preterist position becomes shaky: "And this gospel of the kingdom will be preached in all the world as a witness to all the nations, and then the end will come."

Futurist Confidence

Walvoord writes: "Jesus, having described the signs relating to the destruction of Jerusalem, which some of them would live to see, and the general signs of the progress of the present age, then reveals in detail the specific signs which will be *unmistakable evidence* that *the second coming of Christ* and the end of the age is near."[60]

Of Matthew 24:14 House and Ice write: "If we look closely at Matthew 24:14 we notice that there are two phrases which modify 'shall be preached' — 'in the whole world' and 'to all the nations.' In the first phrase, the adjective 'whole' indicates that it is the world in its totality that is in view."[61] They then parallel the next phrase to that of Matthew 28:19, arguing for a universal proclamation of the gospel. They ask, are preterists are "saying that the gospel was preached before A.D. 70 in the Western hemisphere?"[62]

By keeping in mind the time indicator ("this generation"), the audience (the disciples who ask when the Temple would be destroyed), and the harmony of the preceding signs with the first century experience, we may note that House and Ice's observation is not well taken. Consider the following:

(1) The word "world" here is the Greek word οἰκουμένη (*oikumene*). It very often means the Roman Empire:

> "And it came to pass in those days that a decree went out from Caesar Augustus that all the *world* should be registered" (Luke 2:1).
> "One of them, named Agabus, stood up and showed by the Spirit that there was going to be a great famine throughout all the *world*, which also happened in the days of Claudius Caesar" (Acts 11:28).
> Acts 24:5 is quite relevant to our point: "For we have found this man [Paul] a plague, a creator of dissension among all the Jews

---

[60] Walvoord, *Prophecy Knowledge Handbook*, 386-387. Emphasis mine.
[61] House and Ice, *Dominion Theology*, 298.
[62] Ibid.

throughout the *world*, and a ringleader of the sect of the Nazarenes."

When did Paul stir up Jews in the western hemisphere?

(2) The phrase "all the nations" is epexegetical, referring to those nations in that particular οἰκουμένη (*oikumene*), i.e., those nations subsumed *under the imperial authority of Rome.* The "world" to which the "gospel of the kingdom was preached" (the Roman Empire) is provided a "witness" to all of its particular "nations."

(3) It is important to remember the contextual setting again. The whole discourse results from Christ's reference to the Jewish Temple's destruction and the disciples's concern with the end of the Jewish age (Matt. 24:2-3). The "witness" throughout "all the nations" of the *oikumene* testifies especially *against the Jews*. It witnesses to the coming of the *kingdom* of Christ, which is presented to and rejected by the Jews.[63]

We must remember that the Jews are scattered throughout the Roman Empire: "Now there were dwelling in Jerusalem Jews, devout men, from *every nation under heaven*" (Acts 2:5). In fact, "the Jews, since the Babylonish captivity, had been scattered over all the world. They were as ubiquitous in the Roman empire in the first century as they are now throughout Christendom."[64] This is so much the case that pagan writers complain of the breadth and depth of the Jewish influence.[65]

We should remember that John Baptist and Christ preach to the Jews that "the kingdom of heaven is at hand" (Matt. 3:1ff; Mark 1:15). Hence, the gospel of Christ's redemptive kingdom is "to the Jew first" (Matt. 10:5-6; Rom. 1:16; 2:9,10). Here the King, Jesus Christ (cp. Acts 17:7; Rev. 1:5), promises a universal testimony of the "good news," i.e., "gospel" (εὐαγγέλιον *euaggelion*), of the kingdom to the "world"-wide Jewish presence. According to Acts, the disciples teach "all the Jews throughout the nations" (Acts 21:21[66]) and cause dissension "among all the Jews throughout the world οἰκουμένη, *oikumene*]" (Acts 24:5).

The Jews continually seek signs from Christ,[67] so finally, he gives this

---

[63] Cp. Mark 1:15 and Matt. 4:17 (where Jesus preaches the kingdom to the Jews) with John 19:12, 15, 21; Matt. 27:41-42; Mark 15:30-32; Luke 23:35-38 (where the Jews reject his kingship).

[64] Schaff, *History of the Christian Church*, 1:85. See my *Before Jerusalem Fell*, 211ff for more evidence.

[65] Tacitus, *Histories* 5:5; Juvenal, *Fourteenth Satire* 11:96ff. See also Josephus *Against Apion* 2:28ff; *Wars* 3:3; and *Antiquities* 14:7:2.

[66] The Greek of Acts 21:21 is: τοὺς; κατὰ τὰ ἔθνη πάντας Ἰουδαίους (*tous kata ta ethne pantas Ioudaious*). The translation cited is from Marshall, *Interlinear Greek English New Testament*, 566.

[67] Matt. 12:38; 16:1; Mark 8:11; Luke 11:16, 29-30; John 2:18; 6:30. Cp. 1 Cor. 1:22.

conclusive sign: his judgment on the Temple, Jerusalem, and Israel (cf. later exposition of Matt. 24:30). As the disciples spread out over the nations of the Roman Empire, they leave a testimony to the Jews in all nations that Jesus is the Christ. The Jews must turn and be saved, or they will perish with that generation (Acts 2:29-41). Their flaming Temple confirms his prophetic word. Of this verse Lightfoot comments that "Jerusalem was not to be destroyed before the gospel was spread over all the world . . . . [A]ll men, as many as ever heard the history of Christ, should understand that dreadful wrath and severe vengeance which was poured out upon that city and nation by which he was crucified."[68]

(4) This interpretation is further strengthened by the parallel in Mark 13:8-10, which provides additional insight into Christ's meaning: "These are the beginnings of sorrows. But watch out for yourselves, for they will deliver you up to councils, and you will be beaten in the synagogues. And you will be brought before rulers and kings for My sake, for a testimony to them. And the gospel must first be preached to all the nations." The Lord is referring to the Jewish opposition to the disciples by "councils" and "synagogues"; the Book of Acts demonstrates this actually happens in the first century.

Preterist Vindication

Now let me point out the fulfillment of the Matthew 24:14 prophecy in the first century. How is "the gospel of the kingdom preached in the whole world"? In Acts 2:5 Luke records the composition of the crowd hearing Peter's pentecostal sermon: "Now there were dwelling in Jerusalem Jews, devout men, from every nation under heaven." Using House and Ice's approach we could dispute Luke's record: surely there were no representatives from the "western hemisphere," were there? (House and Ice would have a problem taking this approach to Acts 24:5, as well.) Yet Luke records that men are there "from every nation under heaven" — and the western hemisphere is under heaven. Obviously he does not mean to include the western hemisphere; to press his words thus is patently wrong. Here in Acts 2:5 we have a gathering to hear the witness of the gospel, a gathering that meets the requirements of Matthew 24:14, at least *representationally*. But there is more.

In Romans 1:8 Paul writes: "First, I thank my God through Jesus Christ for you all, that your faith is spoken of throughout the whole world." Their faith is the Christian faith; Paul says it is being spoken of throughout the "whole world." Turner attempts to reduce this to a proclamation "among

---

[68] John Lightfoot, *Commentary on the New Testament from the Talmud and Hebraica* 4 vols. (Peabody, Mass.: Hendrikson, 1989 [1658]), 2:313.

other Christians."[69] Even if this were so, however, the point remains: it is being spoken of "throughout the whole world" where Christians would be a witness. Furthermore, we could use Turner's interpretive approach to understand Matthew 24:14.

Later Paul mentions gospel preachers: "Their sound has gone out to all the earth, and their words to the ends of the world" (Rom. 10:18). He speaks of "the gospel which has come to you, as it has also in all the world. . . . [T]he gospel which you heard, which was preached to every creature under heaven" (Col 1:6, 23). Turner discounts these references on the basis that Paul still longs "to take the gospel to previously unreached regions (Spain)."[70] But the point remains: if Paul can state Romans 10:18 and Colossians 1:6 and 23 as *fact* in his lifetime, why may we not see these as *fulfillments* of Matthew 24:14?

Matthew 24:14 is no hindrance at all to the preteristic viewpoint. In fact, it harmonizes beautifully with many other Scriptures — much more easily than does dispensationalism's view that must run roughshod over the clear statement of Matthew 24:34.

The Abomination of Desolation

We come now to the most famous and least understood portion of the Olivet Discourse — the abomination of desolation passage (Matt. 24:15-28). The dispensationalist holds that this episode "is still future."[71] While discussing Matthew 24:15-26, Walvoord comments: "One of the sources of confusion among interpreters of the Olivet Discourse is their attempt to find complete fulfillment of the entire Olivet Discourse in connection with the destruction of Jerusalem."[72] According to dispensationalists, the abomination of desolation has been *near* for *almost 2,000 years* (this is due to their doctrine of imminency[73]). For several years now dispensationalists have been excited

---

[69] Turner, "The Structure and Sequence of Matthew 24:1-41," *GTJ*, 8.

[70] Ibid.

[71] Walvoord, *Prophecy Knowledge Handbook*, 387.

[72] I agree that it is an error to discover the fulfillment of the *entire* Olivet Discourse in A.D. 70. I do firmly believe, though, that the events up through verse 33 has found such fulfillment (cf. Matt. 24:34). See discussion below.

[73] The events of Matt. 24:15ff do not begin until after the ever imminent rapture: "It should be noted that the signs [in Matt. 24] are in relation to the second coming of Christ at the end of the Tribulation, not to the Rapture of the church which has no signs and is imminent until it occurs." Walvoord, *Prophecy Knowledge Handbook*, 392. But they are especially close now: "Those who read the Book of Revelation [which speaks of the same events as the Olivet Discourse] today and are captured by its graphic revelation should sense that while these events have not yet been fulfilled, they could be very quickly, and the time for preparation for the end-time events is now," ibid., 645-646.

by reports that Jews are presently preparing the stones for the rebuilding of the Temple.[74] Supposedly this is setting the stage for the abomination of desolation.

While dealing with the abomination of desolation, Walvoord offers a table of the "Predicted Order of Prophetic Events Related to Israel." These events are supposed to surround that prophetically significant time, but this table seems quite incredible.[75] What are some of these "predicted" and "prophetic" events allegedly revealed in Scripture? As an illustration of the naivete of such tabular apocalypticism, I will list two: "2. United Nations recognizes Israel as a nation and allows 5,000 square miles of territory. . . ." "4. [T]he United States becomes her principal benefactor and supplier of military aid and money." Unfortunately, he neglects to provide us with the Bible verses relating to the United Nations, the 5,000 square miles of territory, the United States, and so forth. Those who do not find the United Nations and the United States in Bible prophecy will not be impressed by his table, including even progressive dispensationalists who bemoan such.[76]

Abomination

Therefore when you see the 'abomination of desolation,' spoken of by Daniel the prophet, standing in the holy place (whoever reads, let him understand). . . . (Matt. 24:15)

In the Old Testament an "abomination" especially relates to the desecration of worship, either by outright false worship (Deut. 7:25; 27:15) or by the profaning of true worship (Lev. 7:18; Deut. 17:1). Here in Matthew 24:15 Christ mentions "the holy place" as involved in "the abomination of desolation." Despite Walvoord and other dispensationalists, we may apply this pas-

---

[74] For recent examples, see: Chuck Stewart and Don Missler, *The Coming Temple: Center Stage for the Final Countdown* (Costa Mesa, Calif.: Calvary Chapel, 1990); Thomas Ice and Randall Price, *Ready to Rebuild: The Imminent Plan to Rebuild the Last Days Temple* (Eugene, Ore.: Harvest House, 1992); and Ken Sidey, "For the Love of Zion," *Christianity Today* 35 (December, 16, 1991), 46ff.

[75] Walvoord, *Prophecy Knowledge Handbook*, 382-383. Several years ago I noted a non-dispensationalist premillennial theologian suggesting a similar scenario of detailed historic expectations. See my review of J. Barton Payne's *Biblical Prophecy for Today* in *Christianity Today*, 23 (November 3, 1978), 42.

[76] "This type of dispensationalism also popularized apocalyptic readings of the Bible in terms of current history." Darrell L. Bock, "Charting Dispensationalism," *Christianity Today*, 38 (September 12, 1993), 26-28.distinguishes his name from the distinguishes his name from the names of those of the "circumcision." In Acts 1:19 Luke speaks of Jews' language as "*their* proper tongue." These indicate he is a non-Jew.

sage to the destruction of Jerusalem and the Temple in A.D. 70. Actually the burden of proof is on the dispensationalist to prove the case for a *futurist* interpretation. The more natural reading of the text is the preterist. This is so for several reasons:

(1) As Jesus utters these prophetic words a Temple is standing in a "holy city" (Jerusalem is the holy city, Matt. 4:5; 27:53). His audience could imagine no other referent. To suppose a future *rebuilt* Temple here *must be proved*, not assumed.

(2) Christ speaks these words in response to the disciples's observations on that very Temple: "His disciples came to Him to show Him the buildings of *the Temple*" (Matt. 24:1). This action prompts this discourse (Matt. 23:38-24:3).

(3) Christ points to that Temple: "see ye not all these things." He then speaks of its destruction: "not one stone shall be left on another that shall not be thrown down" (Matt. 24:2). This surely involves "desolation" and, as we will show, includes abominable acts. Interestingly, when speaking of Jerusalem's destruction, Josephus uses the word ἠρημώθη (*eremothe*) in *Wars* 6:10:1. This is the verbal form of the noun "desolation" (ἐρήμωσις, *eremoseos*) that Christ uses in Matthew 24:15. Josephus, like Christ, also applies Daniel's prophecy to this event: "In the very same manner Daniel also wrote concerning the Roman government, and that our country should be made desolate by them" (*Antiquities* 10:11:7).

(4) And of course, the specific time-frame demands an A.D. 70 reference for the "abomination": "Assuredly, I say to you, this generation will by no means pass away till all these things are fulfilled" (Matt. 24:34).

To assist in interpreting this difficult verse, it is helpful to compare the Gentile Luke's parallel account in Luke 21:21 with Matthew's very Jewish account.[77] As often happens, Luke uses language more easily understood by the Gentile. Rather than employing the obscure Old Testament phrase "abomination of desolation" (from Dan. 9:27 as recorded in Matthew 24:15), Luke writes: "But when you see Jerusalem *surrounded by armies, then know that its desolation* is near" (Luke 21:20). If it were not for the pressure of an intricate, pre-conceived system (dispensationalism), merely laying the passages side-by-

---

[77] The name Λουκᾶς (*Loukas*) is Greek, not Hebrew. In Col. 4:11, 14 Paul distinguishes his name from the names of those of the "circumcision." In Acts 1:19 Luke speaks of Jews' language as "*their* proper tongue." These indicate he is a non-Jew.

side would quickly convince the casual reader that the *same* events are in view. But dispensationalists make a radical distinction between Luke 21:20 and Matt. 24:15, holding that Luke's statement points to the A.D. 70 event and that Matthew's speaks of an event in our future.[78]

The Holy Place

The "abomination of desolation" is so dreadful it will prompt desperate flight from the area. This horrible episode will occur "in the holy place." The reference to "the holy place" might seem to speak of just the Temple itself and nothing more. Surely the Temple is involved, *but the reference is broader, speaking of both the city and the Temple.* Several problems present themselves to the narrow Temple-only view:

(1) Luke clearly interprets the phrase as the surrounding of the city "Jerusalem" (Luke 21:21). And Jerusalem itself is a holy place,[79] being the capital of the "holy land" (Zech. 2:12).[80]

(2) The prophecy calls for flight from all of Judea (the region surrounding Jerusalem), not just the Temple environs. This is why Christ weeps over Jerusalem just before uttering this prophecy (Matt. 23:37). Christ is warning of Jerusalem's devastating destruction, not just the Temple's desecration by profane actions. The rising storm of war, not the spread of ritual heresy, prompts flight from the region.

(3) The original Old Testament context mentions both "the city and the sanctuary" (Dan. 9:26). Daniel 9:25 even calls Jerusalem "the holy city" (whereas Matthew speaks of "the holy place"). In fact, the original prophecy pivots on the rebuilding of the *city* (Dan. 9:25). To limit the reference solely to the Temple is surely unwarranted. The preceding context of Matthew agrees with Daniel in involving *both* the *city* and the *Temple* (Matt. 23:37-38).

Josephus on Jerusalem's Destruction

The phrase "the abomination of desolation" summarily designates the events leading up to the destruction of Jerusalem and the Temple by the Roman armies. The holy city/place where the Jews worship God in his Temple will suffer abomination and desolation. Josephus gives us a clear record of

---

[78] See: Walvoord, *Prophecy Knowledge Handbook*, 386; Pentecost, *Thy Kingdom Come*, 249.

[79] Neh. 11:1, 18; Isa. 48:2; 52:1; 66:20; Dan. 9:16, 24; Joel 3:17.

[80] For Jewish references to Israel as the "holy land," see: 2 Baruch 63:10; 4 Ezra 13:48; 2 Maccabees 1:7.

this occurring in Jerusalem's last days, especially after the surrounding of Jerusalem.[81] It is particularly distressing to the Jew that abominable Gentiles[82] would ultimately enter the Temple of God, as do the Romans (see below).

When the Jewish War finally comes to Jerusalem all hell breaks loose — and I mean this somewhat literally. Demonism seems to be a real factor in the Jewish War, as a comparison of Revelation 9 and Matthew 12:41-45 shows. The Idumeans stir up revolution within Jerusalem, bringing war into the Temple itself (*Wars* 4:5): "the outer Temple was all of it overflowed with blood; and that day, as it came on, saw eight thousand five hundred dead bodies there" (*Wars* 4:5:1). The inner strife is so bad that Josephus calls it "a sedition begotten by another sedition"; he says Jerusalem is "like a wild beast grown mad, which for the want of food from abroad, fell now upon eating its own flesh" (*Wars* 5:1:1). Hence, Christ's dire warning to flee without turning back (Matt. 24:16-18). Once Titus begins encircling the city, it will not take him long to seal it off from the outer world (Matt. 24:16-20).

As Titus begins his final march to Jerusalem, the Zealots "seize upon the inner court of the Temple, and lay their arms upon the holy gates, and over the holy fronts of that court." They even partake of the "the great abundance of what was consecrated to sacred uses" causing such an uproar that the "Temple was defiled everywhere with murders" (*Wars* 5:1:2). They "went over all the buildings, and the Temple itself, and fell upon the priests, and those that were about the sacred offices" (*Wars* 5:1:3).

Finally, Titus builds "a wall round about the whole city" (*Wars* 5:12:1), causing those within the Temple to perform additional sacrilege: John of Gischala "emptied the vessels of that sacred wine and oil [cp. Rev. 6:6] which the priests kept to be poured on the burnt-offerings, and which lay in the inner court of the Temple, and distributed it among the multitude, who, in their anointing themselves and drinking, used each of them above a hin of them" (*Wars* 5:13:6). Titus's victory is complete: "the Romans upon the flight of the seditious into the city, and upon the burning of the holy house itself, and of all the buildings lying round about it, brought their ensigns to the Temple, and set them over against its eastern gate; and there did they offer

---

[81] I highly recommend reading Josephus's *Wars of the Jews*, especially Books 4-7, in conjunction with the Olivet Discourse and Revelation. For a few examples, see my *Before Jerusalem Fell*, ch. 14.

[82] Cf. Acts 10:28; 11:2-3; cf. Eph. 2:14. The Roman historian Tacitus touches on the Jewish exclusivism, when he complains of the Jews's "stubborn loyalty and ready benevolence towards brother Jews. But the rest of the world they confront with the hatred reserved for enemies.... They have introduced the practice of circumcision to show that they are different from others," *Histories* 5:5.

sacrifices to them, and there did they make Titus imperator, with the greatest acclamations of joy" (*Wars* 6:6:1). Although the "abomination of desolation" involves the destruction of Jerusalem (beginning with its encircling), it culminates in this final abominable act within in the Temple itself.

Where Eagles Dare

Remarkably this very conclusion seems to be in Christ's mind when he states: "For wherever the carcass is, there the *eagles* will be gathered together" (Matt. 24:28 NKJV). Josephus describes the marching order of the Roman troops, mentioning the prominence of their eagle ensigns: "Then came the ensigns encompassing the *eagle*, which is at the head of every Roman legion, the king, and the strongest of all birds, which seems to them a signal of dominion, and an omen that they shall conquer all against whom they march; these sacred ensigns are followed by the trumpeters" (*Wars* 3:6:2; cf. 5:2:1). The Roman ensigns — to which Titus's soldiers offer sacrifices in the holy of holies — are *eagles*.[83] Tertullian (A.D. 160-220) writes of the Roman ensigns: "The camp religion of the Romans is all through a worship of the standards, a setting the standards above all gods" (*Apology* 16). Certainly this gathering of eagles is a grievous abomination.

Conclusion

In Matthew 24:2 the Lord points to the Temple buildings, asking his disciples (Matt. 24:1): "Do you not see all these things?" What he prophetically declares in the following verses has direct relevance to the Jewish Temple of the first century. As he concludes this section of the Olivet Discourse, he does so with a firm pronouncement: "Assuredly, I say to you, this generation will by no means pass away till all these things are fulfilled" (Matt. 24:34). Both these architectural and temporal indicators require a first century focus for the passage.

The "abomination of desolation" prophecy finds fulfillment in A.D. 70, during the August/September destruction of the Temple by the armies of the Roman general Titus. The abomination of desolation is not something we should fear today. The constant expectation of its breaking forth in our day is misguided. This horrible judgment of God punctuates the *beginning of Christ's kingdom* on earth, not the *end of the "Church Age."* But there is more in Matthew 24. We now turn to that.

---

[83] "The eagle was adopted as the standard of the legion, and was carried by the first maniple of the first cohort." Sir Paul Harvey, *The Oxford Companion to Classical Literature* (Oxford: Clarendon, 1937), 49.

CHAPTER THREE

THERE WILL BE GREAT TRIBULATION
Matthew 24:21-36

For then there will be great tribulation, such as has not been since the beginning of the world until this time, no, nor ever shall be. And unless those days were shortened, no flesh would be saved; but for the elect's sake those days will be shortened.

Matthew 24:21-22

Introduction

In our study of the precursory signs of the great tribulation, we saw that the past fulfillment approach of preterism easily accounts for all the elements of the prophecy recorded in Matthew 24:1-20. But our study is not over. We must now enter the section of Matthew 24 where we find some of the seemingly most difficult statements for preteristic fulfillment. I hope to show that upon close examination, these verses do not form any barrier to a first century fulfillment of the Lord's prophecy. Indeed, they fit beautifully in the preteristic scheme — when understood in terms of their biblical context.

Matthew 24:21-22 reads: "For then there will be great tribulation, such as has not been since the beginning of the world until this time, no, nor ever shall be. And unless those days were shortened, no flesh would be saved; but for the elect's sake those days will be shortened." Futurists almost universally deem this prophetic datum fatal to preterism. By way of introduction let us consider some bold statements futurists make regarding these two verses.

The Greatness of the Great Tribulation

Charles C. Ryrie argues of the great tribulation: "the fact that this period is yet future will be even more evident as the characteristics of the period are

63

given . . . . First, it is a unique period."[1] Then he cites Matthew 24:21.

Gleason L. Archer points to our text as indicating "a level of horrible and overwhelming destruction surpassing anything ever known before."[2]

Douglas Moo comments that it is "the greatest distress in world history."[3] Who among us would argue that A.D. 70 was the greatest distress in world history, considered simply in terms of human loss?

Charles L. Feinberg speaks of World War I and II, then asks, "who can legitimately equate them with . . . Matthew 24:21?"[4] The point being that if two World Wars did not meet up to Matthew 24:21, surely the Jewish War with Rome did not.

David L. Turner writes that "the stress on the unparalleled nature of this judgment (24:21-22) does not seem to be exhausted by the A.D. 70 destruction, as severe as it was."[5]

John F. Walvoord calls it a "time of unprecedented trouble," a trial that "would exceed any judgment of the past or the future."[6] In fact, "never in the history of the world has there been [the] destruction of human life described here."[7] What is more, "the trials and difficulties of that day would be so severe that it would exterminate the entire human race if it were not for the fact that they are cut short by the return of Jesus Christ."[8] "Interpreted literally, the tribulation clearly eclipses anything that the world has ever known by way of destruction."[9]

In his refutation of postmillennialism Anthony Hoekema cites Matthew 24 as indicating "a great tribulation such as has not been from the beginning of the world and never will be." Hoekema presents this passage as virtually conclusive proof the end times will necessarily be grievous.[10] William

---

[1] Charles C. Ryrie, *The Basis of the Premillennial Faith* (Neptune, N.J.: Loizeaux, 1953), 141.

[2] Gleason L. Archer, in Archer, *et al.*, *The Rapture: Pre, Mid, or Post-tribulational?* (Grand Rapids: Zondervan, 1984), 109.

[3] Douglas J. Moo, in Archer, *et al.*, *The Rapture*, 165.

[4] Charles L. Feinberg, *Millennialism: The Two Major Views* (3rd ed: Chicago: Moody, 1980), 167.

[5] David L. Turner, "Structure and Sequence of Matthew 24:1-41: Interaction with Evangelical Treatments," *Grace Theological Journal* 10:1 (Spring 1989): 13.

[6] John F. Walvoord, *Prophecy Knowledge Handbook* (Wheaton, Ill.: Victor, 1990), 521, 564.

[7] Ibid., 556.

[8] John F. Walvoord, *The Nations, Israel, and the Church in Prophecy* (3 vols. in one: Grand Rapids: Zondervan, 1988), 2:110.

[9] Ibid., 3:129.

[10] Anthony Hoekema, *The Bible and the Future* (Grand Rapids: Eerdmans, 1979), 178.

Hendriksen concurs with his fellow amillennialist: "Jesus is here speaking about a tribulation that will characterize 'those days,' a tribulation such as has never been and never again shall be, *a very brief period of dire distress that shall occur immediately before his return*. . . . It should hardly be necessary to add that justice is not done to the concept of this tribulation, which immediately precedes 'the end' of the world's history and which surpasses any other distress in its intensity, if it is referred solely to the sorrows experienced during the fall of Jerusalem."[11]

At this point I admit the statement by our Lord seems to require something quite beyond the events of A.D. 70 — *but only when taken out of its context,* both near (Matt. 24) and far (Old Testament language). The Lord does say there "has not been [such a judgment] since the beginning of the world until this time, no, nor ever shall be." His warning speaks of the danger "no flesh would be saved." How are we to reconcile such dramatic statements to the A.D. 70 event?

The Preterist Interpretation

As a matter of fact, reconciliation is possible. And this is much more consistent with both the language and the expectation of Scripture than the futurist approaches to Matthew 24:1-34. Let me list five arguments against the futurist understanding of Matthew 24:21-22 while establishing the preterist approach.

1. The Time Frame

An immediate response to the futurist claims lays ready at hand: Just twelve verses later Christ says "all these things" will befall "this generation" (Matt. 24:34). And he says this in the context dealing with the destruction of the very Temple then standing (Matt. 23:36-24:3). There is no way around these facts. We know as a matter of indisputable historical record that Titus destroys the Temple in August/September, A.D. 70.[12] As Jesus bears his cross to Calvary he exhorts the "daughters of Jerusalem" to weep for themselves because of this coming judgment (Luke 23:28-31, cp. Rev. 6:16). Revelation mentions the Great Tribulation in a similar time-constrained context: "And I said to him, 'Sir, you know.' So he said to me, 'These are the ones who come out of the great tribulation, and washed their robes and made them white in the blood of the Lamb'" (Rev. 7:14). This is preceded and followed by time statements tying the event to the first century (Rev. 1:1, 3; 22:6-10). There is

---

[11] William Hendriksen *The Gospel of Matthew* (Grand Rapids: Baker, 1973), 860. Emphasis his.

[12] Josephus, *Wars* 7:1:1.

no getting around the clarity of these time statements either in Matthew 24 or in Revelation.[13]

2. The Jewish Setting

It is fundamentally important for us to understand this passage from the Jewish perspective in Christ's day. The Jewish War with Rome from A.D. 67 to 70 causes the deaths of tens of thousands of the Jews in Judea and the enslaving of untold thousands more. The Jewish historian Flavius Josephus, an eye-witness to the Jewish War, reports that 1,100,000 Jews perished in the siege of Jerusalem (*Wars* 6:9:3). Though many historians doubt this figure, Arndt accepts them as valid, given the flood of refugees.[14] J. L. von Mosheim, the great ecclesiastical historian, writes that "throughout the whole history of the human race, we meet with but few, if any, instances of slaughter and devastation at all to be compared with this."[15]

But as awful as are the Jewish loss of life and the utter devastation of "the holy city" Jerusalem, the Jews lament even more the final destruction of the Temple of God and the absolute cessation of the sacrificial system. The covenantal significance of the loss of the Temple stands as the most dramatic outcome of the War. It is an unrepeatable loss in that the Temple has never been rebuilt. Therefore, any Jewish calamity after A.D. 70 pales in comparison to the redemptive-historical significance of the Temple's loss.

Josephus mourns the devastation of Jerusalem in several places employing words similar to our Lord's: "Whereas the war which the Jews made with the Romans hath been the greatest of all those, not only that have been in our times, but, in a manner, of those that ever were heard of" (*Wars*, Preface, 1). "The misfortunes of all men, from the beginning of the world, if they be compared to these of the Jews, are not considerable as they were" (*Wars*, Preface, 4). "Neither did any other city ever suffer such miseries. . . from the beginning of the world" (*Wars* 5:10:5).

3. The Divine Perspective

We must further understand the significance of A.D. 70 from the divine perspective. The Jewish War is God's holy judgment upon the Jews for their wickedly crucifying his Son.[16] This is clear in the ending of the Parable of the Vineyard:

---

[13] See also Chapter 5 below for a discussion of the Revelation references.

[14] W. F. Arndt *The Gospel According to St. Luke* (St. Louis: Concordia, 1956), 421-22.

[15] John Laurence von Mosheim, *Historical Commentaries on the State of Christianity*, 2 vols., (New York: Converse, 1854), 1:125.

[16] The New Testament strongly emphasizes first century Jewish culpability for

Then last of all he sent his son to them, saying, "They will respect my son." But when the vinedressers saw the son, they said among themselves, "This is the heir. Come, let us kill him and seize his inheritance." And they caught him, and cast him out of the vineyard, and killed him. Therefore, when the owner of the vineyard comes, what will he do to those vinedressers? They said to Him, "He will destroy those wicked men miserably, and lease his vineyard to other vinedressers who will render to him the fruits in their seasons" (Matt. 21:37-41).

Luke 19:41-44 is also relevant:

Now as he drew near, he saw the city and wept over it, saying, "If you had known, even you, especially in this your day, the things that make for your peace! But now they are hidden from your eyes. For the days will come upon you when your enemies will build an embankment around you, surround you and close you in on every side, and level you, and your children within you, to the ground; and they will not leave in you one stone upon another, because you did not know the time of your visitation."

4. The Noahic Flood

What is more, just a few verses after Matthew 24:21-22 the Lord mentions the Noahic Flood (vv. 38-39), which destroys the *entire* world except one family. Even the strong dispensational statements cited earlier see their Great Tribulation as stopping far short of leaving only *one family* alive.

Obviously we should not interpret Christ's language literally after all. It is dramatic hyperbole, well justified by the gravity of the situation. Not every Jew dies in the Jewish War, but its devastation is such that it takes an act of God to prevent the destruction of *all* of Israel (cp. Matt. 24:22).[17]

5. Prophetic Parlance

This unique-event language of Christ is common stock-in-trade in prophetic writing. Lane comments on Mark 13:19, the parallel verse to Matthew

---

the crucifixion of Christ: Acts 2:22-23; Acts 3:13-15a; Acts 5:30; 7:52; 1 Thess. 2:14-15. They demand that the Romans crucify Him: Matt. 20:18-19; 27:11-25; Mark 10:33; 15:1; Luke 18:32; 23:1-2; John 18:28-31; 19:12, 15; Acts 3:13; Acts 4:26-27.

[17] It was limited to three and one-half years: Spring A.D. 67-August/September A.D. 70. See my *The Beast of Revelation* (Tyler, Tex.: Institute for Christian Economics, 1989).

24:21: "The severity of the distress that will accompany the destruction of Jerusalem is vividly suggested through Semitic hyperbole. Characteristically, oracles of judgment are couched in language that is universal and radical. The intention is to indicate that through human events God intervenes powerfully to modify the course of history. The entire world feels the vibrations of that intervention."[18] This is most interesting to the preterist, for it dismantles the futurist argument. The Old Testament has many such statements that support our view that the language is hyperbolic.

Regarding the woe of the tenth plague upon Egypt, the Scripture says: "Then there shall be a great cry throughout all the land of Egypt, *such as was not like it before, nor shall be like it again*" (Exo. 11:6). According to dispensationalists the Great Tribulation affects the entire earth. Consequently, it affects Egypt. But this passage says Egypt will *never again* experience such a terrible event as the tenth plague, which occurs hundreds of years before Christ. Yet the future Great Tribulation is supposed to be the worst ever for everyone — including Egyptians.

In a prophecy regarding the Babylonian captivity and the destruction of Jerusalem God employs language reminiscent of Christ's: "And I will do among you what *I have never done, and the like of which I will never do again*, because of all your abominations" (Eze. 5:9). Even dispensationalists admit this prophecy is about the Babylonian captivity of the distant past.[19] And this is specifically about Jerusalem, which is very prominent in the Matthew 24 passage.

Daniel speaks of the Babylonian captivity in similar language: "And he has confirmed his words, which he spoke against us and against our judges who judged us, by bringing upon us a great disaster; for *under the whole heaven such never has been done as what has been done to Jerusalem*" (Dan. 9:12).

Clearly, the unique-event language is common parlance in prophetic literature. We must not interpret it in a woodenly literal manner, as is obvious from all the evidence above.

False Christs

As we continue our survey of Matthew 24:1-36, we return to a familiar theme. In verses 23-26 we again hear a warning regarding false prophets, a warning reminiscent of that in verse 11.

---

[18] William L. Lane, *The Gospel of Mark* (NICNT) (Grand Rapids: Eerdmans, 1974), 471.

[19] Walvoord, *Prophecy Knowledge Handbook*, 160. J. Dwight Pentecost, *Thy Kingdom Come* (Wheaton, Ill.: Victor, 1990), 180. Charles Dyer, "Ezekiel," in John F. Walvoord and Roy B. Zuck, eds., *The Bible Knowledge Commentary: Old Testament* (Wheaton, Ill.: Victor, 1985), 1236.

Christ reiterates to his followers a warning against falling for false escape promises regarding the coming A.D. 70 era tribulation: "Then if anyone says to you, 'Look, here is the Christ!' or 'There!' do not believe it. For false christs and false prophets will arise and show great signs and wonders, so as to deceive, if possible, even the elect. See, I have told you beforehand. Therefore if they say to you, 'Look, he is in the desert!' do not go out; or 'Look, he is in the inner rooms!' do not believe it" (Matt. 24:23-26).

False Expectations

It is one of the most basic instincts of man to avoid affliction and danger. As Josephus says of the false prophecies during the Jewish War: "Now, a man that is in adversity does easily comply with such promises; for when such a seducer makes him believe that he shall be delivered from those miseries which oppress him, then it is that the patient is full of hopes of such deliverance."[20] Man has a God-created will to live, for "He has put eternity in their hearts" (Eccl. 3:11). With the onset of the great tribulation, anxiety might overcome many; false messianic expectations might easily tempt them.

As is evident from the Lord's High Priestly Prayer, however, his people should expect preservation in temptation, not deliverance *from* it: "I do not pray that You should take them out of the world, but that You should keep them from the evil one" (John 17:15). In essence, the Lord is warning against the notion of an imminent return — a position the wisdom of which history has borne out for the past nineteen centuries. His people could expect only false Christs during the first century. The Lord's glorious, bodily return will be in the distant future: "But while the bridegroom was *delayed*, they all slumbered and slept" (Matt. 25:5). "For the kingdom of heaven is like a man traveling to a *far* country, who called his own servants and delivered his goods to them. . . . After a *long time* the lord of those servants came and settled accounts with them" (Matt. 25:14, 19).

Just before his ascension Christ deals with the problem of imminence among his often-confused disciples: "They asked Him, saying, 'Lord, will You at this time restore the kingdom to Israel?' And he said to them, 'It is not for you to know times [χρόνος, *chronos*] or seasons which the Father has put in his own authority" (Acts 1:7). It is particularly the time factor that is at issue in their question. This is evident in that: (1) The time element "at this time" is placed early in the Greek sentence for emphasis. (2) The disciples suspect it may be "at this time." (3) Christ's answer focuses only on the time element. The *chronos* time-reference in Christ's answer indicates a long period of time of uncertain duration. It speaks "of a rather long period of time composed

---

[20] Josephus, *Wars* 6:5:2.

of several shorter ones."[21] In fact, "times" is found in the plural, thereby multiplying its effect.

False Messiahs

Unfounded hope for escape during the perilous times of the first century is fertile ground for messianic expectations. So Christ expressly warns against such. I have already provided biblical evidence for false Christs arising during the apostolic era, let me now bring in some extra-biblical evidence. These data — as every other in Matthew 24:1-34 — have a direct historical relevance to the pre-A.D. 70 era.

In John Lightfoot's encyclopedic research in Jewish Talmudic literature, we find records of rabbinic interpretations that fuel false Messianic fervor in the first century. Isaiah 56:7 reads: "Before she travailed, she gave birth; before her pain came, she delivered a male child." Based on this, the rabbis argue "that the Messias should be manifested before the destruction of the city."[22] Christ's followers are not to fall for such, Jesus warns.

Micah 5:3 reads: "Therefore He shall give them up, until the time that she who is in labor has given birth; then the remnant of his brethren shall return to the children of Israel." From this the rabbis deduce that "the Son of David will not come, till the wicked empire [of the Romans] shall have spread itself over all the world nine months." Clearly a Messianic hope is in the air as the fateful events of the A.D. 60s unfold on the scene of history.

Josephus records for us the following incidents that occur before the outbreak of the Jewish War with Rome. "There was also another body of wicked men gotten together, not so impure in their actions, but more wicked in their intentions, who laid waste the happy state of the city [Jerusalem] no less than did these murderers. These were such men as deceived and deluded the people under pretense of divine inspiration, but were for procuring innovations and changes of the government; and these prevailed with the multitude to act like madmen, and went before them into the wilderness, as pretending that God would there shew them the signal of liberty" (*Wars* 2:13:4).

Josephus also mentions that "there was an Egyptian false prophet that did the Jews more mischief than the former; for he was a cheat, and pretended to be a prophet also, and got together thirty thousand men that were deluded by him; these he led round about from the wilderness to the mount which was

---

[21] William F. Arndt and F. Wilbur Gingrich, *A Greek-English Lexicon of the New Testament* (4th ed.: Chicago: University of Chicago, 1957), 896.

[22] Babylonian Joma, fol. 10.1. Cited in: John Lightfoot, *A Commentary on the New Testament from the Talmud and Hebraica*, 4 vols., (Peabody, Mass.: Hendrickson, rep. 1989 [1658]), 1:318-319.

called the Mount of Olives, and was ready to break into Jerusalem by force from that place" (*Wars* 2:13:5).

Of the events during the Jewish War itself, he writes: "A false prophet was the occasion of these people's destruction, who had made a public proclamation in the city that very day, that God commanded them to get up upon the temple, and there should received miraculous signs of their deliverance. Now, there was then a great number of false prophets suborned by the tyrants to impose upon the people, who denounced this to them, that they should wait for deliverance from God" (*Wars* 6:5:2).

The rabbinic expectations of the sudden appearance of the Messiah fuel the multiplication of and merge with deceptions by false prophets during the Jewish War. This is precisely the scenario Jesus warns about. Interpreting the cause of the Jewish War, Josephus observes: "What did elevate them in undertaking this war was an ambiguous oracle that was also found in their sacred writings, how, 'about that time, one from their country should become governor of the habitable earth.' The Jews took this prediction to belong to themselves in particular; and many of the wise men were thereby deceived in their determination" (*Wars* 6:5:4).

Again we see how the prophecies of Matthew 24 find fulfillment in the first century. In that these prophecies are for that era (Matt. 24:34), why should we opt for a futurist approach to the matter?

Like Lightning

Quite emphatically the Lord warns his disciples he will not come in a visible, bodily manner in those days. He twice states that any report of his physical presence would be erroneous: "Then if anyone says to you, 'Look, here is the Christ!' or 'There!' do not believe it" (Matt. 24:23). "Therefore if they say to you, 'Look, He is in the desert!' do not go out; or 'Look, He is in the inner rooms!' do not believe it" (Matt. 24:26). Clearly these statements discourage their expecting any visible return in that day; he expressly declares that any command to look for Him in some limited particular location would be a mistake.

Christ Comes in Judgment

Yet there will be a "coming" of Christ in that day: "For as the lightning comes from the east and flashes to the west, so also will the coming of the Son of Man be" (Matt. 24:27). This, however, is a spiritual judgment-coming, rather than a bodily coming.

The Sanhedrin who abuse Him during the ecclesiastical trials leading up to his crucifixion will witness such a judgment-coming. Notice what Christ says to his abusers: "The high priest answered and said to Him, 'I adjure You by the living God that You tell us if You are the Christ, the Son of God.' Jesus said to him, 'It is as you said. Nevertheless, I say to you, hereafter you will see the Son of Man sitting at the right hand of the Power, and coming on the clouds of heaven'" (Matt. 26:63-64).

Here the Lord informs the high priest and the other members of the Sanhedrim that they will see his coming. The coming they will witness is like the one Isaiah attributes to Jehovah against Egypt: "The burden against Egypt. Behold, the LORD rides on a swift cloud, and will come into Egypt" (Isa. 19:1). The LORD did not physically ride down into Egypt on a cloud. Neither is the "coming of the Son of Man" against the Sanhedrim and their nation a physical coming. Nor is the "coming as lightning" mentioned in Matthew 24:27 a publicly visible, physical coming. It is manifestly a judgment-coming against those who call down his blood upon them and their children (Matt. 27:25).

In Matthew 24:27 the Lord speaks of his judgment-coming against Jerusalem (cf. Matt. 23:37-24:2) as analogous to "the lightning [that] comes from the east and flashes to the west." Dispensationalists generally teach that this speaks of the Second Coming. Some see the analogy to lightning in the visibility of his Second Coming, the lightning suggesting "a splendorous, visible event,"[23] a "very visible event."[24] Others see the analogy in the speed of his Coming, comparing it to the velocity of lightning: his coming will be "sudden and interventionist,"[25] "sudden, like a stroke of lightning."[26] Certainly lightning is a "splendorous" event — and very fast. But is that the aspect of lightning Jesus has in mind here?

The Significance of Lightning

Two alternative interpretations are more likely, given the surrounding context, the full statement of Christ, and the total biblical background. Probably both are involved. The local context demands this coming occur in "this generation" (Matt. 24:34) for it concerns events associated with the destruction of the Temple (Matt. 24:2). I cannot see how any interpretive approach other than preterism can account for this temporal delimitation. Unless we argue that Christ physically appeared at the destruction of the Temple, this

---

[23] Louis A. Barbieri, Jr., "Matthew," in John F. Walvoord and Roy B. Zuck, eds, *The Bible Knowledge Commentary: New Testament* (Wheaton, Ill.: Victor, 1983), 77.

[24] Walvoord, *Prophecy Knowledge Handbook*, 389.

[25] H. Wayne House and Thomas D. Ice, *Dominion Theology: Blessing or Curse?* (Portland, Ore.: Multnomah, 1988), 295.

[26] Warren W. Wiersbe, *The Bible Exposition Commentary*, 2 vols., (Chicago: Moody, 1989), 1:89.

must be a spiritual judgment coming.

First, notice the fuller statement of Christ with its specific contextual addendum: It is said to flash (ἐξέρχεται, *exerchetai,* "come forth") from east to west. Elsewhere when Christ says Satan falls from heaven "like lightning" (Luke 10:18), the direction is clearly in view (given the spatial imagery of Scripture: heaven being up and hell being down). This probably is involved here, in that the destroying armies come toward Jerusalem from an easterly direction. Josephus's record of the march of the Roman armies through Israel shows they wreaked havoc on Jerusalem by approaching it from the east.

Second, in the wider biblical context lightning is that which terrifies (Eze. 19:16; 20:18), because it is so violently destructive: "He also gave up their cattle to the hail, And their flocks to fiery lightning. He cast on them the fierceness of His anger, wrath, indignation, and trouble, By sending angels of destruction among them" (Psa. 78:48-49). Here the "fiery lightning" is equivalent to "angels of destruction." There are numerous examples of such lightning imagery in Scripture.[27] Lightning is a nerve shattering feature of a violent storm; frequently the Scripture speaks of catastrophic wars as storms (e.g., Isa. 28:2; 29:6; Eze. 38:9).

Matthew 24 surely involves the idea of terrifying desolation in that the Lord clearly speaks of destruction (v. 2), war (vv. 6-7), sorrow (v. 8), desolation (v. 15), flight from danger (vv. 16-20), great tribulation (v. 21), and death (v. 28). Obviously the calamitous storm that falls upon Israel during the Jewish War is visible. Yet it is not Christ Himself who is corporally present. Rather he directs the Roman armies by his providence, just as God directs Cyrus as a bird of prey under his sovereign providence (Isa. 46:10-11). Jesus provides a parabolic description of the destruction of Jerusalem in Matthew 22:2-15: "But when the king heard about it, he was furious. And he sent out *his* armies, destroyed those murderers, and burned up their city" (Matt. 22:7).

The visibility of lightning seems merely to be a side-effect that allows the mention of direction. Nevertheless, even if he intends to emphasize visibility here, that does not indicate it portrays the Second Advent. If Christ intends visibility, our view still fits, for on this approach the false Christs the Jews vainly look for are in various hidden localities (Matt. 24:26). But overshadowing these will be the awesome and public Israel-wide destruction by the very visible Roman armies, whom the true Christ sends to do his bidding. Nevertheless, the other interpretations I suggest above are superior to this view.

---

[27] 2 Sam. 22:15; Job 36:32; Psa. 18:14; 140:6; Eze. 21:10; Zech. 9:14; Rev. 11:19; 16:18.

A Carcass for Eagles

In verse 28 we read of birds of prey consuming the carcasses: "For wherever the carcass is, there the eagles will be gathered together." This seems to speak of the dreadful devastation Rome wreaks upon Israel. The furious soldiers who cruelly ravage the people will destroy national, political Israel. Josephus often mentions the rage of the Roman troops: "The army now having no victims either for slaughter or plunder, through lack of all objects on which to vent their rage. . ." (*Wars* 7:1:1). The imagery is familiar enough to an agrarian people: the ugly, rotting corpse of an animal blanketed by bickering birds of prey.

On another occasion in Scripture a dead body symbolizes Israel: the vision of the dry bones in Ezekiel 37.[28] She is morally, spiritually, and covenantally dead in the eyes of God. Before the Olivet Discourse Christ symbolically portrays his death-dealing curse on Israel by cursing the fig tree (Matt. 21:19-20). Shortly thereafter he speaks a parable about his rejection, which the Pharisees foolishly agree should be recompensed by the destruction of those responsible (Matt. 21:33-41). Then he speaks of Himself as the "Stone which the builders rejected" (Matt. 21:42). Following immediately upon this Christ says: "And whoever falls on this stone will be broken; but on whomever it falls, it will grind him to powder" (Matt. 21:44). Ultimately, upon Israel comes "all the righteous blood shed on the earth, from the blood of righteous Abel to the blood of Zechariah, son of Berechiah, whom you murdered between the temple and the altar" (Matt. 23:35).

This judgment comes through the providential instrument of God, the Roman army. Israel is judicially dead; the Roman armies will devour her carcass. This is why Jesus weeps over Jerusalem (Matt. 23:37); this is why God leaves her house desolate (Matt. 23:38). The Spirit of God, which is her life, departs. Consequently, God will totally destroy her capital city and holy Temple.

The Scripture views the body as a wondrous creation by God, inspiring awe among God's people (Psa. 139:13-16; Eccl. 10:5). Because God wonderfully fashions man's body (Gen. 2:7), God's people treat the body with the utmost respect, carefully preparing it for burial (John 19:40)[29]. Only the bodies of vile sinners are denied proper preparation for burial, having their corpses

---

[28] The mysterious reference to Michael and Satan contending for the body of should probably be understood in this manner (Jude 9), as many reformed commentators note. The body of Moses is the nation of Israel, much like the body of Christ is the Church.

[29] See also: Gen. 23:19; 47:30; 49:29; 50:5; Jer. 16:4. Cf. Tacitus, *The Histories* 5:6: "Rather than cremate their dead, the prefer to bury them." Cf. Mishnah, *Shabbath* 23:5; Sanhedrin 6:5.

cremated instead (Gen. 23:19; Lev. 21:9;[30] 1 Sam. 31:12). The death-dealing judgment of God on covenant rebellion often causes a tragic loss of burial arrangements, resulting in animals devouring the bodies of the deceased. This is an aspect of covenantal curse: "Your carcasses shall be food for all the birds of the air and the beasts of the earth, and no one shall frighten them away" (Deut. 28:26).[31]

Now why does the Lord portray this judgment with eagles preying upon the carcass? It is interesting that our Lord chooses the word "eagles" (ἀετός, *aetos*) here. He could choose a more generic term such as ὄρνεον (*orneon*, "fowl"), as John employs in a similar context in Revelation 19:21. Instead, Christ chooses the term that reminds us of the symbol of the Roman Empire: the ensigns the legions carry before them into battle. Josephus mentions the Roman eagle Herod affixes to the Temple gate to the chagrin of the Jews (*Antiquities* 17:6:3).

As I note in the preceding chapter, Josephus records the act that lies behind the imagery here: "The Romans, now that the rebels had fled to the city, and the sanctuary itself and all around it were in flames, carried their standards into the temple court and, setting them up opposite the eastern gate, there sacrificed to them, and with rousing acclamations hailed Titus as imperator" (*Wars* 6:6:1). The Roman ensigns bear the eagle as the symbol of Rome: "Next [came] the ensigns surrounding the eagle [ἀετός, *aetos*], which in the Roman army precedes every legion, because it is the king and the bravest of all the birds; it is regarded by them as the symbol of empire" (*Wars* 3:6:2; cf. Suetonius, *Galba* 13). These were "sacred emblems" (ibid.).

Thus, as Jerusalem collapses to her "death" the marauding armies of Rome pour into the city on that fateful day to devour the corpse. Jerusalem is so stripped of her valuables that Josephus writes: "So glutted with plunder were the troops, one and all, that throughout Syria the standard of gold was depreciated to half its former value" (*Wars* 6:6:1). The soldiers gather as bickering eagles over a corpse, picking it apart and gorging on its valuables.

The Collapse of the Universe?

As I continue the exposition of Matthew 24, I will note some remarkable concessions made by recent dispensationalists. These indicate the unwinding of dispensationalism's literalistic hermeneutic, a major element of the historic dispensational system.

---

[30] The burning of these adulteresses is after they have died by stoning or some other such means.

[31] See also: Gen. 40:19; 1 Sam. 17:44; 1 Kgs. 14:11; 16:4; 21:24; Psa. 79:2; Jer. 7:33; Jer. 15:3; 16:4; 19:7; Eze. 39:17; Rev. 6:8; 19:21.

Classic Dispensationalism and Matthew 24:29

Classic dispensationalists deem the following words conclusive of the futurity of the Great Tribulation, linking its conclusion with the Second Advent: "Immediately after the tribulation of those days shall the sun be darkened, and the moon shall not give her light, and the stars shall fall from heaven, and the powers of the heavens shall be shaken" (Matt. 24:29).

If we interpret this verse in a woodenly literal sense, the astronomical phenomena are too catastrophic for A.D. 70. At this juncture in our study, I will list some sample explanations of Matthew 24:29 by literalistic dispensationalists. Then I will consider both the proper interpretation of the passage and some recent dispensational concessions indicating the strength of the preterist argument.

Walvoord: "There will be other unusual phenomena occurring in connection with the second coming of Christ (. . .Matt. 24:29)." "The Second Coming will be preceded by many supernatural events in the skies. . . . (Matt. 24:29)."[32]

Wiersbe: "Those who have confused those two 'sign events' have ended up believing that Jesus Christ returned in A.D. 70!" "The cosmic changes mentioned in Matthew 24:29 precede the return of Jesus Christ to the earth."[33]

Ice: "Matthew 24:29 says 'the sun will be darkened.'. . . The question must be raised: Did the sun literally not shine over the land of Egypt and at the same time shine in the land of Goshen during the ninth plague (Exodus 10:21-29)? Of course. . . . The point is clear: If these events are to happen literally, in a manner corresponding to the Exodus events, then the whole preterist view is wrong. . . ."[34]

Hindson: "The reference to the events **Immediately after the tribulation,** such as the sun being darkened and the stars falling, etc., refer to the cataclysmic events that will accompany Christ's return at the end of the Tribulation to establish his Millennial Kingdom on earth."[35]

Barbieri: "**Immediately** following **the distress of** that period, the Lord will return. His return will be accompanied by unusual displays in the heavens (v. 29. . .)."[36]

Clearly dispensationalism views Matthew 24:29 as referring to a literal, astronomical catastrophe associated with the Second Advent. Just as clearly,

---

[32] Walvoord, *Prophecy Knowledge Handbook,* 333, 389.

[33] Wiersbe, *Bible Exposition Commentary,* 1:88, 89.

[34] House and Ice, *Dominion Theology,* 318, 319.

[35] Edward E. Hindson, "Matthew," Hindson and Woodrow Michael Kroll, *Liberty Commentary on the New Testament* (Lynchburg, Vir.: Liberty Press, 1978), 79.

[36] Barbieri, "Matthew," p. 78.

such events do not occur in A.D. 70 — if interpreted literally. How shall we understand this passage?

Stellar Imagery and National Devastation

Once again we must briefly mention the controlling exegetical factor of the passage — a factor absolutely precluding the imposition of an a priori literalism. Just five verses after the statement before us, Jesus unambiguously asserts: "Assuredly, I say to you, this generation will by no means pass away till all these things are fulfilled" (Matt. 24:34).

How then shall we understand verse 29? Rather than interpreting it in a woodenly literal manner, we must interpret it covenantally. That is, we should let Scripture interpret Scripture. I will argue that this passage speaks of the A.D. 70 collapse of geo-political Israel. Let us note that there is biblical warrant for speaking of national catastrophe in terms of cosmic destruction.

Isaiah 13 speaks of remarkably similar events accompanying Babylon's collapse in the Old Testament era. Indisputably, Isaiah has in view the fall of Babylon: "The burden against Babylon which Isaiah the son of Amoz saw" (Isa. 13:1). "Behold, I will stir up the Medes against them. . . . And Babylon, the glory of kingdoms, the beauty of the Chaldeans' pride, will be as when God overthrew Sodom and Gomorrah" (Isa. 13:17, 19). But how does Isaiah describe Babylon's fall? As cosmic destruction: "For the stars of heaven and their constellations will not give their light; the sun will be darkened in its going forth, and the moon will not cause its light to shine. . . . Therefore I will shake the heavens, and the earth will move out of her place" (Isa. 13:10, 13).

The biblical prophet describes the historical fall of Edom with celestial imagery: "Their slain shall be thrown out; their stench shall rise from their corpses, and the mountains shall be melted with their blood. All the host of heaven shall be dissolved, and the heavens shall be rolled up like a scroll; all their host shall fall down as the leaf falls from the vine. . . . For My sword shall be bathed in heaven; indeed it shall come down on Edom" (Isa. 34:3-5).

Elsewhere Ezekiel describes the fall of Egypt in history: "'Son of man, take up a lamentation for Pharaoh king of Egypt, and say to him. . . . When I put out your light, I will cover the heavens, and make its stars dark; I will cover the sun with a cloud, and the moon shall not give her light. All the bright lights of the heavens I will make dark over you'" (Eze. 32:2, 7-8).

Such imagery, then, indicates that the God of the heavens (the Creator of the sun, moon, and stars) is moving in judgment against a nation (blotting out its light). When a national government collapses in war and upheaval it is often poetically portrayed "as a cosmic catastrophe — an undoing of Creation."[37]

---

[37] Dyer, "Jeremiah," *Bible Knowledge Commentary*, 1135.

In fact, the Old Testament applies this vivid poetic language to Israel's historical judgment. Jeremiah portrays the destruction of Jerusalem by the Babylonians in like terms: "At that time it will be said to this people and to Jerusalem, 'A dry wind of the desolate heights blows in the wilderness toward the daughter of My people. . . . I beheld the earth, and indeed it was without form, and void; and the heavens, they had no light. I beheld the mountains, and indeed they trembled, and all the hills moved back and forth . . . . For this shall the earth mourn, and the heavens above be black, because I have spoken" (Jer. 4:11, 23-24, 29). Similarly the prophet Joel threatens Israel's Old Testament judgment: "Blow the trumpet in Zion, and sound an alarm in My holy mountain. . . . The earth quakes before them, the heavens tremble; the sun and moon grow dark, and the stars diminish their brightness" (Joel 2:1, 10).

Consequently, we may easily apply Matthew 24:29 to the destruction of Jerusalem in A.D. 70. Christ draws the imagery in his prophecy from Old Testament judgment passages that sound as if they are world-ending events. And in a sense it is "the end of the world" for those nations God judges. So is it with Israel in A.D. 70.

Dispensational Hermeneutic Concessions

Although it was not so twenty years ago, today there is no hermeneutic reason why dispensationalists may dismiss out-of-hand the preterist interpretation of Matthew 24:29. Even Dallas Seminary's *dispensational Bible Knowledge Commentary* admits such stellar catastrophic language is applicable to historical judgments. Let me cite some explanations of a few Old Testament cosmic destruction passages from this commentary. I will parenthetically list the author and page number from the commentary. The statements below undermine the literalistic hermeneutic of dispensationalism and cripple the argument against a preterist view of Matthew 24.

On Jeremiah 4:23-28: "Jeremiah pictured God's coming judgment as a cosmic catastrophe — an undoing of Creation. Using imagery from the Creation account (Gen. 1) Jeremiah indicated that no aspect of life would remain untouched. God would make Judah **formless and empty**. . . . God's imagery was so awesome that some might have though he would totally destroy the land of Israel" (Charles Dyer, 1136).

On Isaiah 13:10: "The statements in 13:10 about the heavenly bodies (**stars. . . sun . . .moon**) no longer functioning may figuratively describe the total turnaround of the political structure of the Near East. The same would be true of **the heavens** trembling **and the earth** shaking (v. 13), figures of speech suggesting all-encompassing destruction" (John A. Martin, 1059).

On Ezekiel 32:11-16 (cp. vv. 3-8): "This third section of Ezekiel's lament drops the figurative description of Egypt's destruction (vv. 3-8) and portrays Egypt's fall to Babylon literally" (Charles H. Dyer, 1291).

On Joel 2:10-11: "The army's approach is accompanied by cosmic disorder. The entire world, from **earth** below to **sky** above, quivers (cf. **shakes** and **trembles**) before the thunderous battle cry of the divine Commander. This cosmic response is a typical poetic description of the Lord's theophany as Warrior. . . If the army in Joel 2:1-11 was in Joel's **day**, it may foreshadow the army in chapter 3" (Robert B. Chisolm, Jr., 1417).

Strangely, the same commentary set interprets Matthew 24:29 by reference to Isaiah 13:10, which serves as evidence "His return will be accompanied by unusual displays in the heavens (v. 29; cf. Isa. 13:10; 34:4. . . .)" (Louis A. Barbieri, Jr., 78). But why may we not interpret these stellar phenomena in Matthew 24:29 like those in Isaiah, Jeremiah, Ezekiel, and Joel? The devastation of Jerusalem is a divine judgment tantamount to the destruction of the world. In fact, Jerusalem's fall is the collapse of the Jews's world, as it were.

The Sign of the Son of Man in Heaven

We turn now to consider the meaning of Matthew 24:30: "And then shall appear the sign of the Son of man in heaven: and then shall all the tribes of the earth mourn, and they shall see the Son of man coming in the clouds of heaven with power and great glory." This verse, along with all other verses leading up to it from Matthew 24:1, applies to the A.D. 70 destruction of the Temple.

It is easy to see how futurists jump to the conclusion that this is referring to the Second Advent — when we omit the historical episode designate (Matt. 24:2) and the time qualifier (Matt. 24:34). But we should not omit these. Let us see how the several elements of this verse fit nicely into the preterist understanding of the whole passage.

Grammatical Considerations

Here I prefer the Authorized Version (KJV) to most other translations (including the New King James Version). It follows the Greek word order more closely and translates the passage so accurately: "Then shall appear the sign of the Son of Man in heaven" is the translation of the Greek, which reads: καὶ τότε φανήσεται τὸ σημεῖον τοῦ υἱοῦ τοῦ ἀνθρώπου ἐν οὐρανῷ (*kai tote phanesetai to semeion tou huiou tou anthropou en ourano*, Matt. 24:30a).[38]

---

[38] A word for word translation would be: *kai* = and, *tote* = then, *phanesetai* = shall appear, *to* = the, *semeion* = sign, *tou* = of the, *huiou* = son, *tou* = of the, *anthropou* = man, *en ourano* = in heaven. See the American Standard Version and A. Marshall, *The Interlinear Greek-English New Testament* (2d ed.: Grand Rapids: Zondervan, 1959), 108.

I believe it is somewhat misleading to translate the phrase: "then shall appear the Son of Man in the sky." To understand this verse in such a manner not only requires a restructuring of the text, but is patently anti-contextual. It is important to note that the "sign" is what "shall appear": "then will appear[39] the sign." The Son of Man does not appear; the sign appears. Then Christ defines what the sign signifies: it is the sign "of the Son of Man" (a descriptive genitive).

What Christ teaches here is extremely important to redemptive history. He is responding to the question of his disciples regarding when the end of the "age" (αἰῶνος, *aionos*) will occur (Matt. 24:3). In essence, his full answer is: When the Romans lay waste the Temple (vv. 6 and 15 anticipate this) and pick apart Jerusalem (v. 28); that is, when the government of Israel utterly collapses (v. 29), then it will be evident he who prophesies this destruction is "in heaven." The "sign" is not a visible token in heaven (or the sky): the "Son of Man," whom the first century Jews reject, is in heaven, as the "sign" indicates. But what is "the sign"?

The Smoking Temple

The Temple's final destruction (which is the main topic of the discourse, Matt. 23:38-24:3) serves as the sign that the Son of Man is in heaven. It is his curse upon "these things" (Matt. 24:2) that causes this woe; it is his wrath as the Son of Man in heaven that sovereignly brings judgment: "Daughters of Jerusalem, do not weep for Me, but weep for yourselves and for your children. For indeed the days are coming in which they will say, 'Blessed are the barren, the wombs that never bore, and the breasts which never nursed!' Then they will begin to say to the mountains, 'Fall on us!' and to the hills, 'Cover us!' For if they do these things in the green wood, what will be done in the dry?" (Luke 23:28-31). He prophesies it; the Jews will experience the fulfilling of his powerful word.

The idea of Matthew 24:30 is parallel in some respects to that of Acts 2:19: "I will show wonders in heaven above and signs in the earth beneath: blood and fire and vapor of smoke." Those elements marking the total collapse of Jerusalem — blood, fire, and smoke — serve as the sign that the Son of Man is at God's right hand.

Interestingly, smoke serves as a sign for Israel's armies in the Old Testament: "Now the appointed signal between the men of Israel and the men in ambush was that they would make a great cloud of smoke rise up from the city" (Jdgs. 20:38). In Scripture the bellowing of smoke clouds from a scene

---

[39] The Greek φαίνω (*phaino*, "appear") may indicate "perceive, recognize," and not just "personally appear." See: 2 Cor. 13:7; Luke 24:11.

of judgment often serves as evidence of that judgment (Gen. 19:28; Josh. 18:20; 20:40; Psa. 37:20; Isa. 14:31; 34:10; Rev. 14:11; 18:9).

In another context employing slightly different terminology, Christ tells the Sanhedrin who condemn Him: "I say to you, hereafter you will see the Son of Man sitting at the right hand of the Power, and coming on the clouds of heaven" (Matt. 26:64). In the smoky destruction of Jerusalem these Jewish leaders should see the Son of Man's position of power in his cloud-judgment (see below).

The sign, then, signifies that the Son of Man is in heaven, where he comes from (John 3:13, 31; 6:42; 17:5) and ascends to (Mark 16:19; Luke 24:51; John 14:2, 4). Despite the disbelief of the Jews (John 6:32-42) who seek signs from heaven (Matt. 16:1; Mark 8:11; Luke 11:16), Christ is from heaven. The era of racial focus (the Jews), geographical delimitation (the Promised Land), and typological ministry (the Temple and its services) is fading away (John 4:21-23; Heb. 12:27-28). The destruction of the Temple is the final, conclusive sign: the Son of Man is in heaven so that he might be Lord of all nations (Matt. 28:19-20; Acts 2:21; Rev. 1:5) in spiritual worship (John 4:24; Phil. 3:3).

Heaven Above

The Greek word for "heaven" here is οὐρανὸς *(ouranos)*, which may be translated either "heaven" (the abode of God) or "sky" (the cloudy atmosphere above the ground). Here it is best to translate it as "heaven." This fits better with the redemptive historical significance of the earthly Temple's removal and the ascending to heaven of the True Temple, Jesus Christ (cf. John 2:18-22; cp. Matt. 12:6).

If one disputes this translation, however, the preterist utility of the verse still remains. Suppose we translate the verse: "then shall appear the sign of the Son of man in the sky." In this case we would apply *the sign in the sky* to the *place where the smoke ascends* from Jerusalem's smoldering remains. That is, if the verse is not informing us of the ultimate reality that Jerusalem's destruction is proof the Son of Man is in heaven, then it would be teaching that the smoke-sign in the sky is an indication of his visitation of Jerusalem in wrath. Either way, preterism sufficiently accounts for Matthew 24:30a, though the initial translation is much preferred.

Consider one of the options Dallas Seminary's commentary suggests: "Exactly what the sign of the Son of Man will be is unknown . . . . Some believe the sign may involve the heavenly city, New Jerusalem, which may descend at this time and remain as a satellite city suspended over the earthly city Jerusalem throughout the Millennium (Rev. 21:2-3)."[40] This is a strange

---

[40] Barbieri, "Matthew," p. 78. J. Dwight Pentecost holds this strange conception of the New Jerusalem, see: Pentecost, *Things to Come*, 577-580.

interpretation, to say the least.

The Mourning of the Tribes

In Matthew 24:30b we read: "Then all the tribes of the earth will mourn, and they will see the Son of Man coming on the clouds of heaven with power and great glory." As with the word ouranos (mentioned above), so the word γῆ, *(ge,* translated "earth") contains two basic ideas. The word may have either a general referent: *the tangible ground, the earth.* Or it may have a specific referent: *a particular land area, a nation.*

The Arndt-Gingrich *Lexicon* gives the following possible meanings of γῆ *(ge):* 1. Soil, earth (see: Mark 4:5, 8, 20). 2. Ground (see: Matt. 10:29; 15:35). 3. Bottom of the sea (not in Scripture). 4. Land, region, country, native land (see: Matt. 10:15; 11:24). 5. The earth, globe (Acts 10:12; 2 Pet. 3:5). Of course, which meaning we choose is a matter of contextual exegesis.

The Rabbis are particularly careful in their description of "the land" (ἡ γῆ, *he ge).* Edersheim notes that "Palestine was to the Rabbis simply 'the land,' all other countries being summed up under the designation of 'outside the land.'"[41] Elsewhere he comments:

> The pilgrim who, leaving other countries, entered Palestine, must have felt as if he had crossed the threshold to another world. Manners, customs, institutions, law, life, nay, the very intercourse between man and man, were quite different. All was dominated by the one all-absorbing idea of religion. It penetrated every relation of life. Moreover, it was inseparably connected with the soil, as well as the people of Palestine, at least so long as the Temple stood. Nowhere else could the Shekhinah . . . dwell or manifest itself; nor could, unless under exceptional circumstances, and for 'the merit of the fathers,' the spirit of prophecy be granted outside its bounds. To the orthodox Jew the mental and spiritual horizon was bounded by Palestine. It was 'the land'; all the rest of the world, except Babylonia, was 'outside the land.' No need to designate it especially as 'holy'; for all here bore the impress of sanctity, as he understood it.[42]

---

[41] Alfred Edersheim, *Sketches of Jewish Social Life* (Grand Rapids: Eerdmans, 1972 [1876]), 14. See Mishnah tractates: Orlah 3:9; Gittim 1:2; Abodah Zarah 1:8; Mikwaoth 8:1. Kelim 1:6 notes that "there are ten degrees of holiness. The Land of Israel is holier than any other land."

[42] Alfred Edersheim, *The Life and Times of Jesus the Messiah* (Grand Rapids: Eerdmans, rep. n.d. [1883]), Bk. 1, ch. 7.

The context of Matthew 24 — involving the Scribes and Pharisees (23:1ff), Temple (24:2), Judea (24:16), and "this generation" (24:34) — strongly suggests that the proper translation of verse 30b is "the tribes of the land." The reference to "the tribes" reinforces this view in that it is a common designate for the Twelve Tribes of Israel.[43] The Septuagint "with few exceptions . . . has φυλή [*phule*, "tribe"], so that this becomes a fixed term for the tribal system of Israel."[44] Indeed, the Old Testament text from which Christ draws this wording shows the tribes of Israel are in view (cf. Zech. 12:10-14).

So then, the mourning will befall the Jewish tribes in Israel; they will endure the brunt of God's wrath and judgment for their rejection of Christ. They must flee the area if they are to preserve their lives (Matt. 24:16). After this fearful flight they shall mourn the loss of their beloved land, government, homes, friends, and Temple.

Here again, though, we may allow a less restrictive translation for argument's sake. Even if some insist on the translation "earth, world" in Matthew 24:30b, the preterist view is unharmed. Instead of locating the mourning in Israel where the scene of judgment focuses, this translation would speak of the widespread Jewish mourning throughout the world upon hearing the news. Surely the Jews throughout the world of the day would mourn Jerusalem's fall and the Temple's destruction. Though the other translation is contextually preferable.

The Clouds of Heaven

The final phrase in Matthew 24:30c is: "They will see the Son of Man coming on the clouds of heaven with power and great glory."

We must again recall Christ's interchange with the Sanhedrin at his ecclesiastical trial before his crucifixion: "The high priest answered and said to Him, 'I adjure You by the living God that You tell us if You are the Christ, the Son of God.' Jesus said to him, 'It is as you said. Nevertheless, I say to *you*, hereafter you will see the Son of Man sitting at the right hand of the Power, and coming on the clouds of heaven'" (Matt. 26:63-64). Here Christ informs the Sanhedrin that they will see his coming. As I argue above, this is not a physical, visible coming, but a judgment-coming upon Jerusalem. They "see" it in the sense we "see" how a math problem works: with the "eye of understanding" rather than the organ of vision.

Again we must recall that the "coming" the Sanhedrin (Matt. 26:64) and

---

[43] Gen. 49:28; Exo. 24:4; Eze. 47:13; Matt. 19:28; Luke 22:30; Acts 26:7; Rev. 21:12.

[44] Christian Maurer "φυλή (*phule*)," Gerhard Kittel and Gerhard Friedreich, eds., 10 vols., *Theological Dictionary of the New Testament*, trans. by Geoffrey W. Bromiley (Grand Rapids: Eerdmans, 1974), 9:246.

Israel at large (Matt. 24:30) will witness is like Jehovah's coming against Egypt in the Old Testament: "The burden against Egypt. Behold, the LORD rides on a swift cloud, and will come into Egypt" (Isa. 19:1). The LORD did not physically ride on a cloud down into Egypt. I agree with Dallas Seminary's *Bible Knowledge Commentary*: Isaiah 19:1 speaks of "the impending Assyrian advance" under "God's judgment."[45] Likewise, neither is it exegetically necessary that the "coming of the Son of Man" be a physical coming that the Sanhedrin will see. Because Israel rejects her Messiah (Matt. 23:37; John 1:11; Acts 26:7), he judges her.

The Great Jubilee

I move now Matthew 24:31: "And He will send His angels with a great sound of a trumpet, and they will gather together His elect from the four winds, from one end of heaven to the other."

Dispensational Confusion

The surface appearance in this verse of an eschatological rapture or the Second Advent seems amenable to the dispensational system: "they will gather together His elect from the four winds," at the "trumpet" sound issued by "angels." Yet classic dispensationalism has such a pandemonium of theological qualifications, historical compartments, redemptive peoples, eschatological phenomena, revelational programs, law principles, and so forth, that this passage really expresses the system's weaknesses, rather than demonstrating its strength.

Walvoord writes of this verse: "Some[46] have taken the elect here to refer specifically to the elect living on earth, but it is more probable that this event will include all the elect, or the saved, including Old Testament saints, saved Israel, the church,[47] and the saints of the Tribulation period leading up to the Second Coming. Some will need to be resurrected from the dead, such as the martyrs (Rev. 20:4-6) and the Old Testament saints (Dan. 12:2). The church was resurrected, or translated, earlier, at the time of the Rapture. At the second coming of Christ no child of God will be left unresurrected or unrestored, but all will share in the millennial kingdom."[48]

Notice the multiplying of peoples here. The general resurrection of amillen-

---

[45] John A. Martin, "Isaiah," *Bible Knowledge Commentary: Old Testament*, 1065.

[46] One of the "some" is J. Dwight Pentecost, who teaches that this verse speaks of the "regathering of Israel." Pentecost, *Things to Come*, 282; Pentecost, *Thy Kingdom Come*, 255.

[47] Pentecost comments: "the reference to 'his elect' (v. 31) could not possibly refer to the church." Pentecost, *Thy Kingdom Come*, 255.

[48] Walvoord, *Prophecy Knowledge Handbook*, 390.

nialism and postmillennialism divides people into two classes: the saved and the lost. But when talk of the resurrection arises, dispensationalists must account for various classes of peoples in their respective programs, resurrections, judgments, rewards, eternal destinies, and so forth.

For example, notice the following partial listing of judgments by Walvoord: "According to the Scriptures a series of judgments is related to Christ's return. . . . [T]he martyred dead of the great Tribulation will be judged and rewarded [Rev. 20:4]. In addition, Israel will be judged (Eze. 20:33-38), and the Gentiles will be judged (Matt. 25:31-46). These judgments precede and lead up to the millennial kingdom."[49] Thus, "while all the righteous will be raised before the Millennium, individuals will retain their identities and their group identifications such as Gentile believers and believers in Israel in the Old Testament, the church of the New Testament, and saints of the Tribulation."[50]

Of Matthew 24:31 Walvoord defines the elect in terms of the various dispensationally imposed categories: "Old Testament saints, saved Israel, the church, and the saints of the Tribulation period." Fortunately, the timing of this resurrection is such that it does not have to account for another group of the righteous: those who die in the millennium after conversion to Christ.[51] Walvoord explains that the "first resurrection" language of Revelation 20 actually "supports the conclusion that the resurrection of the righteous is by stages." These stages include the church at the Rapture, the two witnesses in the Tribulation, the Tribulation martyrs soon after Christ's return to earth, and the Old Testament saints.[52]

Postmillennial Jubilee

A more reasonable interpretation of Matthew 24:31 is to view it as a symbolical trumpeting in of the ultimate Jubilee Year. This is the time of the forgiveness of man's ultimate debt; it is the "day of salvation." By employing imagery drawn from the Year of Jubilee in Leviticus 25, the Lord here speaks of the final stage of redemption. This redemptive culmination begins in his earthly ministry, as we may surmise from such passages as Mark 1:15: "The time is fulfilled, and the kingdom of God is at hand. Repent, and believe in

---

[49] John F. Walvoord, "Revelation," *Bible Knowledge Commentary: New Testament*, 980.

[50] Ibid.

[51] "In the millennial kingdom it will be a time of great joy and rejoicing and deliverance for the people of God, but death and sin will still be present." Walvoord, *Prophecy Knowledge Handbook*, 119. In fact, Walvoord seems oblivious to the fate of deceased millennial saints, for he never mentions them in his Revelation exposition in *Bible Knowledge Commentary*.

[52] Walvoord, "Revelation," *Bible Knowledge Commentary*, 980.

the gospel." It is sealed at the destruction of Jerusalem, which we see in Mark 9:1: "Assuredly, I say to you that there are some standing here who will not taste death till they see the kingdom of God present with power." The levitical Jubilee law is a ceremonial law symbolically portraying the coming of full forgiveness in the Messiah and the incorporation of the nations into the one people of God (see: Matt. 8:11-12; Rom. 11:11-25; Eph. 2:12-21).

The Old Testament Jubilee Year follows after seven consecutive sabbath years. The sabbath year is a God-ordained year of rest for the land held every seventh year. The Year of Jubilee occurs after the passing of seven sevens, or after the forty-ninth year. It is the culmination of all of the sabbatical tokens of rest.[53]

In the Year of Jubilee, Israel experiences release from bondage and debt:

> And you shall consecrate the fiftieth year, and proclaim liberty throughout all the land to all its inhabitants. It shall be a Jubilee for you; and each of you shall return to his possession, and each of you shall return to his family. That fiftieth year shall be a Jubilee to you; in it you shall neither sow nor reap what grows of its own accord, nor gather the grapes of your untended vine. For it is the Jubilee; it shall be holy to you; you shall eat its produce from the field. In this Year of Jubilee, each of you shall return to his possession. And if you sell anything to your neighbor or buy from your neighbor's hand, you shall not oppress one another (Lev. 25:10-14).

The typology of redemption contained in the Jubilee legislation lends it a beautiful prophetic utility. Isaiah employs Jubilee imagery to prophesy of the coming ultimate Jubilee:

> The Spirit of the Lord GOD is upon Me, because the LORD has anointed Me to preach good tidings to the poor; He has sent Me to heal the brokenhearted, to proclaim liberty to the captives, and the opening of the prison to those who are bound; to proclaim the acceptable year of the LORD, and the day of vengeance of our God (Isa. 61:1-2).

The Lord Jesus Himself introduces the fulfillment of the Jubilee Law in his ministry, when he preaches from Isaiah 61 at the Temple:

And He was handed the book of the prophet Isaiah. And when He

---

[53] Daniel's Seventy Weeks, which lead up to Christ, is also clearly framed in terms of the Jubilee law. See pages 13-14 above.

had opened the book, He found the place where it was written: "The Spirit of the LORD is upon Me, because He has anointed Me to preach the gospel to the poor. He has sent Me to heal the brokenhearted, to preach deliverance to the captives and recovery of sight to the blind, to set at liberty those who are oppressed, to preach the acceptable year of the LORD." Then He closed the book, and gave it back to the attendant and sat down. And the eyes of all who were in the synagogue were fixed on Him. And He began to say to them, "Today this Scripture is fulfilled in your hearing" (Luke 4:17-21).

Thus, Christ's ministry introduces "the Acceptable Year of the Lord" (Luke 4:19), "the Day of Salvation" (2 Cor. 6:6), which the righteous of the Old Testament longed to see (Matt. 13:17).

This is why the Lord mentions the sounding of the "trumpet" in Matthew 24: it was the means for announcing the Jubilee.[54] According to Matthew 24:31, when the Temple order collapses, Christ's "angels" will go forth to all nations joyfully trumpeting the gospel of salvific liberation: "And He will send His angels with a great sound of a trumpet, and they will gather together His elect from the four winds, from one end of heaven to the other."

The word for "angel" here is ἄγγελος (*aggelos*) in the Greek. It can be translated "messengers," signifying human messengers, as in several places in Scripture.[55] It does not seem to refer to the supernatural heavenly beings here. Rather the idea here is that those who know Christ as Savior will go forth into all the earth proclaiming the message of full salvation, the removal of man's sin debt to God. But even if we apply this to angels, it could then refer "to the supernatural power which lies behind such preaching."[56] Then it would teach that the angels of God attend our faithful proclamation.

It is particularly after the fall of Jerusalem that the Church is freed from its bondage to Judaism. This occurs so that she might become a truly universal Church, rather than a racially-focused, geographically-confined people. A major problem plaguing the pre-A.D. 70 church is Zionism, as is evident in Acts 10, 11, 15, Galatians, and Hebrews.[57] This is a serious threat to the

---

[54] The clarion call to salvation or the strong word of God may be expressed as a "voice like a trumpet." See: Isa. 58:1; Jer. 6:17; Rev. 1:10; 4:1.

[55] Matthew 11:10; Mark 1:2; Luke 7:24, 27; 9:52. See: LXX at 2 Chron. 36:15-16; Hag. 1:13; Mal. 2:7.

[56] R. T. France, *Matthew (Tyndale New Testament Commentaries)* (Downers Grove, Ill.: Inter-Varsity Press, 1985), 345. This is one of the better commentaries for studying the Olivet Discourse.

[57] For more information see my *Before Jerusalem Fell: Dating the Book of Revelation*

universality and advance of the Christian message.

Through gospel preaching by faithful messengers, God gathers the elect into his kingdom from the four corners of the world. The phrase "from one end of heaven to the other" does not indicate the place of the action in heaven above; it often signifies nothing more than "horizon to horizon" (Deut. 30:4; Neh. 1:9; cp. Matt. 8:11; Luke 13:28-29). Rather, it speaks of evangelistic activity spreading throughout the earth; it parallels "from the four winds," that is, the four points of the compass.

The "gathering together" (ἐπισυνάξουσιν, *episunaxousin*) involves both the local assembling of the saints in microcosm (Heb. 10:25; Jms. 2:2) and the universal assembling of the saints in macrocosm (2 Thess. 2:1; cp. Matt. 22:7-13). The proclamation of the gospel is to be worldwide, as confidently expected in the Old Testament (Psa. 22:27; Isa. 45:22; Mic. 5:4) and the New Testament (Matt. 28:19-20; Luke 13:29; Acts 13:39).

Conclusion

We must realize the significance of the collapse of Jerusalem in A.D. 70; it effectively removes a major hindrance to the spread of the Christian faith. We see this particularly in two respects: (1) The Jewish ceremonial laws confuse many early Christians. Circumcision is particularly troublesome in that some deem it necessary for salvation (Acts 15; Gal. 5:1-6; Phil. 3:1-3). The growing danger exists that Christianity will be a mere sect of Judaism, as the Romans originally assume. With the Temple's destruction, this tendency will subside. (2) The first persecutors of the faith are the Jews (Acts 8:1ff). With the A.D. 70 demise of the Jews's strength and the dissipation of their energy, Christianity receives much less resistance from them. Jewish persecution of Christians does not cease entirely (Polycarp is a dramatic case in point), but it does decline significantly.

The Key Text

In this conclusion to our study of Matthew 24, I arrive at the passage containing the verse I deal with in our introduction. We come now to verses 31-36, which include the all important key text for the understanding of this section of the Olivet Discourse: verse 34. At this point I want to consider this verse in its immediate setting, in order to throw additional light on it.

Matthew 24:31-36 reads:

> And He will send His angels with a great sound of a trumpet, and
> they will gather together His elect from the four winds, from one

---

(Tyler, Tex.: Institute for Christian Economics, 1989), chs. 8, 13.

end of heaven to the other. Now learn this parable from the fig tree: When its branch has already become tender and puts forth leaves, you know that summer is near. So you also, when you see all these things, know that it is near, at the very doors. Assuredly, I say to you, this generation will by no means pass away till all these things are fulfilled. Heaven and earth will pass away, but My words will by no means pass away. But of that day and hour no one knows, no, not even the angels of heaven, but My Father only.

The Great Prophet and Prophetic Signs

A simple reading of Matthew 24:34 provides an unambiguous assertion that *all* of the things Christ the Great Prophet mentions up to this point — that is, everything in verses 4 through 34 — are to occur *in the very generation of the original disciples*: "Assuredly, I say to you, this generation will by no means pass away till all these things are fulfilled" (24:34). Here "this generation" is identical to "this generation" of Matthew 23:36. In Matthew 23 the Lord rebukes the Scribes and Pharisees of his own day (Matt. 23:13-16, 23, 25, 27, 29). Then in Matthew 23:36 he assures them: "I say to you, all these things will come upon this generation." We may not catapult these woes two thousand years into the future.

Neither may we project the events of Matthew 24:4-34 into the distant future. In fact, the whole impetus to this discourse is Christ's reference to the destruction of the historical Temple to which the disciples point (Matt. 23:38 - 24:1-3). Here we must remind ourselves that a series of divinely ordained signs will precede the approaching destruction of the Temple (24:4ff). The first few signs are general indicators of the final judgment on the Temple: "All these are the beginning of sorrows" (24:8). All of these signs do, in fact, come to pass in the era before A.D. 70. Just as surely as fig leaves indicate approaching summer (24:32), so the events of Matthew 24:4-32 signify the destruction of the Temple.

Christ's Second Advent Unknown

This matter of the historical signs is important in another way. Following his prophecy of the Temple's demise the Lord turns to consider his glorious Second Advent (24:36ff). He specifically says there will be no such signs of that distant event: "But of that day and hour no one knows. . . . As in the days before the flood, they were eating and drinking, marrying and giving in marriage, until the day that Noah entered the ark, and did not know until the flood came and took them all away, so also will the coming of the Son of Man be. . . . Watch therefore, for you do not know what hour your Lord is coming" (24:36-42). With these words the Lord looks beyond the signs just given for "this generation" (αὖτη, *haute*, near demonstrative, Matt. 24:34) to the event of "that day" (ἐκείνης, *ekeines*, far demonstrative) (24:36). Thus, the Lord's attention turns to his Second Advent at the end of history. Although he provides signs regarding the events coming upon his own "generation," he carefully distinguishes his eschatological coming by the fact of its signlessness.

Contextual evidence suggests that Christ is distinguishing two different comings. One coming is his *coming upon Jerusalem* in temporal judgment to end the old covenant era; the other is his coming at the Second Advent in final judgment to end history (24:36ff). These two "comings" are theologically related while historically distinct. Consider the following:

(1) By all appearance Matthew 24:34 functions as a concluding statement; it seems to end the preceding prophecy: "Truly I say to you, this generation will not pass away until all these things take place." Consequently, the following events relate to some episode not in *this generation*. Thus, all prophecies before verse 34 are to occur in this generation.

(2) He contrasts the near and far in verse 36: "This generation" versus "that day." It would be more appropriate for Christ to speak of "this day" rather than "that day" if he is referring to the time of "this generation."

(3) The grammatical structure of the new section suggests a change of subject: Περί δὲ (*peri de*, "but of" or "but concerning"). Of this verse, the Arndt-Gingrich-Danker *Lexicon* comments that this structure appears "at the beginning of a sentence" and "is connected with the verb that follows."[58] Indeed, France insists verse 36 "marks a deliberate change of subject."[59]

(4) Before verse 34 Christ mentions signs pointing to the A.D. 70 coming: "wars and rumors of wars" (v. 6), "famines and earthquakes" (v. 7), "false prophets" (v. 11), and so forth. Accordingly, we may know the time of its approach; it is a predictable event. After verse 34, signs are replaced by elements of surprise, indicating the coming in that section is unknown and therefore unpredictable: "they did not understand" (v. 39), "you do not know" (v. 42), "if the head of the house had known" (v. 43), "coming at an hour

---

[58] William F. Arndt, Wilbur Gingrich, and Frederick W. Danker, *A Greek-English Lexicon of the New Testament and Other Early Christian Literature* (2d. ed.: University of Chicago Press, 1979), 645.

[59] R. T. France, *Matthew (Tyndale New Testament Commentaries)* (Downers Grove, Ill.: InterVarsity, 1985), 347.

when you do not think He will" (v. 44), "he does not expect him" (v. 50), and "you do not know" (25:13)

(5) Even Christ Himself does not know the time of the Second Advent (v. 36). In the earlier section, however, he clearly knows the time of the A.D. 70 judgment, for he tells his disciples that certain signs may come but "the end is not yet" (v. 6). He also tells them these things will certainly happen in "this generation."

(6) In the early section of Matthew 24 the time frame is short: "this generation." In the following section (and through Matt. 25) the time frame is much longer: "But if that evil servant says in his heart, 'My master is delaying his coming'" (Matt. 24:48). "But while the bridegroom was delayed, they all slumbered and slept" (Matt. 25:5). "After a long time the lord of those servants came and settled accounts with them" (Matt. 25:19).

(7) The character of the first section dramatically differs from that of the second. In the first section all is chaotic, laden with war and persecution. In the second section all appears tranquil, marrying and eating and drinking.

(8) In the first section Christ urges flight from the area (Matt. 24:16-20), clearly implying there will be time to flee. In the second section no opportunity for flight exists, all befalls men suddenly (Matt. 24:48-51).

Some, nevertheless, will try to squeeze datable signs from the text. The classic illustration of this is Edgar Whisenant's writings. Of verse 36, Whisenant argues:

> In all four gospels, Jesus never deviated from the day and the hour as the limitation on his church's Rapture. God says what He means and means what He says. You don't have to help God say what God means to say. Jesus said that only the day and the hour was un-known.... The Greek words used by Jesus imply that, we can know the week, month, and year, but we cannot know the day nor hour.[60]

Even dispensationalists more cautious than Whisenant fall to temptation here. Walvoord writes: "Though they will not know the day nor the hour, they will be able to comprehend the approximate time because the length of the

---

[60] Edgar C. Whisenant, *88 Reasons Why the Rapture Could be in 1988* (Nashville: World Bible Society, 1988), 6.

total period is forty-two months (Rev. 13:5)."[61] Barbieri is a little more vague, but still offers indicators: "The precise moment of the Lord's return cannot be calculated by anyone. . . . But the period before his coming will be like the time *in the days of Noah*."[62] Pentecost agrees: "While no one knows the specific day or hour in which Jesus Christ will return, people who properly understand and interpret the signs will know that they are living in the last days."[63]

There are problems with seeking signs for Christ's eschatological coming, however. First, the whole point of Jesus's instruction here is that men ought always to be ready: "Watch therefore, for you do not know what hour your Lord is coming" (Matt. 24:42). If he suggests there are historical signs that will point to the particular era (within forty-two months, a decade, or whatever), and if these signs are to precede a still future (to us) eschatological event, then his whole point is undermined. For then his first hearers and those following them for the next nineteen hundred years or so would be under no compulsion to readiness. The signs pointing to Christ's coming would still lay off hundreds of years in the future.

Second, in Revelation we find the forty-two month period that Walvoord brings into the discussion. But the temporal indicators there specifically tie the forty-two months to the first century. According to the Apostle John, the forty-two months of Revelation 11 are to happen "soon," they are "near" (Rev. 1:1, 3; 22:6, 10). In fact, John draws the words in Revelation 11:1-2 from Luke's version of the Olivet Discourse found in Luke 21:24; this has to do with the A.D. 67-70 destruction of Israel (cp. Rev. 11:1-2; Luke 21:20-24; Matt. 24:15-17). Notice that the reference to "gentiles" and "tread under foot" in Revelation 11:1-2 show John's dependence upon the Lord's words in Luke 21:24. Both texts relate the action to Jerusalem for a set time, as well.

> And they will fall by the edge of the sword, and be led away captive into all nations. And Jerusalem will be trampled by Gentiles until the times of the Gentiles are fulfilled. (Luke 21:24)

> But leave out the court which is outside the temple, and do not measure it, for it has been given to the Gentiles. And they will tread the holy city under foot for forty-two months. (Rev. 11:2).

Third, both the terms "day" and "hour" appear in Scripture in a non-

---

[61] Walvoord, *Prophecy Knowledge Handbook*, 389.
[62] Barbieri, "Matthew," *Bible Knowledge Commentary*, 78, 79.
[63] Pentecost, *Thy Kingdom Come*, 256.

literal way. The Greek ἡμέρα (*hemera*, "day") may be used in a non-literal sense of an era, such as the Christian era: "Behold, now is the accepted time; behold, now is the day of salvation" (2 Cor. 6:2b). And even ὥρα (*hora*, "hour") may stand for an expansive period of time: "Little children, it is the last hour; and as you have heard that the Antichrist is coming, even now many antichrists have come, by which we know that it is the last hour" (1 Jn. 2:18). Apparently the two words in Matthew 24 indicate we cannot know the extent of the longer ("day") or shorter ("hour") time before his Return.

The Lord's Second Advent is absolutely undatable. Christ does not suggest it may merely be imprecisely datable.

Conclusion

Although the Olivet Discourse is a favorite of date-setting populists, it should not be so. These verses, so often set in our near future, actually occur in our distant past. The relevance of Matthew 24:1-34 is to the first century. Furthermore, Christ specifically decries the possibility of dating his Second Coming (Matt. 24:36ff).

Many contemporary Christians believe beyond any doubt that we are living in the very last days before Christ's Return. Yet our parents and grandparents living through World Wars I and II seemingly had even clearer "signs." Hear the words of an earlier prophetic writer. Writing in 1918 Arthur W. Pink sounds the alarm:

> Brethren, the end of the Age is upon us. All over the world, reflecting minds are discerning the fact that we are on the eve of another of those far-reaching crises which make the history of our race.... Those who look out on present conditions are forced to conclude that the consummation of this dispensation is at hand.... The sands in the hour glass of this Day of Salvation have almost run out. The signs of the Times demonstrate it. 'But,' it may be asked, 'Have not other ages, as well as the present been crowded with signs of distress?' Undoubtedly. . . . They unduly magnified the evil, and erred in their calculations. . . . But today, the Signs are so plain they cannot be mis-read, though the foolish may close their eyes and refuse to examine them. What these Signs are we have shown at length in chapter six and if the evidence there furnished has not convinced the reader that the Lord is at hand, then there is little hope that any further arguments drawn from Scripture will do so.[64]

---

[64] A. W. Pink, *The Redeemer's Return* (Ashland, Ky.: Calvary Baptist Bookstore, rep. n.d. [1918]), 318-319.

Pink was wrong then; his contemporary sympathizers are wrong today. And for the same reasons: they are mis-reading the text. Pink eventually realized his error and changed his views. I am hopeful that many more Christians will exercise such wisdom.

CHAPTER FOUR

THE MAN OF LAWLESSNESS
2 Thessalonians 2:1-8

Let no one deceive you by any means; for that Day will not come unless the falling away comes first, and the man of sin is revealed, the son of perdition, who opposes and exalts himself above all that is called God or that is worshiped, so that he sits as God in the temple of God, showing himself that he is God.

2 Thessalonians 2:3-4

Introduction

In this chapter I will consider one of the more difficult passages of Scripture, rivaling Daniel 9 in its interpretive controversy: 2 Thessalonians 2. This famous eschatological reference contains Paul's reference to the Man of Lawlessness (Nestle's Text), or Man of Sin (Majority Text).

The passage is noted for its exceptional difficulty. The great church father Augustine writes of a certain portion of the passage: "I confess that I am entirely ignorant of what he means to say." New Testament Greek scholar Vincent omits interpreting the passage in his four volume lexical commentary: "I attempt no interpretation of this passage as a whole, which I do not understand." Renowned Greek linguist Robertson despairs of the task of interpreting these verses because the prophecy is "in such vague form that we can hardly clear it up." Morris urges "care" in handling this "notoriously difficult passage." Bruce notes that "there are few New Testament passages which can boast such a variety of interpretations as this." Best confesses: "we must acknowledge our ignorance." Ladd laments: "There are no darker words in the entire Pauline corpus than these, and any interpretation must be at best a hypothesis."[1] Even some dispensationalists admit it is an "extremely puz-

---

[1] Augustine, *City of God*, 20:19. Marvin R. Vincent, *Word Studies in the New Testament* (Grand Rapids: Eerdmans, rep. 1946 [1887]), 4:67. A. T. Robertson, *Word Pic-*

95

zling passage of Scripture that has been a thorn in the flesh of many an expositor."[2]

But as with the hotly debated Daniel 9:24-27 passage, so here: an exceedingly difficult prophecy becomes a key text for dispensationalism. Note the following comments by dispensationalists.

Constable observes that "this section of verses contain truths found nowhere else in the Bible. It is key to understanding future events and it is central to this epistle." Culver deems it "the cornerstone of the doctrine of the Antichrist," "a foundational text." According to Walvoord, the Man of Lawlessness revealed here is "the key to the whole program of the Day of the Lord." While attempting to prove the pretribulation rapture, Feinberg suggests "probably the strongest argument in support of this view is the identification of the Man of Sin (1 Thess. 2:3 [*sic*]) with the prince who makes the covenant with many and begins Daniel's seventieth week (Dan. 9:27)."[3]

Of 2 Thessalonians 2 Chafer notes: "though but one passage is found bearing upon the restraining work of the Holy Spirit, the scope of the issues involved is such as to command the utmost consideration." Pentecost agrees: "One of the important considerations accompanying a study of the tribulation period is the relation sustained by the Holy Spirit to that period and the work He will accomplish in it. . . . Much of the question of the Spirit's relation to the tribulation is determined by the interpretation of 2 Thessalonians 2:7-8."[4]

Ryrie and Feinberg employ 2 Thessalonians 2:4 as one of the few passages used "to clinch the argument" for the rebuilding of the Temple, while Thomas confidently asserts: "This evidently is a Jewish temple to be rebuilt in Jerusalem in the future. Dependence of these words on Daniel 9:26-27; 11:31,

---

tures in the New Testament 4:51. Leon Morris, *The First and Second Epistles to the Thessalonians* (*NICNT*) (Grand Rapids: Eerdmans, 1959), 213. F. F. Bruce, *New Testament History* (Garden City, N.Y.: Anchor, 1969), 309. Ernst Best, *Commentary on First and Second Thessalonians* (London: Black, 1977), 301. George Eldon Ladd, *A Theology of the New Testament* (Grand Rapids: Eerdmans, 1974), 560.

[2] E. Schuyler English, *Rethinking the Rapture* (Neptune, N.J.: Loizeaux, 1954), 72.

[3] Thomas L. Constable, "2 Thessalonians," in John F. Walvoord and Roy B. Zuck, eds., *Bible Knowledge Commentary: New Testament* (Wheaton: Victor, 1983), 717. Robert Duncan Culver, *Daniel and the Latter Days* (2d. ed.: Chicago: Moody, 1977), 71, 75. John F. Walvoord, *Prophecy Knowledge Handbook* (Wheaton, Ill.: Victor, 1990), 493. Lewis Sperry Chafer, *Systematic Theology*, 7 vols., (Dallas: Dallas Seminary, 1948), 6:85.Paul D. Feinberg, "The Case for the Pretribulation Rapture Position," in Gleason L. Archer, Jr., *et al*, *The Rapture: Pre-, Mid-, or Post-Tribulational?* (Grand Rapids: Zondervan, 1984), 61.

[4] J. Dwight Pentecost *Things to Come* (Grand Rapids: Zondervan, 1958), 259.

36, 37; 12:11 (cf. Matt 24:15; Mark 13:14) demands such a reference."[5] Ice and Price, who hold that "two additional Temples . . . will be built in the future,"[6] write: "The apostle Paul gives us perhaps the clearest passage relating to the third Temple in *2 Thessalonians 2:3,4.*"[7]

Because of its enormous difficulties, 2 Thessalonians 2 generates lively debate in eschatological studies. In the pessimistic eschatologies of amillennialism, premillennialism and dispensationalism, this passage frequently appears as evidence of worsening world conditions that lead up to a final apostasy within the Church. When countering the optimism of postmillennialism, amillennialist Hoekema refers to this passage in a mere two sentences,[8] confident it offers a self-evident refutation of postmillennialism. Hendriksen interprets this 2 Thessalonians 2:3 as pointing "to the fact that, by and large, the visible Church will forsake the true faith."[9] Dispensationalist Culver comments that this passage stands "in spite of this postmillennial doctrine of Christianity."[10]

Surely we go astray when establishing our eschatological program on 2 Thessalonians 2. Yet, though a perplexing passage requiring caution, I believe there is sufficient data in it at least to remove it from our future.

The Historical Setting

The Thessalonian epistles are among Paul's earliest writings, vying with Galatians (depending on the North/South Galatia debate[11]) and James as the earliest written portions of the New Testament. Paul writes these within just a few weeks of each other, and not long after his visit to Thessalonica (1

---

[5] Charles C. Ryrie, *The Basis of the Premillennial Faith* (Neptune, N.J.: Loizeaux, 1953), 151. See also: Charles Lee Feinberg in Feinberg, ed., *Prophecy and the Seventies* (Chicago: Moody, 1971), 181. Robert L. Thomas, "2 Thessalonians," in vol. 2, Frank E. Gaebelein, ed., *Expositor's Bible Commentary* (Grand Rapids: Zondervan, 1978), 322.

[6] Thomas Ice and Randall Price, *Ready to Rebuild: The Imminent Plan to Rebuild the Last Days Temple* (Eugene, Ore.: Harvest, 1992), 52.

[7] Ibid., 199.

[8] Anthony A. Hoekema, *The Bible and the Future* (Grand Rapids: Eerdmans, 1979), 178.

[9] William Hendriksen, *I and II Thessalonians* (NTC) (Grand Rapids: Baker, 1955), 171.

[10] Culver, *Daniel and the Latter Days*, 71.

[11] Donald Guthrie, *New Testament Introduction* (3rd ed.: Downer's Grove, Ill.: InterVarsity Press, 1970), 457-465. D. A. Carson, Douglas J. Moo, and Leon Morris, *An Introduction to the New Testament* (Grand Rapids: Zondervan, 1992), 290-294.

Thess. 2:17).[12] On his Second Missionary Journey (Acts 16-18) Paul travels from Philippi to Thessalonica, then to Berea, and Athens for brief visits. He then moves on to Corinth, where he writes the Thessalonian epistles. At Corinth he is alone until Silas and Timothy arrive (Acts 18:1, 5).

In 1 Thessalonians Paul mentions he has just been to Philippi (2:2), and to Athens (3:1) where Timothy arrives (3:6). The salutations of the letters mention Paul, Timothy, and Silas together (1 Thess. 1:1; 2 Thess. 1:1). Archaeologically we know that the Gallio of Acts 18:12-17 was proconsul in Corinth from A.D. 51-53. Thus, the dates of the letters would be about A.D. 51-52. Luke's record of the place and circumstances of Paul's writing in Acts provides background information extremely helpful in casting light on the obscure passage before us.

During Paul's visit to Thessalonica he preaches to the Jews that Jesus is the Messiah (Acts 17:1-3). Though some Jews believe, his preaching riles others to mob action (17:4-5). The mob even drags "some of the brethren to the rulers of the city" complaining: "These who have turned the world upside down have come here too. Jason has harbored them, and these are all acting contrary to the decrees of Caesar, saying there is another king — Jesus" (17:6-7). After taking security from Jason and the others, the civil rulers let them go (17:9), allowing Paul to depart safely to Berea. The Jews do not so easily quiet, however, for "when the Jews from Thessalonica learned that the word of God was preached by Paul at Berea, they came there also and stirred up the crowds" (17:13). This results in the immediate dismissal of Paul to Athens (17:14-15).

Paul stays in Athens only three or four weeks.[13] He soon travels to Corinth (Acts 18:1), where he remains for eighteen months (18:11). But again serious Jewish antipathy arises. Interestingly, at Corinth Paul meets Aquila and Priscilla, Christians who are among the Jews Claudius Caesar banishes from Rome (18:2). According to Roman historian Suetonius: "As the Jews were indulging in constant riots at the instigation of Chrestus, [Claudius] banished them from Rome."[14] This reference to "Chrestus" is undoubtedly a Latin variant for the name "Christ."[15]

---

[12] William Hendriksen, *I and II Thessalonians* (NTC) (Grand Rapids: Baker, 1955), 15. Guthrie, *New Testament Introduction*, 566-567, 579. John A. T. Robinson, *Redating the New Testament* (Philadelphia: Westminster, 1976), 53.

[13] F. F. Bruce, *The Book of the Acts* (NICNT) (Grand Rapids: Eerdmans, rep. 1980 [n.d.]), 364.

[14] Suetonius, *Claudius* 25:4. Cp. Dio Cassius, *History* 60:6; Orosius, *History*, 7:6:15ff.

[15] Michael Grant, ed., Suetonius, *The Twelve Caesars*, trans. by Robert Graves (London: Penguin, 1979), 202. See: Bruce, *New Testament History*, 297-299; Richard L. Niswonger, *New Testament History* (Grand Rapids: Zondervan, 1988), 113-114.

Upon meeting these saints, who had suffered from Jewish riots against Christians in Rome, Paul sets about boldly preaching to the Jews in Corinth: "Jesus is the Christ" (Acts 18:5; cp. 17:3). Again the Jews violently oppose his message, organizing resistance[16] against him and blaspheming to such an extent that he determines to turn from the Jews to the Gentiles (18:6). Matters worsen for him because of his remarkable success with a certain prominent Jewish leader, Crispus "the ruler of the synagogue" (18:8). Though Paul seldom baptizes, he baptizes Crispus (1 Cor. 1:14-16; Acts 18:8). Due to the intensity of the opposition, the Lord promises his special protection so that he will remain in Corinth (18:9-11).

All of this explains the strong language against the Jews in the Thessalonian epistles. It uncovers some of the more subtle concerns therein. In his first letter he writes:

> For you, brethren, became imitators of the churches of God which are in Judea in Christ Jesus. For you also suffered the same things from your own countrymen, just as they did from the Jews, who killed both the Lord Jesus and their own prophets, and have persecuted us; and they do not please God and are contrary to all men, forbidding us to speak to the Gentiles that they may be saved, so as always to fill up the measure of their sins; but wrath has come upon them to the uttermost (1 Thess. 2:14-16).

He complains of Satanic resistance to his ministry, which according to the context, probably indicates Jewish opposition (1 Thess. 2:18, cp. 15-16[17]). He seems to allude to Jewish opposition in 2 Thessalonians 1:4ff, where he mentions the Thessalonians's perseverance and afflictions for their faith (1:4ff; cp. Acts 17:4-6). This also may be motivating his request that the Thessalonians pray for his deliverance from such "unreasonable and wicked men" (3:2; cf. Acts 17:4-6, 13; 18:6; 1 Thess. 2:14-16).

This Jewish context is important for understanding the situation confronting Paul. Below I will show that 2 Thessalonians contains strong allusions to the Olivet Discourse, which speaks of the destruction of the Temple and the

---

[16] The Greek term ἀντιτασσομένων (*antitassomenon*, "opposed") in Acts 18:6 is a military term and indicates organized resistance.

[17] Cf. Matt. 12:43-45; John 8:44; Rev. 2:9; 3:9. In 2 Corinthians Paul mentions Satanic blinding to the gospel (4:4) in the context of making reference to the veil blinding the Jews regarding the New Covenant (3:15; cp. Heb. 8:8-13). He then discusses his own grievous persecution (4:7-18). See my *Before Jerusalem Fell: Dating the Book of Revelation* (3d. ed. Atlanta: American Vision, 1999), ch. 13.

judgment of the Jews (cp. Matt. 23:35—24:2; cp. Acts 17:3; 18:5).[18] As Carson notes, the Olivet Discourse "is undoubtedly a source of the Thessalonian Epistles."[19]

Our Gathering Together

> Concerning the coming of our Lord Jesus Christ and our being gathered to him, we ask you, brothers, not to become easily unsettled or alarmed by some prophecy, report or letter supposed to have come from us, saying that the day of the Lord has already come. (2 Thess. 2:1-2)

Paul's statement "concerning the coming of our Lord Jesus Christ and our gathering together to Him" (2 Thess. 2:1) is the *crux interpretum* of this passage. I believe he is here speaking of the A.D. 70 judgment on the Jews — the very judgment emphasized in the first portion of the Olivet Discourse, the Book of Revelation, and numerous other passages of Scripture.

Though he speaks of the Second Advent just a few verses before (1:10), he is not dealing with that event here. Of course, similarities exist between the Day of the Lord upon Jerusalem in A.D. 70 and the universal Day of the Lord at the Second Advent. The one is a temporal betokening of the other, being a distant adumbration of it.[20] The Second Advent provides a final hope for the *eternal resolution* to their suffering; the A.D. 70 Day of the Lord affords an approaching *temporal resolution* (cp. Rev. 6:10). Orthodox scholars from each of the millennial schools agree that Christ brings these two events into close connection in the Olivet Discourse. Indeed, Christ's disciples almost certainly confuse the two (Matt. 24:3). The same connection seems to exist here, as well.

There are several reasons why we believe that Paul is speaking of two distinct comings here in 2 Thessalonians. (1) In 2 Thessalonians 1:10 Paul employs a different word for the *coming* of Christ (ἔλθη, *elthe*) than he does in

---

[18] Page attempts to draw the parallel with Revelation 20, comparing the restraint and deception of Satan and the flaming coming of Christ with the deception, restraint, and coming here. Sydney H. T. Page, "Revelation 20 and Pauline Eschatology," *Journal of the Evangelical Theological Society* 23:1 (March, 1980): 31-44.

[19] D. A. Carson, "Matthew," in Frank E. Gaebelein, ed., *The Expositor's Bible Commentary*, 12 vols. (Grand Rapids: Zondervan, 1984), 8:489. See also: G. Henry Waterman, "The Sources of Paul's Teaching on the 2nd Coming of Christ in 1 and 2 Thessalonians," *Journal of the Evangelical Theological Society* 18:2 (June, 1975): 105-113.

[20] There are various Days of the Lord in Scripture. For example, upon Babylon (Isa. 13:9, cp. v.1) and Egypt (Jer. 46:10, cp. vv. 2, 11-14; Eze. 30:36).

2:1 (παρουσία, *parousia*). (2) There the Second Advental judgment brings "everlasting destruction from the presence of the Lord" (1:9); here a temporal "destruction" (2:8). (3) There the Second Advent includes "his mighty angels" (1:7); here the temporal judgment does not mention these mighty angels (2:1-12).

(4) Furthermore, the "gathering together to Him" of 2 Thessalonians 2:1 picks up on the Lord's reference in Matthew 24:31. The word translated "gather together" here is ἐπισυνάξουσιν (*episunagoge*). We find this word elsewhere only in Hebrews 10:25, where it speaks of a worship assembly. But its cognate verb form appears in Matthew 24:31, where the *gathering* relates to "this generation" (Matt. 24:34). There it signifies calling the elect into the church by the trumpeting of the archetypical Great Jubilee (cf. 2 Thess. 1:11; 2:14).[21] Here it functions in the same way: with the coming destruction of Jerusalem and the Temple, from that point on Christians will be "gathered together" in a *separate* and *distinct* "assembly" (ἐπισυνάξουσιν, *episunagoge* — the Church is called a συναγωγὴν (*sunagoge*) in James 2:2. After Jerusalem's destruction, God no longer tolerates Temple worship — indeed, he makes it impossible. Though Christians frequently worship at the Temple prior to A.D. 70, they never will again.[22]

The Day of Christ / the Lord here fulfills Joel 2:31-32, which Peter applies to first century Jerusalem in Acts 2:16-21. In Acts 2 Peter identifies tongues as a sign of covenantal curse,[23] which points to Jerusalem's coming destruction in blood, fire, and smoke (Acts 2:19-21, 40). This explains why it is at *Jerusalem* (and nowhere else) Christians sell their property and share the proceeds (Acts 2:44-45): Jerusalem is on the eve of destruction (Matt. 24:2-34; Luke 23:28-30).[24]

---

[21] See Chapter 3 discussion of Matthew 24:29ff. Cp. J. Marcellus Kik, *An Eschatology of Victory* (Nutley, N.J.: Presbyterian and Reformed, 1971), 144-150. David Chilton, *The Great Tribulation* (Tyler, Tex.: Institute for Christian Economics, 1987), 25-28.

[22] Acts 1:4; 1:8; 18:21; 20:16; 24:11. Even in this early post-commission Christianity, believers continued to gravitate toward the Jews: engaging in Jewish worship observances (Acts 2:1ff.; 21:26; 24:11), focusing on and radiating their ministry from Jerusalem (Acts 2-5), frequenting the Temple (Acts 2:46; 3:1ff.; 4:1; 5:21ff.; 21:26; 26:21) and attending the synagogues (13:5, 14; 14:1; 15:21; 17:1ff.; 18:4, 7, 19, 26; 19:8; 22:19; 24:12; 26:11).

[23] For a study of the contra-Jewish function of tongues, which are so detailed in 1 Corinthians, see: Kenneth L. Gentry, Jr., *Crucial Issues Regarding Tongues* (Placentia, Calif.: author), 1997 [1982]). O. Palmer Robertson, *The Final Word: A Biblical Response to the Case for Tongues and Prophecy Today* (Edinburgh: Banner of Truth, 1993), 41-49. David G. Hagopian, ed., *Always Reforming: A Dialogue of Differences within the Reformed Tradition* (Phillipsburg, N.J.: Presbyterian and Reformed, 1999).

[24] David Chilton, *Productive Christians in an Age of Guilt Manipulators* (Tyler, Tex.:

Paul consoles his readers by denying the false report that "the day of Christ had come" (2 Thess. 2:2). Apparently there is an unusual reason for this epistle so soon after the first one: some unscrupulous deceivers forge letters from Paul and falsely claim charismatic insights about eschatological concerns. In his earlier letter he corrects the Thessalonians's grief over deceased loved ones, who worry that their deaths preclude their sharing in the resurrection (1 Thess. 4:13-17). Now new eschatological deceptions are troubling the young church (2 Thess. 2:1-3a): Some think the Day of the Lord had come,[25] so they quit working (2 Thess. 3:6-12). In another context and due to the catastrophic upheaval expected in the approaching judgment of Israel, Paul suggests that the Corinthians forgo marriage for a while (1 Cor. 7:26-29). But here in 2 Thessalonians 2 incorrect doctrinal instruction is tempting the Thessalonians to stop all necessary labor, thinking the time had come.

The word "trouble" (θροέω, *throeo*; 2:2) is in the present infinitive form, which signifies a continuing state of agitation. This word appears elsewhere only in the Olivet Discourse (Mark 13:7; Matt. 24:6), where it sits in a similar theological context: one warning of *deception* and *trouble* regarding the *coming* Day of Christ. "Take heed that no one *deceives* you. For many will come in My name, saying, 'I am He,' and will deceive many. And when you hear of wars and rumors of wars, do not be *troubled*; for such things must happen, but *the end is not yet*" (Mark 13:5-7). The Olivet Discourse parallels are instructive.

The Man of Lawlessness

Don't let anyone deceive you in any way, for that day will not come until the rebellion occurs and the man of lawlessness is revealed, the man doomed to destruction. He will oppose and will exalt himself over everything that is called God or is worshiped, so that he sets himself up in God's temple, proclaiming himself to be God. Don't you remember that when I was with you I used to tell you these things? And now you know what is holding him back, so that he may be revealed at the proper time. For the secret power of lawlessness is already at work; but the one who now holds it back will continue to do so till he is taken out of the way. (2 Thess. 2:3-

---

Institute for Christian Economics, 1981), 168-170.

[25] Greek: ἐνέστηκεν (*enesteken*). A. M. G. Stephenson, "On the meaning of ἐνέστηκεν ἡ ἡμέρα τοῦ κυρίου in 2 Thessalonians 2:2," *Texte und Untersuchungen zur Geschichte der altchristlichen Literatur* 102 (1968) 442-451. William F. Arndt and F. Wilbur Gingrich, *A Greek-English Lexicon of the New Testament* (4th ed.: Chicago: University of Chicago, 1957), 266. See: Morris, *First and Second Thessalonians*, 215. Note the agreement among the following translations: NASB, NKJV, NEB, TEV, Moffatt's New Translation, Weymouth, Williams, Beck.

7)

The deception these unprincipled men are promoting worries Paul: "Let no one deceive you by any means" (v. 3a). He uses the strengthened form for "deception" (ἐξαπατήσῃ, *exapatese*) with a double negative prohibition. To avoid the deception and to clarify the true beginning of the Day of the Lord upon Jerusalem, Paul informs them: "that Day will not come unless the falling away comes first, and the man of lawlessness is revealed, the son of perdition" (2 Thess. 2:3). Before the Day of the Lord "is come" two events must occur: the falling away and the revelation of the man of lawlessness. It is not necessary for these to occur in the chronological order presented, as even dispensationalists admit.[26] Verse nine is clearly out of order and should occur in the midst of verse eight, if strict chronology is important.

The Falling Away

The word "falling away" is ἀποστασία (*apostasia*). It occurs only here and in Acts 21:21 in the New Testament. Historically the word may apply either to a *political* or to a *religious* revolt.[27] But to which does it refer here? Does it point to a future worldwide apostasy from the Christian faith, as per pessimistic eschatologies? Based on this passage, amillennialist William Hendriksen argues that "by and large, the visible Church will forsake the true faith." Dispensationalist Constable comments: "This rebellion, which will take place within the professing church, will be a departure from the truth that God has revealed in His Word."[28]

Or does the ἀποστασία (*apostasia*) refer to a political rebellion of some sort? We can make a good case for its referring to the Jewish apostasy/rebellion against Rome.

Interestingly, Josephus calls the Jewish War an ἀποστασία (*apostasia*) against the Romans: "And now I perceived innovations were already begun, and that there were a great many very much elevated, in hopes of a *revolt* [ἀποστασία, *apostasia*] from the Romans" (*Life* 4). "When John, the son of Levi, saw some

---

[26] Constable, "2 Thessalonians," 718. Non-dispensationalist Marshall comments: "The argument is difficult to follow, partly because of the way in which Paul tackles the theme in a non-chronological manner." I. Howard Marshall, *1 and 2 Thessalonians* (NBC) (Grand Rapids: Eerdmans, 1983), 185

[27] For political *apostasia* see the Septuagint at Ezra 4:12, 15, 19; Neh. 2:19; 6:6; 1 Esd. 2:23. See also: 1 Macc. 13:16; 2 Macc. 5:11. For religious *apostasia* see the Septuagint at Josh. 22:22; 2 Chr. 29:19; and 33:19, and in the New Testament Acts 21:21.

[28] Hendriksen, *I and II Thessalonians* (NTC), 170. Constable, "2 Thessalonians," 718.

of the citizens much elevated upon their *revolt* [ἀποστασία, *apostasia*] from the Romans, he labored to restrain them; and entreated them that they would keep their allegiance to them" (ibid., 10).

Probably Paul merges the religious and political concepts, though emphasizing the outbreak of the Jewish War resulting from their apostasy against God.[29]

We may infer this from 1 Thessalonians 2:16. There Paul says the Jews "always fill up the measure of their sins [i.e., religious *apostasia* against God]; but *wrath has come upon them to the uttermost* [i.e., the result of political *apostasia* against Rome]." The *apostasia* (revolt) Paul mentions will lead to the military devastation of Israel (Luke 21:21-22; 23:28-31; Acts 2:16-20). The filling up the measure of the fathers' sins (Matt. 23:32; 1 Thess. 2:16; Rev. 18:5) leads to Israel's judgment, thereby vindicating the righteous slain in Israel (Matt. 23:35; cf. Matt. 24:2-34). The *apostasia* of the Jews against God is centuries long, culminating in their rejecting the Messiah (Matt 21:37-39; 22:2-6). This leads to God's providential judgment via their *apostasia* against Rome (Matt. 21:40-42; 22:7). Paul's emphasis must be on the revolt against Rome in that it is future and datable, whereas the revolt against God was ongoing and cumulative. This is necessary to dispel the deception over which Paul expresses concern. Due to this final apostasy and the consequent destruction of Jerusalem, Christianity and Judaism are forever separated.[30]

Identifying the Man of Lawlessness

According to many Church Fathers, the Man of Lawlessness is Nero Caesar, who also is the Beast of Revelation.[31] The difficulty of this passage lies in the fact that Paul "describes the Man of Sin with a certain reserve" (Origen, *Celsus* 6:45). Apparently this is for fear of incurring "the charge of calumny

---

[29] Daniel Whitby suggests the apostasy growing among Jewish converts to Christianity, as they return to Judaism. This occurs about the same time. Hebrews (written in the A.D. 60s) shows a deep concern about widespread defections among Jewish converts. Daniel Whitby, *A Commentary on the New Testament*, vol. 4, in Patrick, Lowth, Arnald, Whitby, and Lowman, *A Critical Commentary and Paraphrase on the Old and New Testaments and the Apocrypha* (Philadelphia: Carey and Hart, 1848), 813.

[30] See my *Before Jerusalem Fell*, 293-298. Cf. Benjamin B. Warfield, "The Prophecies of St. Paul" in *Biblical and Theological Studies*, ed. by Samuel G. Craig, (Philadelphia: Presbyterian and Reformed, 1952), 473-475.

[31] E.g., Augustine, *City of God* 20:19; Chrysostom cited in Alford, *Greek Testament*, 2:80. If I am correct in equating him with the beast, we could add: Victorinus, *Apocalypse* 17:16; Lactantius, *On the Death of the Persecutors* 2; Sulpicius Severus, *Sacred History* 2:28, 29. See my *The Beast of Revelation* (Tyler, Tex.: Institute for Christian Economics, 1989).

for having spoken evil of the Roman emperor" (Augustine, *City of God* 20:19). Thus, Paul becomes very obscure in order to hide his prophecy from the Roman authorities. Josephus does the same when speaking about Daniel's fourth kingdom, which applies to Rome (Josephus, *Ant.* 10:10:4). Paul and his associates had already suffered at the hands of the Thessalonian Jews for "acting contrary to the decrees of Caesar, saying there is another king — Jesus" (Acts 17:7). Wisdom demands discreetness in his reference to imperial authority; his recent (1 Thess. 2:17) personal ministry among them allows it: they are to "remember" that while with them he "told [them] these things" (2:5). His personal instruction would allow them to know much more than we can from his discrete allusions in his letters.

Apparently something is presently (*ca.* A.D. 52) "restraining" the Man of Lawlessness: "you *know* what *is restraining* [κατέχον, *katechon*; present participle], that he may be revealed in his own time" (2:6). This strongly suggests the preterist understanding of the whole passage. The *Thessalonians themselves know* what is *presently restraining* the Man of Lawlessness; in fact the Man of Lawlessness is alive and waiting to be "revealed."[32] This implies that for the time-being Christians can expect some protection from the Roman government. The Roman laws regarding *religio licita* are currently in Christianity's favor, while considered a sect of Judaism and before the malevolent Nero ascends the throne. Paul certainly profits from the protection afforded by the Roman judicial apparatus (Acts 18:12ff.) and makes important use of these laws in A.D. 59 (Acts 25:11-12; 28:19) as a shield from the malignancy of the Jews. And he expresses no ill-feelings against Rome, when writing Romans 13 in A.D. 57-59 — during the early reign of Nero, the famous *Quinquennium Neronis*.[33]

While Paul writes 2 Thessalonians 2, he is under the reign of Claudius Caesar, who has just banished Jews from Rome for persecuting Christians (Suetonius, *Claudius* 24:5; cp. Acts 18:2). Paul even employs a word play on Claudius's name. The Latin word for "restraint" is *claudere*, which is related to "Claudius."[34] Interestingly, Paul shifts between the neuter and masculine forms of the "the restrainer" (2 Thess. 2:6, 7). This suggests he may be including

[32] The view that the Roman government was the restrainer is called by Schaff "the patristic interpretation." Philip Schaff, *History of the Christian Church* (3rd ed: Grand Rapids: Eerdmans, 1910), 1:377n. It was held by Tertullian, *On the Resurrection of the Flesh* 24 and *Apology* 32; Irenaeus, *Against Heresies* 5:25-26; Augustine, *City of God* 20:19; Lactantius, *Divine Institutes*, 7:15.

[33] Trajan, *Epistle* 5; cp. Suetonius, *Nero* 19. See: B. W. Henderson, *The Life and Principate of the Emperor Nero* (London: Methuen, 1903), ch. 3.

[34] Bruce, *New Testament History*, 310. John A. T. Robinson, *Redating the New Testament* (Philadelphia: Westminster, 1976), 17-18. John Lightfoot, *A Commentary on the*

both the imperial law and the present emperor in his designation "restrainer." While Claudius lives, Nero, the Man of Lawlessness, is powerless to commit wide-ranging public lawlessness. Christianity is free from the imperial sword until the Neronic persecution erupts in November, A.D. 64.

Early in Nero's reign careful tutors hide his evil from the public eye. Eventually he breaks free of their restraints and is publicly "revealed" for what he really is. Roman historians write of Nero: "Other murders were meant to follow. But the emperor's tutors, Sextus Afranius Burrus and Lucius Annaeus Seneca, prevented them. . . . They collaborated in controlling the emperor's perilous adolescence; their policy was to direct his deviations from virtue into licensed channels of indulgence" (Tacitus, *Annals* 13). "Although at first his acts of wantonness, lust, extravagance, avarice and cruelty were gradual and secret . . . yet even then their nature was such that no one doubted that they were defects of his character and not due to his time of life" (Suetonius, *Nero* 26). "Gradually Nero's vices gained the upper hand: he no longer tried to laugh them off, or hide, or deny them, but openly broke into more serious crime" (*Nero* 27, cp. 6). "After this, no considerations of selection or moderation restrained Nero from murdering anyone he pleased, on whatever pretext" (*Nero* 37).

The Mystery of Lawlessness

Remarkably imperial law so checks the Jews that they do not kill James the Just in Jerusalem until about A.D. 62. This is after the death of the Roman procurator Festus and before the arrival of Albinus (Josephus, *Ant.* 20:9:1). About this time, Paul writes Philippians from prison with confidence he will be released (Phil. 1:25). But with the outbreak of the Neronic Persecution (Nov., A.D. 64) the "*mystery* of lawlessness" becomes the "*revelation* of the Man of Lawlessness." During Paul's second Roman imprisonment he is sure he will die (2 Tim. 4:6ff).

The evil "mystery of lawlessness" is "already working," though restrained in Claudius's day (2 Thess. 2:7). This could be an allusion to the evil conniving and plotting of Nero's mother Agrippina, who (apparently) poisons Claudius so that Nero can ascend the imperial throne.[35] The cunning machinations to secure imperial authority for Nero are in gear. Or it could suggest that the true nature of lawlessness is already mysteriously at work in the imperial cultus and its rage for worship, though it has not yet jealously broken

---

New Testament from the Talmud and Hebraica, vol.2 (Peabody, Mass.: Hendrickson, rep. 1989 [1658]), 312.See: J. R. V. Marchant and Joseph F. Charles, *Cassell's Latin Dictionary* (New York: Cassell, n.d.), 101-2: "Claudius" "1. claudo. . . *to shut, close, opp. aperire*).

[35] Tacitus, *Annals* 12:62ff; Suetonius, *Claudius* 44.

out upon the Christian community. Either of these possibilities are suggestive of preterism.

Showing That He is God

The Roman emperor, according to Paul, "exalts himself above all that is called God or that is worshiped" (2 Thess. 2:4a). Just a few years before Paul writes, the public receives warning of the evil potential of emperor worship, when the emperor Caligula (a.k.a. Gaius) attempts to place his image in the Temple in Jerusalem (Josephus, *Ant.* 18:8:2-3).

The Temple of God. The phrase "so that he sits as God in the temple of God, showing himself that he is God" is interesting. When ὥστε (*hoste*, "so that") is followed by an infinitive (καθίσαι, *kathisai*, "to sit"), it indicates a *purpose intended* — not necessarily a *purpose accomplished*.[36] As Moule puts it: "Strictly speaking the Infinitive should indicate only the *potential* result, representing the inherent qualities of the situation and not necessarily the actual consequences."[37]

Earlier it was Caligula's *intention* to sit in "the temple of God" in Jerusalem to "show himself that he is God." In fact, Philo tells us that "so great was the caprice of Caius [Caligula] in his conduct toward all, and especially toward the nation of the Jews. The latter he so bitterly hated that he appropriated to himself their places of worship in the other cities, and beginning with Alexandria he filled them with images and statues of himself."[38]

The Worship of Nero. Soon after Paul writes, that sort of desire arises again — in the megalomania of Nero Caesar. The Roman dramatist and statesman Seneca (B.C. 4—A.D. 65) convinces Nero that he is destined to become the very revelation of the divine Augustus and of the god Apollo.[39] Speaking as Apollo, Seneca praises Nero: "He is like me in much, in form and appearance, in his poetry and singing and playing. And as the red of morning drives away dark night, as neither haze nor mist endure before the sun's rays, as everything becomes bright when my chariot appears, so it is when Nero ascends the

---

[36] As in Luke 4:29, where the Jews led Jesus to a hill "so as to cast him down" (ὥστε κατακρημνίσαι αὐτόν, *hoste katakremnisai auton*). Best, *Commentary on First and Second Thessalonians*, 286-290. H. E. Dana and Julius R. Mantey, *A Manual Grammar of the Greek New Testament* (Toronto: Macmillan, 1955), 214. Robert W. Funk, ed., F. Blass and A. DeBrunner, *A Greek Grammar of the New Testament and Other Early Christian Literature* (Chicago: University of Chicago Press, 1961), § 391 (3).

[37] C. F. D. Moule, *An Idiom-Book of New Testament Greek* (2d ed.: Cambridge: Cambridge University Press, 1960), 141.

[38] Philo, *Legatio ad Caium* 43, as cited by Eusebius, *Ecclesiastical History* 2:6:2.

[39] Seneca, *On Clemency* 1:1:6; *Pumpkinification* 4:15-35.

throne. . . . He restores to the world the golden age."[40]

Suetonius remarks of Nero that "since he was acclaimed as the equal of Apollo in music and of the Sun in driving a chariot, he had planned to emulate the exploits of Hercules as well."[41] An inscription from Athens speaks of him as: "All powerful Nero Caesar Sebastos, a new Apollo."[42]

On copper coins struck in Rome and at Lugdunum, Nero's image appears as Apollo playing the lyre, his head radiating the light of the sun. One type has Genius (a Roman tutelary deity) sacrificing over an altar on the reverse side; another has Apollo on the reverse. As Bo Reicke notes of Nero's Apollo fascination: "All this was more than pomp and show: Nero strove with deadly seriousness to play the role of Augustus and Apollo politically, the former primarily from 54 to 61, the latter from 62 to 68."[43]

As early in his reign as 55 the senate erects a huge statue of Nero in Rome's Temple of Mars.[44] The statue is the same size as that of Mars in Mars's own Temple.

We see that the populace actually worships Nero, based on inscriptions found in Ephesus; these refer to him as "Almighty God" and "Saviour."[45] We find reference to Nero as "God and Savior" in an inscription at Salamis, Cyprus.[46] Indeed, as his megalomania increased, the tendency to worship him as ruler of the world became stronger, and in Rome his features appeared on the colossus of the Sun near the Golden House, while his head was represented on the coinage with a radiate crown. Members of the imperial house also began to receive unheard of honours: . . . Nero deified his child by Poppaea and Poppaea herself after their deaths. All this was far removed from the modest attitude of Augustus."[47]

Regarding the imperial development of the emperor cult, Caligula (Gaius) and Nero "abandoned all reserve"[48] in promoting emperor worship. In fact,

---

[40] Ethelbert Stauffer, *Christ and the Caesars* (Philadelphia: Westminster Press, 1955), 52.

[41] Suetonius, *Nero* 53.

[42] Mary E. Smallwood, *Documents Illustrating the Principates Gaius Claudius and Nero* (Cambridge: University Press, 1967), p. 52 (entry #145).

[43] Bo Reicke, *The New Testament Era: The World of the Bible from 500 B.C. to A.D. 100* (Philadelphia: Fortress, 1968), p. 70.

[44] See: Tacitus, *Annals* 13:8:1.

[45] James J. L. Ratton, *The Apocalypse of St. John* (London: R and T Washbourne, 1912), 48.

[46] Smallwood, *Documents Illustrating the Principates Gaius Claudius and Nero*, 142.

[47] H. H. Scullard, *From the Gracchi to Nero* (2nd ed.: New York: Barnes and Noble, 1963), 371.

[48] Eduard Lohse, *The New Testament Environment*, trans. by John E. Steely (Nashville: Abingdon, 1976), p. 220.

"Caligula and Nero, the only two of the Julio-Claudians who were direct descendants of Augustus, demanded divine honors while they were still alive."[49]

Perhaps we may best see this demand for worship by Nero in the following incident. In A.D. 66 Tiridates, King of Armenia, approaches Nero in devout and reverential worship, according to Roman historian Dio Cassius (A.D. 150-235):

> Indeed, the proceedings of the conference were not limited to mere conversations, but a lofty platform had been erected on which were set images of Nero, and in the presence of the Armenians, Parthians, and Romans Tiridates approached and paid them reverence; then, after sacrificing to them and calling them by laudatory names, he took off the diadem from his head and set it upon them. . . .
>
> Tiridates publicly fell before Nero seated upon the rostra in the Forum: "Master, I am the descendant of Arsaces, brother of the kings Vologaesus and Pacorus, and thy slave. And I have come to thee, my god, to worship thee as I do Mithras. The destiny thou spinnest for me shall be mine; for thou art my Fortune and my Fate.[50]

Dio Cassius notes also the fate of one senator who does not appreciate Nero's "divine" musical abilities: "Thrasaea was executed because he failed to appear regularly in the senate, . . . and because he never would listen to the emperor's singing and lyre-playing, nor sacrifice to Nero's Divine Voice as did the rest."[51] This senator fails to worship the Man of Lawlessness and is summarily executed.

In A.D. 67 Nero goes to Greece, where he remains for more than a year performing as a musician and an actor in the Grecian festivals. Arthur Weigall gives the response of the Greeks, as he comments upon Dio Cassius's history of Rome: "Soon Nero was actually deified by the Greeks as 'Zeus, Our Liberator.' On the altar of Zeus in the chief temple of the city they inscribed the words 'to Zeus, our Liberator' namely Nero, for ever and ever; in the temple of Apollo they set up his statue; and they called him 'The new Sun, illuminating the Hellenes,' and 'the one and only lover of the Greeks of all time.'"[52]

When Nero returns to Rome from Greece in A.D. 68, it is to the trium-

---

[49] Joseph Ward Swain, *The Harper History of Civilization*, Vol. 1 (New York: Harper, 1958), p. 229.

[50] Dio Cassius, *Roman History* 62:5:2.

[51] Ibid., 62:26:3.

[52] Arthur Weigall, *Nero: Emperor of Rome* (London: Thornton Butterworth, 1933), 276.

phant praise of the city as he enters the Palace and Apollo's Temple on the Palatine. Dio Cassius records the scene: "The city was all decked with garlands, was ablaze with lights and reeking with incense, and the whole population, the senators themselves most of all, kept shouting in chorus: 'Hail, Olympian Victor! Hail, Pythian Victor! Augustus! Augustus! Hail to Nero, our Hercules! Hail to Nero, our Apollo! The only Victor of the Grand Tour, the only one from the beginning of time! Augustus! Augustus! O, Divine Voice! Blessed are they that hear thee.'"[53]

Finally the future emperor Titus actually accomplishes this "intention" when he completes the devastation of Jerusalem set in motion by Nero. Titus invades the Temple in A.D. 70 and his soldiers worship Rome within: "And now the Romans . . . brought their ensigns to the temple, and set them over against its eastern gate; and there did they offer sacrifices to them, and there did they make Titus imperator, with the greatest acclamations of joy" (Josephus, *Wars* 6:6:1).

By September, A.D. 70, the very Temple of which Paul speaks in 2 Thessalonians 2:4 is forever gone. This fact also supports the preterist understanding of the passage.[54] In fact, it parallels Matthew 24:15 and functions as Paul's treatment of the "abomination of desolation," which is to occur in "this generation" (Matt. 24:34).

The Persecution of Christians. Not only so, but Nero openly "opposes" (2 Thess. 2:4) Christ by persecuting his followers. He even begins the persecution by presenting himself in a chariot as the sun god Apollo. He does this while burning Christians at the stake for illumination at his self-glorifying party.

We find the earliest evidence for Nero's persecuting wrath upon the Christians in an epistle from Clement of Rome to the Corinthians (designated 1 Clement). In 1 Clement 5 the writer mentions the persecution of the apostles. Then in section 6 Clement tells us that "unto these men were gathered a vast multitude of the elect, who through many indignities and tortures, being the victims of jealousy, set a brave example among ourselves."

The great Christian apologist Tertullian (A.D. 150-230) defends Christianity by challenging men to search the archives of Rome for the proof that

---

[53] Dio Cassius, *Roman History* 62:20:5.

[54] W. G. Kümmel, *Introduction to the New Testament*, trans. by Howard Clark Kee (17th ed.: Nashville: Abingdon, 1973), 267. The dispensationalist idea of a rebuilt Temple here has to be read eisegetically into the text, in that the reference to the Temple in 2 Thess. 2:4 (1) is written while the Jewish Temple is still standing as the obvious referent, (2) lacks any allusion to a rebuilding of the Temple, and (3) if speaking of a rebuilt Temple, would be contrary to the clear, divinely ordained disestablishment of the Temple (e.g., John 4:21; Matt. 23:38—24:2; Heb.8:13; 12:18-29).

Nero persecuted the Church: "And if a heretic wishes his confidence to rest upon a public record, the archives of the empire will speak, as would the stones of Jerusalem. We read the lives of the Caesars: At Rome Nero was the first who stained with blood the rising faith."[55]

Roman historian Tacitus gives a most detailed and terrifying account of the beginning of the persecution:

> But by no human contrivance, whether lavish distributions of money or of offerings to appease the gods, could Nero rid himself of the ugly rumor that the fire was due to his orders. So to dispel the report, he substituted as the guilty persons and inflicted unheard-of punishments on those who, detested for their abominable crimes, were vulgarly called Christians. . . .
>
> So those who first confessed were hurried to the trial, and then, on their showing, an immense number were involved in the same fate, not so much on the charge of incendiaries as from hatred of the human race. And their death was aggravated with mockeries, insomuch that, wrapped in the hides of wild beasts, they were torn to pieces by dogs, or fastened to crosses to be set on fire, that when the darkness fell they might be burned to illuminate the night. Nero had offered his own gardens for the spectacle, and exhibited a circus show, mingling with the crowd, himself dressed as a charioteer or riding in a chariot. Whence it came about that, though the victims were guilty and deserved the most exemplary punishment, a sense of pity was aroused by the felling that they were sacrificed no on the altar of public interest, but to satisfy the cruelty of one man.[56]

In a list of the "positive" contributions of Nero as emperor, Roman historian Suetonius (A.D. 70-160) notes that he persecuted Christians: "During his reign many abuses were severely punished and put down, and no fewer new laws were made: a limit was set to expenditures: "Punishment was inflicted on the Christians, a class of men given to a new and mischievous superstition."[57]

---

[55] Tertullian, *Scorpion's Sting*, 15.
[56] Tacitus, *Annals* 15:44.
[57] Suetonius, *Nero* 16.

The Lord Will Consume

> And then the lawless one will be revealed, whom the Lord Jesus will overthrow with the breath of his mouth and destroy by the splendor of his coming. The coming of the lawless one is according to the working of Satan, with all power, signs, and lying wonders. (2 Thess. 2:8-9)

As just indicated, the lawless one is eventually revealed. The *mystery* form of his character gives way to a *revelation* of his lawlessness in Nero's wicked acts. This occurs after the restrainer (Claudius, who maintained *religio licita*) is "taken out of the way," allowing Nero the public stage upon which to act out his horrendous lawlessness.

According to Hendriksen, verse eight destroys the preterist's identification of the Man of Lawlessness with the Roman emperor, because that verse ties the events to the era of the Second Advent: "The fact is an insurmountable obstacle in the path of the 'Roman emperor' theory."[58] The strong preteristic indications in the passage heretofore, however, demand a different understanding of this destructive coming of Christ.

As I show in the discussion of verse 1, Matthew 24:30 is most relevant here: "Then the sign of the Son of Man will appear in heaven, and then all the tribes of the earth will mourn, and they will see the Son of Man coming on the clouds of heaven with power and great glory." Christ specifically applies that verse to the first century (Matt. 24:34). We may similarly interpret other verses: Revelation 1:7[59] (cp. Rev. 1:1, 3); Matthew 26:63-65; and Mark 9:1. Christ comes in judgment upon Jerusalem in the A.D. 67-70 events.

In the judgment-coming against Jerusalem there is also judgment for the Man of Lawlessness, Nero. "It is somewhat remarkable that the flames of war consumed almost at the same time the Temple of Jerusalem and the Capitol of Rome."[60] For the beleaguered Christians there is hope and comfort in the promise of relief from Jewish opposition (2 Thess. 2:15-17) and Nero. Not only does Jerusalem collapse within twenty years, but Nero himself dies a violent death in the midst of the Jewish War (June 8, A.D. 68). His death occurs in the Day of the Lord, which is Christ's judgment-coming against Jerusalem. Paul tells us that he will die by the breath of Christ. This is like the Old Testament prophecy of the Lord's destroying Assyria with his coming and the breath of his mouth (Isa. 30:27-31). It is also reminiscent of the

---

[58] Hendriksen, *I and II Thessalonians*, 173.

[59] See chapter 6 below.

[60] Edward Gibbon, *The Decline and Fall of the Roman Empire*, ed. by Frank C. Bourne (New York: Dell, 1963), 276 (ch. 14).

language reflecting Babylon's crushing of Israel (Mic. 1:3-5). In fact, by God's providence Nero's death stops the Jewish War briefly so that Christians trapped in Jerusalem can escape (cp. 1 Thess. 1:10).[61] The Man of Lawlessness/Beast, Nero Caesar, dies in the Day of the Lord with the Great Harlot, Jerusalem (Rev. 19:17-21; cf. Rev. 22:6, 10, 12).

Lying Signs and Wonders

Before closing, perhaps a brief note regarding the "lying signs and wonders" by the Man of Lawlessness is in order. The imperial arrogance to divine pretensions could well manufacture false miracles or spread rumors of such among a superstitious people as confirmation of the emperor's supremacy. Notice that Paul speaks of these as "*lying* wonders" (2 Thess. 2:9). One example available to us a short while after Nero's death is the calling of Vespasian "the miracle worker" (Tacitus, *Histories* 4:81), because by him "many miracles occurred" (Suetonius, *Vespasian* 7).

As I show in the previous section, Nero, the Man of Lawlessness himself, becomes the enemy of Christianity due to his persecution beginning in November, A.D. 64, after several years of relatively stable government. This persecution involves the emperor directly: he rides in a chariot (apparently in mimicry of Apollo the sun god, as was his practice[62]) *while burning Christians at the stake.* Of that year's ending, Tacitus provides interesting material: "As the year ended omens of impending misfortune were widely rumored — unprecedentedly frequent lightning; a comet (atoned for by Nero, as usual, by aristocratic blood); two-headed offspring of men and beasts, thrown into the streets or discovered among the offerings to those deities to whom pregnant victims are sacrificed" (*Annals* 15). Such "signs" among a superstitious people provide the context for understanding Paul's prophecy.

Conclusion

Though 2 Thessalonians 2 is a notably difficult passage, several feastures of the text suggest a preterist understanding of 2 Thessalonians 2:

First, obvious parallels exist between Matthew 24 and Revelation 13. As Carson notes, the Olivet Discourse "is undoubtedly a source of the Thessalonian Epistles."[63] These tie 2 Thessalonians to the same era of ac-

---

[61] See: Josephus *Wars* 4:11:5. Cp. Luke 21:18, 20-24, 27-28; Eusebius, *Ecclesiastical History* 3:5:3; Epiphanius, *Heresies* 29:7. See also: Rev. 7:1-17 in Gentry, *Before Jerusalem Fell*, 243-244.

[62] Suetonius writes of Nero: "Because of his singing he had been compared to Phoebus Apollo and because of his chariot-riding to the Sun-God" (*Nero*, 53).

[63] Carson, "Matthew," 8:489.

complishment: the late A.D. 60s up to A.D. 70. Matthew 24:34 demands a first century accomplishment: "Truly I say to you, *this generation* will not pass away until all these things take place." So does Revelation: "The Revelation of Jesus Christ, which God gave Him to show to His bond-servants, the things which must *shortly take place*, and He sent and communicated it by His angel to His bond-servant John. . . . Blessed is he who reads and those who hear the words of the prophecy, and heed the things which are written in it; for the time is *near*" (Rev. 1:1, 3).

Second, writing almost twenty years prior to its destruction, Paul relates a number of these actions to the Temple still standing. The Temple is an enormously important structure in the nexus between Judaism and Christianity. His A.D. 50s audience would naturally think of the famous Herodian Temple of their own era. Since A.D. 70 this Temple no longer exists.

Third, the present restraint of the Man of Lawlessness (2:6) indicates a contemporary relevance to Paul's original audience. Clearly Paul's letter is an occasional letter, dealing with matters relevant to the Thessalonians (e.g., 2 Thess. 2:2-3). For Paul to suggest something continuing for 2000 years seems quite a stretch of the imagination.

Fourth, the knowledge of the Thessalonians regarding the restrainer (2:6). They seem to understand what is relatively obscure to us. If they understand it sufficiently well, it would appear that this phenomenon must be within their own sphere of reference.

Fifth, Paul speaks about the Man of Lawlessness's present operation in mystery form during his day (2:7). Only a strained interpretation would allow that this continues for 2000 years.

Sixth, when all things are considered as a whole, a relevant overall correspondence of the prophecy's features exists within the Thessalonians's contemporary situation. As with Matthew 24 (analyzed in the preceding two chapters) and Revelation (to be studied in the next two chapters), we find a contemporary relevance to this prophetic writing.

Once again the fulfillment of another dreadful prophecy of Scripture does not haunt our future. Its accomplishment lies in our distant past. Second Thessalonians 2 is a relevant warning of events looming during the lives of Paul's original audience.

CHAPTER FIVE

A SCARLET BEAST FULL OF BLASPHEMY
Revelation 13:1-18

I saw a beast rising up out of the sea, having seven heads and ten horns, and on his horns ten crowns, and on his heads a blasphemous name. . . . And it was granted to him to make war with the saints and to overcome them. And authority was given him over every tribe, tongue, and nation.

Revelation 13:1, 7

Introduction

Undoubtedly the Revelation of John is the leading book of the Bible for eschatological study. Popular prophecy works make abundant reference to Revelation to demonstrate that we are today on the brink of Armageddon and about to witness the rise of the beast/Antichrist.[1]

Dispensational scholar John F. Walvoord writes: "Those who read the Book of Revelation today and are captured by its graphic revelation should sense the fact that while these events have not yet been fulfilled, they could be very quickly, and the time for preparation for end-time events is now."[2] Elsewhere he refers to Revelation's prophecy thus: "Our present world is well prepared for the beginning of the prophetic drama that will lead to Armageddon. Since the stage is set for this dramatic climax of the age, it must mean that Christ's coming for His own is very near. If there ever was an hour when

---

[1] For a comparison of and interaction among four evangelical approaches, including my own, see: C. Marvin Pate, *Four Views on the Book of Revelation* (Grand Rapids: Zondervan, 1998).

[2] John F. Walvoord, *Prophecy Knowledge Handbook* (Wheaton, Ill.: Victor, 1989), 645-6.

men should consider their personal relationships to Jesus Christ, it is today. God is saying to this generation: 'Prepare for the coming of the Lord.'"[3]

Another leading dispensationalist Charles C. Ryrie writes similarly of prophecies from various Scripture passages, but especially Revelation: "But even if the messages of the prophets do not alert you, before finally dismissing them, take a good look again at current events . . . . Have you forgotten how recently the giant of the East has begun to shake himself, along with other emerging nations of the world? . . . How do you account for these unusual events converging in our present day?"[4]

In a "special report" manuscript dealing with Armageddon, best-selling prophecy author Hal Lindsey writes: "This is the most exciting time to be alive in all of human history. We are about to witness the climax of God's dealing with man."[5]

Unfortunately for such best-selling authors, Revelation is as difficult to interpret as it is terrifying to read. Virtually all interpreters concede it is the most perplexing book of the Bible. As Warfield notes: "The boldness of [Revelation's] symbolism makes it the most difficult book of the Bible: it has always been the most variously understood, the most arbitrarily interpreted, the most exegetically tortured."[6] G. R. Beasley-Murray concurs: "Revelation is probably the most disputed and difficult book in the New Testament."[7] George Eldon Ladd agrees: "Revelation is the most difficult of all New Testament books to interpret . . . ."[8] Others beyond number concur.

Even the writer of Revelation himself expresses occasional confusion, requiring angelic interpretation as he writes (Rev. 7:13-14; 17:6-7). Its dramatic events and mysterious characters are designed to strike holy terror into the souls of the readers. Thus, the following dreadful words occur frequently in Revelation: "fear" (10 times); "wrath" (12); "judgment" and related words (13); "war" (8); "torment" (7); "death," "kill," "deadly," and related words (27); "sword" (9); "fire," "burning," and the like (23); "blood" (15); "weep-

---

[3] John F. Walvoord, *Armageddon, Oil and the Middle East: What the Bible says about the future of the Middle East and the end of Western civilization* (2nd ed.: Grand Rapids: Zondervan, 1990), 228.

[4] Charles C. Ryrie, *The Living End* (Old Tappan, N.J.: Revell, 1976), 128-9.

[5] Hal Lindsey and Chuck Missler, *The Rise of Babylon and the Persian Gulf Crisis: A Special Report* (Palos Verdes, Calif.: Hal Lindsey Ministries, 1991), 51.

[6] B. B. Warfield, "The Book of Revelation" in Philip Schaff, ed., *A Religious Encyclopedia*, 3 vols., (New York: Funk and Wagnalls, 1883), 2:80.

[7] G. R. Beasley-Murray, *The Book of Revelation*, in R. E. Clements and Matthew Black, eds., *New Century Bible* (London: Marshall, Morgan, and Scott, 1974), 5.

[8] George Eldon Ladd, *A Commentary on the Revelation of John* (Grand Rapids: Eerdmans, 1972), 10.

ing," "crying," and "mourning" (11); "earthquake," "lightning," "thunder," and "wind" (11).

Despite its difficulty, however, I am convinced that Revelation lives up to its name. It is a "revelation," an "unveiling," of God's truth (Rev. 1:1; 22:6), not an obscuring of that truth. And though revealing a terrifying message, it has, in common with all books of the Bible (2 Tim. 3:16-17), a fundamental usefulness for God's people: "Blessed is he who reads and those who hear the words of this prophecy, and keep those things which are written in it; for the time is near" (Rev. 1:3).

But since Revelation is so widely debated and its imagery so difficult to comprehend by the modern Western mind, I would like to consider at some length three fundamental questions before engaging the identity of the beast. These questions are essential for the understanding of both the beast (this chapter) and the harlot (in the next chapter).

The Date of Revelation's Composition

The question of Revelation's date of composition is one of the most important issues facing the interpreter. Both the *interpretive* and the *practical* questions revolving around the book demonstrate this.

The Importance of the Question

Interpretively, Revelation's date has a tremendous bearing upon its proper understanding. The current majority of biblical scholars is in fundamental disagreement with the majority from seventy-five years ago. The current opinion is the late-date view, which holds that John writes in A.D. 95 or 96, while in exile during the final days of Domitian Caesar. This contradicts the older early-date view, which holds John composes Revelation before the destruction of Jerusalem and the Temple in A.D. 70. The early-date position is held by such worthies from the past as Moses Stuart, B. F. Westcott, F. J. A. Hort, J. B. Lightfoot, Alfred Edersheim, Milton Terry, F. W. Farrar, Philip Schaff, and others.[9]

---

[9] Moses Stuart, *Commentary on the Apocalypse*, 2 vols. (Andover: Allen, Morrill, and Wardwell, 1845). B. F. Westcott, *The Gospel According to St. John* (Grand Rapids: Eerdmans, 1954 [1882]). F. J. A. Hort, *The Apocalypse of St. John: I-III* (London: Macmillan, 1908). J. B. Lightfoot, *Biblical Essays* (London: Macmillan, 1893). Alfred Edersheim, *The Temple: Its Ministry and Services* (Grand Rapids: Eerdmans, rep. 1972 [n.d.]), 141ff. Milton S. Terry, *Biblical Hermeneutics: A Treatise on the Interpretation of the Old and New Testaments* (Grand Rapids: Zondervan, rep. 1974), 467. F. W. Farrar, *The Early Days of Christianity* (New York: Cassell, 1884). Philip Schaff, *History of the Christian Church*, 3 vols., (3rd ed.: Grand Rapids: Eerdmans, rep. 1950 [1910]), 1:834. For a list of additional authors holding the early-date view, see my *Before Jerusalem*

Though still a minority view today, within in the past twenty years a growing number of scholars is returning to a date earlier than A.D. 95-96. Among those we can name liberals C. C. Torrey, Rudolf Bultmann, and John A. T. Robinson; evangelicals C. F. D. Moule and F. F. Bruce; and conservatives Cornelis Vanderwaal and Jay Adams.[10]

Early-date advocates generally believe the prophecies of Revelation deal with the tremendous spiritual, social, political, and cultural issues leading up to and culminating in the destruction of Jerusalem in the ill-fated Jewish War of A.D. 67-70. These issues also include the outbreak of the first Roman persecution of Christianity under Nero Caesar (A.D. 64-68), the extinction of the Julio-Claudian line of emperors when Nero dies (A.D. 68), and the Roman Civil Wars of A.D. 68-69.[11] Thus, Revelation is speaking of the *birth pangs* of the kingdom.

The late-date view, on the other hand, allows for an almost infinite variety of interpretations. Most of these concern events lying in the distant future, events betokening the end of world history. On this position, Revelation would be speaking of the *conclusion* of the kingdom, or of the Church Age.

Thus, the date one assigns Revelation has the potential for placing most of its prophecies, particularly its judgment scenes, either at the *beginning* or at the *end* of Christian history. The issue may literally turn Revelation on its head.

Practically, the dating of Revelation has a great bearing on our current outlook and prospects. Our understanding of Revelation has great social and cultural issues hanging in the balance:

Does Revelation teach that in the long run "the world will progressively harden its heart against the Gospel and plunge itself into destruction"?[12] Or does it inform the *first century* Christians of grave and trying times *they* will face, to prove Christianity can weather the most furious storms, thereby bracing them for the long haul?

Should we, therefore, fortify ourselves for the worst and "live like people

---

Fell: Dating the Book of Revelation (Tyler, Tex.: Institute for Christian Economics, 1989), 30-38.

[10] C. C. Torrey, *The Apocalypse of John* (New Haven: Yale, 1958). John A. T. Robinson, *Redating the New Testament* (Philadelphia: Westminster, 1976). Rudolf Bultmann, cited in Robinson's work (359). C. F. D. Moule, *The Birth of the New Testament* (3rd ed.: New York: Harper and Row, 1982), 174. F. F. Bruce, *New Testament History* (Garden City, N.Y.: Doubleday, 1969), 411. Cornelis Vanderwaal, *Search the Scriptures*, 10 vols., (St. Catharines, Ont.: Paideia, 1979), vol. 10. Jay E. Adams, *The Time is at Hand* (Phillipsburg, N.J.: Presbyterian and Reformed, 1966).

[11] Tacitus, *Histories* 1:2-3.

[12] Ibid., 36.

who don't expect to be around much longer"?[13] Or may we look to the future as lying before a conquering Church, which has *already* endured the Great Tribulation and now seeks victory in the world over the long haul?

Of course, we must determine the rationale for adopting a particular date for Revelation on the *evidence*, not upon our psycho-social predisposition, or our hopes and dreams. Let us now consider the evidence for Revelation's dating. The view I will be defending is that the Apostle John writes Revelation in about A.D. 65 or 66. This is just after the outbreak of the Neronic persecution and just before the eruption of both the Jewish War and the Roman Civil Wars.

Evidence for the Early-date

I will engage just two of the internal indicators of time in Revelation. These evidences are based on Revelation's *self-witness*. In that I hold to the full inspiration and inerrancy of Scripture, I am convinced that this sort of evidence is the most fundamental. For a fuller consideration of both the internal and external evidence (the evidence from tradition), the reader should consult my doctoral dissertation, published under the title *Before Jerusalem Fell: Dating the Book of Revelation*.[14]

The Temple in Revelation 11. In Revelation 11:1, 2 we read:

> And there was given me a reed like unto a rod: and the angel stood, saying, Rise, and measure the temple of God, and the altar, and them that worship therein. But the court which is without the temple leave out, and measure it not; for it is given unto the Gentiles: and the holy city shall they tread under foot forty and two months.

Here we find a Temple standing in a city called "the holy city." Clearly a Christian Jew, such as John, must have in mind historical Jerusalem when he speaks of "the holy city." Jerusalem is frequently called such in Scripture.[15] Not only so, but verse 8 tells us that this is the city where "also our Lord was crucified." This can be no other city than historical Jerusalem, according to the clear testimony of Scripture (Luke 9:22; 13:32; 17:11; 19:28).

Now what Temple stands in Jerusalem? Obviously the Jewish Temple ordained of God for his worship — the famous Temple known as Herod's

---

[13] Hal Lindsey, *The Late Great Planet Earth* (Grand Rapids: Zondervan, 1970), 145.

[14] Kenneth L. Gentry, Jr., *Before Jerusalem Fell: Dating the Book of Revelation* (3d. ed.: Atlanta: American Vision, 1999).

[15] Isa. 48:2; 52:1; Neh. 11:1-18; Matt. 4:5; 27:53.

Temple. This reference to the Temple *must* be that historical structure for three reasons: (1) It is located in Jerusalem, as the text clearly states. The audience could conceive of nothing other than that famous Temple. It is remarkable for its magnificence (Mark 13:1), being praised even in the writings of Roman historian Tacitus.[16]

(2) It will be under assault for forty-two months. We know from history that the Jewish War with Rome lasts from Spring, A.D. 67 until August, A.D. 70 — a period of forty-two months. In February, A.D. 67, Nero commissions his most capable general Flavius Vespasian to engage Israel in war; Vespasian actually enters the Promised Land and engages in battle that Spring.[17] The time-frame correspondence is precise, but for a few days.

(3) Revelation 11:1, 2 parallels Jesus's Olivet Discourse statement in Luke 21:24. In Luke 21:5-7 the disciples specifically point to the Jewish Temple to ask about its future. Jesus tells them that it will soon be destroyed stone by stone. In Luke 21:24 he speaks in terms that seem clearly to form the original source of Revelation 11:1, 2:

> Revelation 11:2b: "it is given unto the *Gentiles*: and the *holy city* shall they *tread under foot* forty and two months."
> Luke 21:24: "*Jerusalem* will be *trampled underfoot* by the *Gentiles* until the times of the Gentiles be fulfilled."

Revelation 11 incorporates the reference to the "nations" (or Gentiles), the trampling under foot, and the city of Jerusalem. In that both contexts mention the Temple, the two passages surely speak of the same event: the looming destruction of Jerusalem.

We know as a matter of clear historical and archaeological record that the Romans destroy the Temple in August/September, A.D. 70. And this is a major apologetic point early Christians drive home against the Jews. Early references to this apologetic against Israel include the writings of Barnabas (A.D. 75-100), Ignatius (A.D. 107), Justin Martyr (A.D. 147), Melito of Sardis (A.D. 160-180), and others.[18]

But while John writes, the Temple is standing, awaiting its approaching doom. How else can he "measure" the Temple (even if he is doing so symbolically) if it no longer exists? If John writes this twenty-five years *after* the

---

[16] Tacitus, *Fragments of the Histories* 1.

[17] Bruce, *New Testament History*, 381-382.

[18] Barnabas, *Epistle* 16; Ignatius, *Magnesians* 10; Justin Martyr, *Apology* 32; 47; 53; Melito of Sardis, *Fragments*; *Sibylline Oracles* 1:360-364, 387-400; Hegissipus, *Commentaries on the Acts*; Clement of Alexandria, *Miscellanies* 1:21; 4:15.

Temple's fall it would be horribly anachronous. The reference to the Temple is architectural evidence that gets us back into an era pre-A.D. 70.

The Seven Kings in Revelation 17. In Revelation 17 John records a vision of the seven-headed beast. Here we discover evidence that he writes Revelation *before* the death of Nero, which occurs on June 8, A. D. 68, well before the Temple's destruction.

Regarding this vision we read in verses 9 and 10: "Here is the mind which hath wisdom. The seven heads are seven mountains, on which the woman sits. And there are seven kings: five are fallen, and one is, and the other is not yet come; and when he comes, he must continue a short space."

Most evangelical scholars recognize that the seven mountains represent the famous seven hills of Rome. John writes to be understood (Rev. 1:3) and specifically points out here that the wise one will understand this particular vision (17:9). The recipients of Revelation live under the rule of Rome, which is universally distinguished by its seven hills. The famed seven hills of Rome are mentioned time and again by ancient pagan writers such as Ovid, Claudian, Statius, Pliny, Virgil, Horace, Propertius, Martial, and Cicero.[19] Christian writers such as Tertullian and Jerome mention the seven hills, as do several of the Sibylline Oracles.[20] How could the original recipients, members in the seven historical churches of Asia Minor and under Roman imperial rule, understand this geographical feature as anything else?

We learn further that the seven heads also represent a *political* situation: Five kings are fallen, the sixth is, and the seventh is yet to come and will remain but a little while. Flavius Josephus, the Jewish contemporary of John, clearly states that Julius Caesar is the first emperor of Rome and that following him in succession are Augustus, Tiberius, Caius, Claudius, and Nero.[21] We learn this also from other first century writings, including 4 Ezra, the Sibylline Oracles, and Barnabas.[22] Roman historians Suetonius and Dio Cassius confirm this just a little later.[23] The text of Revelation says of the seven kings that "five have fallen." These emperors are dead as John writes.

But the verse goes on to say "one is." That is, the sixth one is *then reigning* even as John writes. That would be Nero Caesar, who assumes imperial power upon the death of Claudius in October, A.D. 54 and remains emperor until

---

[19] Ovid, *De Tristia* 1:5:69 and *Elegiae* 4; Claudian, *In Praise of Stilicon* 3:135; Statius, *Sylvae* 1; 2:191; Pliny, *Natural History* 3:5, 9; Virgil, *Aeneid* 6:782 and *Georgics* 2:535; Horace, *Carmen Secularae* 7; Propertius 3:10, 57; Martial 4:64; Cicero, *Ad Atticum* 6:5.

[20] Tertullian, *Apology* 35; Jerome, *Letter to Marcella*; and *Sibylline Oracles* 2:18; 11:114; 13:45; 14:108.

[21] Josephus, *Antiquities* 18; 19.

[22] 4 Ezra 11 and 12; Sibylline Oracles, books 5 and 8; Barnabas 4.

[23] Suetonius, *Lives of the Twelve Caesars*; Dio Cassius, *Roman History* 5.

June, A.D. 68.

John continues: "The other is not yet come; and when he comes, he must continue a short time" (Rev. 17:10). Nero commits suicide on June 8, A.D. 68, as the Roman Civil Wars break out in rebellion against his rule. The seventh king is "not yet come." That would be Galba, who assumes power in June, A.D. 68, but who continues only a "short space." His reign lasts a scant six months, until January 15, A.D. 69.

Upon seeing the symbolic vision, John is perplexed: he "wondered with great wonder" (Rev. 17:1, 7a). An interpretive angel appears for the purpose of showing John the proper understanding (Rev. 17:7): "Why do you wonder? I shall tell you the mystery." Revelation 17:9-10 is the *explication* of the vision, not part of the vision; the angel does not give these word to make the matter more difficult. The inherent difficulty requiring wisdom lay in the fact that the seven heads have a *double* referent: geographical ("seven mountains") and political ("seven kings"). The angel functions here much like the angel in Revelation 7:13, 14 — to *interpret* the visual data.

While John writes, then, Nero is still alive and Galba is looming in the near future. Therefore, we learn much from the political evidence regarding the seven kings and the architectural evidence of the standing Temple. John writes Revelation before the destruction of the Temple in August, A.D. 70, and even the death of Nero Caesar, in June of A.D. 68. The fact of John's banishment in a time of tribulation is evidence the Neronic persecution is underway: "I, John, both your brother and companion in tribulation, and in the kingdom and patience of Jesus Christ, was on the island that is called Patmos for the word of God and for the testimony of Jesus Christ" (Rev. 1:9). As noted above, this persecution begins in November, A.D. 64. Therefore, John writes Revelation in either A.D. 65 or 66, not long after the initial outbreak of the Neronic Persecution and just before the engagement of the Jewish War with Rome, which lies in the near future from John's perspective (Rev. 3:9).

The Relevance to the Original Audience

When interpreting any book of the Bible it is important to recognize the original audience. The evangelical hermeneutic is the grammatical-historical method of interpretation, that is, the concern of the evangelical interpreter is to recognize the grammar of a passage in light of its historical context. Consequently, the recognition of an audience and its historical situation is particularly important when a specific message is given *to them* about *their* situation. This is the case in Revelation.

There are at least three factors in Revelation emphasizing the original audience and their circumstances. These *begin* to move us toward the preterist position, which sees most of Revelation finding fulfillment in the first century. When we combine these with the matter of the *expectation* of Revelation (which I will deal with shortly), the preterist approach becomes justified by sound hermeneutical principle. What are the audience factors?

First, John is writing to particular, historic, individual churches that exist in his day. Revelation 1:4 provides a common epistolary opening: "John to the seven churches which are in Asia: Grace unto you, and peace, from him which is, and which was, and which is to come." In verse 11 he specifically names the seven churches to whom he writes: "What you see, write in a book and send it to the seven churches which are in Asia: to Ephesus, to Smyrna, to Pergamos, to Thyatira, to Sardis, to Philadelphia, and to Laodicea." We know these as actual cities containing historical churches. In chapters 2 and 3 John addresses these seven specific churches with individual exhortations and warnings. Interestingly, the historical, geographical, and political allusions in the letters show that John does, in fact, have in view the specific first century churches, as any good commentary will point out.[24]

Second, John writes to these churches in order to be *understood*. The first sentence of Revelation is its title, which defines his work as a "revelation." The Greek word for "revelation" is ἀποκάλυψις (*apokalupsis*), which means an "opening up, uncovering." John opens divine truth for his original audience; he does not write to them to obscure the truth. Furthermore, in Revelation 1:3 we read: "Blessed is he that reads, and they that hear the words of this prophecy, and keep those things which are written therein." He expects the recipients to read the book to the members of the churches; they are to *understand* and keep its directives. John's message (ultimately from Christ, Rev. 1:1) calls upon each of the seven churches to give careful, spiritual attention to his words (Rev. 2:7, 11, 17, 29; 3:6, 13, 22).

Third, in Revelation John notes that he himself and the seven churches are *already* in general "tribulation" (Rev. 1:9a): "I John, who also am your brother, and companion in the tribulation, and in the kingdom and patience of Jesus Christ, was in the isle that is called Patmos, for the word of God, and for the testimony of Jesus Christ." Revelation 2 and 3 contain allusions to greater problems brewing on the world scene —problems that will soon erupt in the "great tribulation" (Rev. 2:22; 7:14; Matt. 24:21). John is not writing to them of events two thousand years distant.

In addition, Revelation shows a deep concern with the expectant cry of the martyrs and the divine promise of their soon vindication. Revelation 6:9-11 reads:

---

[24] William M. Ramsay, *The Letters to the Seven Churches* Grand Rapids: Baker, rep. 1963 [1904]).

> And when he had opened the fifth seal, I saw under the altar the souls of them that were slain for the word of God, and for the testimony which they held: And they cried with a loud voice, saying, How long, O Lord, holy and true, dost thou not judge and avenge our blood on them that dwell on the earth? And white robes were given unto every one of them; and it was said unto them, that they should rest yet for a little season, until their fellowservants also and their brethren, that should be killed as they were, should be fulfilled.

John is clearly writing to particular first century churches about their very real and quite grave circumstances. We must not overlook the original audience relevance.

The Contemporary Expectation of John

The careful interpreter of Revelation must begin at the first verses of the book and let them lead him to John's intended meaning. The truth of the matter is: *John specifically states that the prophecies of Revelation will come to pass shortly.* The events of Revelation are "shortly to take place" because "the time is near." And as if to insure that we not miss the point, he emphasizes this truth in a variety of ways. Let me briefly note his contemporary expectation.

First, John carefully *varies his manner of expression* as if to avoid any potential confusion. A brief survey of the two leading terms he employs will help to ascertain his meaning.

The first of these terms we come upon in Revelation is the Greek word τάχος (*tachos*), translated "shortly." John explains the very purpose of his writing in Revelation 1:1: "The Revelation of Jesus Christ, which God gave Him to show to His bond-servants, the things which must *shortly* [τάχος, *tachos*] take place; and He sent and communicated it by His angel to His bond-servant John." The Arndt-Gingrich-Danker *Lexicon* lists the following meanings under the τάχος (*tachos*) entry, in the form found in Revelation (ἐν τάχει, *en tachei*): "quickly, at once, without delay, soon, in a short time, shortly."[25]

If you look up Revelation 1:1 in *any* modern translation you will find John expects the events to occur soon. This term also occurs in Revelation 2:16; 3:11; and 22:6, 7, 12, 20. Even a cursory reading of these verses unavoidably leads to the conclusion John expects these things to happen "shortly" — not two thousand years later.

---

[25] William F. Arndt, F. Wilbur Gingrich, and Frederick W. Danker, eds., *A Greek-English Lexicon of the New Testament and Other Early Christian Literature* (2d rev. ed: Chicago: University of Chicago, 1979), 807.

The second term John uses is ἐξγγύς (*eggus*), which means "near" (Rev. 1:3; 22:10). In Revelation 1:3 we read: "Blessed is he who reads and those who hear the words of the prophecy, and heeds the things which are written in it; for the time is *near* ἐγγύς, (*eggus*)." This term literally means "at hand." When used of spatial relationships it means "near," "close to"; when used of temporal relationships ἐγγύς, (*eggus*) signifies "near."[26] In our context it speaks of *temporal* nearness; John anticipates these events beginning at any moment — as all translations agree.

Second, John emphasizes his expectancy by *strategic placement* of these time references. He places his bold time statements in both the introduction and conclusion to Revelation. The statement of expectancy is found twice in the first chapter, both occurring in the first three verses: Revelation 1:1 and 3. The same idea is found four times in his concluding remarks: Revelation 22:6, 7, 12, 20. *It is as if John carefully brackets the entire work to avoid any confusion.* It is important to note that these statements occur in the more historical and didactic sections of Revelation, before and after the major dramatic-symbolic visions.

Third, his temporal expectation receives *frequent repetition.* His expectation appears six times in the opening and closing sections of Revelation, at least twice in the letters to the Seven Churches (Rev. 2:16; 3:11), and elsewhere employing other language (e.g., Rev. 6:10-11; 10:6; 12:12; 16:17; 21:6). According to the unambiguous statement of the text the events are "near." John is telling the seven historical churches (Rev. 1:4, 11; 2:1-3:22; 22:16) in his era to expect these prophetic events momentarily. He repeats the point for emphasis.

A Common Objection

Before I move on to other matters, it might be helpful to consider a common rejoinder that the nearness terminology must be computed "relatively to the divine apprehension" of time. This is necessary in that "God is not limited by considerations of time in the same way man is (cf. 2 Pet. 3:8)."[27] That is, the shortness of time is from God's eternal perspective, not man's temporally delimited experience.

But the validity of such an observation is more apparent than real. I will briefly state contrary considerations. (1) The 2 Peter 3:8 passage is theological statement *about* God. Revelation 1:1, 3 is an address *to* men. Any comparison of the two passages is a mixing of categories.

---

[26] Ibid., 214.

[27] Robert L. Thomas, *Revelation 1-7: An Exegetical Commentary* (Chicago: Moody, 1992), 55, 56.

(2) Peter's statement is also written about the *delay* in Christ's second advent. He warns that scoffers will come asking, "Where is the promise of His coming? For since the fathers fell asleep, all things continue as they were from the beginning of creation" (2 Pet. 3:4). Peter assures his readers that "the Lord is not slack concerning His promise, as some count slackness, but is longsuffering toward us, not willing that any should perish but that all should come to repentance" (2 Pet. 3:9). Thus, Peter is giving a theological explanation of the delay in the second advent. John is not doing that in Revelation.

(3) Revelation is written to seven historical churches (Rev. 1:4, 11; 2; 3) about their very real and dangerous circumstances. John writes to them as those already in "tribulation" (Rev. 1:9). Revelation answers the anguished cry of those who have already perished with the promise of the nearness of their vindication (Rev. 6:9-11). If John is speaking of God's time, he is doing so despite their misery and fear. But there is nothing in the context to indicate such. The book would be a cruel taunting of the recipients.

(4) John writes for the purpose of the original audience's understanding (Rev. 1:3). It is inconceivable that he would expect his readers to understand things 2000 years distant and about men and nations they will never know.

(5) Revelation mentions the approaching destruction of Israel's Temple in Revelation 11:1-2. And we know for a fact that this occurred in the lifetime of his original audience.

(6) We are left to ask ourselves a perplexing question: If John did not mean to express the nearness of the revelational events, how else could he have stated such? He uses terminology that not only has strength when each word is considered alone, but whose force is compounded by variation and repetition.

Given the particular audience and message of imminent expectation I do not see how anyone can escape a preterism of some sort. We now have a foundation upon which to build a case for the identity of the beast of Revelation.

Identifying the Beast

The beast is probably one of the more dreadful images in Scripture. Much has been written about him — most of it worthless. Revelation 13 portrays him as a dangerously evil foe of God's people and of righteousness. In light of Revelation's significance to its first century audience, the beast must be someone relevant to them.

Most commentators agree that the beast imagery in Revelation shifts between the generic and the specific. That is, sometimes the beast pictures a kingdom, sometimes an individual leader of that kingdom. At some places the beast has seven-heads, which are seven kings collectively considered. In Revelation 13:1 John notes that he "saw *a beast* coming up out of the sea, having ten horns and *seven heads.*" Revelation 17:10 specifically notes that the seven heads represent "seven kings." Thus, the *beast* is generically portrayed as a *kingdom.*

But in the very same contexts the beast appears as an individual. John urges his readers to "calculate the number of the beast, for the number is that of *a man*" (Rev. 13:18). In Revelation 17:11 the interpretive angel tells John and his readers "the beast which was and is not, is himself also an eighth, and *is one of the seven.*" This feature, as frustrating as it may be, is recognized by commentators of all schools of interpretation.[28]

His Generic Identity

Generically the beast is the ancient Roman Empire of the first century, under which John writes. According to Revelation 17:9 the seven heads of the beast represent "seven mountains." Perhaps no point is more obvious in Revelation than this: *the seven mountains stand for Rome,* the one city in history known for its seven hills. As I note above, the referent is virtually beyond doubt.

His Specific Identity

But who is the beast *individually* considered? John tells us that it is "a man": "Here is wisdom. Let him who has understanding calculate the number of the beast, for it is the number of a man: his number is 666" (Rev. 13:18). In his personal incarnation, the beast is none other than Nero Caesar, who alone fits the bill. This vile character fulfills all the relevant and necessary requirements of the text of Revelation:

First, the number 666 fits Nero Caesar. In Revelation 13:18 John informs us that the number of the beast is "666." The significance of this number lies in the fact that alphabets serve a two-fold purpose in antiquity. They function both as phonetic symbols, serving the same purpose as our modern alphabet, and as numerals. Our familiar Hindu-Arabic numbering system is a much later development of history, arising in the sixth century. An ancient *Hebrew* spelling of Nero's name is נרון קסר (*Nrwn Qsr*). Archaeological finds document this spelling, which provides us with precisely the numerical value of

---

[28] For example: John F. Walvoord, *The Revelation of Jesus Christ* (Chicago: Moody Press, 1966), 200; Charles Ryrie, *Revelation* (Chicago: Moody, 1968), 82; Leon Morris, *The Revelation of St. John* (1st ed.: Grand Rapids: Eerdmans, 1969), 210-211; R. H. Charles, *A Critical and Exegetical Commentary on the Revelation of St. John*, 2 vols., (Edinburgh: T and T Clark, 1920), 1:349; Philip Mauro, *Things Which Soon Must Come to Pass* (Rev. ed.: Swengel, Penn.: Reiner Publications, n.d.), 402.

666.[29] The numerical valuation is as follows:

Nrwn: N=50; R=200; W=6; N=50. *Qsr:* Q=100; S=60; R=200.

A great number of biblical scholars accept this as the solution to the problem. Is it not remarkable that this most relevant emperor has a name that fits precisely the required sum? This surely is not sheer historical accident.

Second, the textual variant supplements the evidence. If you consult a Bible with marginal references you may notice something of interest regarding Revelation 13:18. Your reference may say something to the effect: "Some manuscripts read 616." The fact is that the number in some ancient manuscripts of Scripture is actually 616. But why this textual change? Is it an accidental slip of the mind, or of the pen by some ancient copiest? Or is it an intentional alteration by some well-meaning scribe?

Surely the different reading is not due to any accident of sight by an early copiest. The numbers 666 and 616 are as different in Greek as 1 and 6 are in English. And this is true whether the number is spelled out in words or written out as alphabetic-numerals: The value 666 appears in abbreviated numerical form as: χ ξ ϛ; 616 appears as: χ ι ϛ. In manuscripts spelling out the value, 666 appears as: ἑξακόσιοι ἑξήκοντα ἕξ, whereas 616 appears as: ἑξακόσιοι δέκα ἕχ. Who could confuse these letter-numerals or words? As textual scholars agree, it must be intentional.[30]

Although we cannot be absolutely certain, we may make a strong and most reasonable case for the following conjecture. John, a Jew, quite naturally uses a Hebrew spelling of Nero's name from which he derives the numerical value 666. But when Revelation begins circulating among those less acquainted with Hebrew, a well-meaning copiest assists the reader by altering the number to 616. This sum is the value of "Nero Caesar" when spelled in Hebrew by transliterating it from its more common Latin spelling. Such a hypothesis satisfactorily explains the rationale for the divergence: so the non-Hebrew might more easily discern the identity of the beast. Such a possibility offers a remarkable confirmation of the designation of Nero.

Third, the beastly image fits Nero Caesar. In Revelation 13 John specifi-

---

[29] D. R. Hillers, "Revelation 13:18 and A Scroll from Murabba'at," *Bulletin of the American Schools of Oriental Research* 170 (April, 1963) 65. The evidence may be seen by consulting the French work edited by Benoit, J. T. Milik, and R. DeVaux, *Discoveries in the Judean Desert of Jordan* II (Oxford: Oxford University Press, 1961), 18, plate 29. See also: Marcus Jastrow, *A Dictionary of the Targumim, the Talmud Babli and Yerushalmi, and the Midrashic Literature* (London: 1903).

[30] See: Bruce M. Metzger, *A Textual Commentary on the Greek New Testament* (London: United Bible Societies, 1971), 751-752.

cally designates the one behind the 666 as a "beast." The Greek word for "beast" speaks of wild, carnivorous animals — animals such as those in the cruel Roman arenas. Because of its natural association, the term is applied figuratively to persons with "a 'bestial' nature, *beast, monster.*"[31]

Not only does John employ the word "beast," but he even symbolically represents this fearsome being with horrible, beastly imagery. This beast is a compound of such destructive carnivores as the leopard, lion, and bear: "Now the beast which I saw was like a leopard, his feet were like the feet of a bear, and his mouth like the mouth of a lion. And the dragon gave him his power, his throne, and great authority" (Rev. 13:2).

As is almost universally agreed, Nero has a "bestial nature." His own countrymen fear and hate him. Roman historian Suetonius (A.D. 70-160) speaks of Nero's "cruelty of disposition" evidencing itself at an early age. He documents Nero's evil, stating that "neither discrimination nor moderation [were employed] in putting to death whosoever he pleased on any pretext whatever."[32] Suetonius notes that Nero "compelled four hundred senators and six hundred Roman knights, some of whom were well to do and of unblemished reputation, to fight in the arena."[33] Nero enjoys homosexual rape and torture. He ruthlessly kills his parents, brother, wife, aunt, and many others close to him and of high station in Rome.[34]

Roman historian Tacitus (A.D. 56-117) speaks of Nero's "cruel nature" that "put to death so many innocent men."[35] Pliny the Elder (A.D. 23-79), a Roman naturalist, describes Nero as "the destroyer of the human race" and "the poison of the world."[36] The Roman satirist Juvenal (A.D. 60-140) documents "Nero's cruel and bloody tyranny."[37] Elsewhere he calls Nero a "cruel tyrant."[38]

Nero so affects the imagination that the pagan writer Apollinius of Tyana (4 B.C.—A.D. 96), a contemporary of Nero, even calls Nero a "beast": "In my travels, which have been wider than ever man yet accomplished, I have seen many, many wild beasts of Arabia and India; but this beast, that is commonly called a Tyrant, I know not how many heads it has, nor if it be crooked of claw, and armed with horrible fangs. . . . And of wild beasts you cannot say that they were ever known to eat their own mother, but Nero has gorged

---

[31] Arndt and Gingrich, *Lexicon*, 361.
[32] Suetonius, *Nero* 7:1.
[33] *Nero* 28-35.
[34] Ibid.
[35] Tacitus, *Histories* 4:7-8.
[36] Pliny, *Natural History* 7:45; 22:92.
[37] Juvenal, *Satire* 7:225.
[38] Ibid., 10:306ff

himself on this diet."[39]

Fourth, the war with the saints. The beast is said to "make war with the saints and to overcome them" (Rev. 13:7). In fact, he conducts blasphemous warfare for a specific period of time — forty-two months: "And he was given a mouth speaking great things and blasphemies, and he was given authority to continue for forty-two months" (Rev. 13:5).

The Neronic persecution initiated in A.D. 64 is the first ever *Roman* assault on Christianity. As Church father Eusebius (A.D. 260-340) notes: "Nero was the *first* of the emperors who showed himself an enemy of the divine religion."[40] Sulpicius Severus (A.D. 360-420) concurs: "He *first* attempted to abolish the name of Christian."[41] In his *Annals*, Roman historian Tacitus points to those who were persecuted as "those who . . . were vulgarly called Christians."[42] Roman historian Suetonius concurs, for in a list of the few "positive" contributions of Nero as emperor, he includes Nero's persecution of Christians: "During his reign many abuses were severely punished and put down, and no fewer new laws were made: . . . . Punishment was inflicted on the Christians, a class of men given to a new and mischievous superstition."[43]

Noted church historian Mosheim writes of Nero's persecution:

> Foremost in the rank of those emperors, on whom the church looks back with horror as her persecutors, stands Nero, a prince whose conduct towards the Christians admits of no palliation, but was to the last degree unprincipled and inhuman. The dreadful persecution which took place by order of this tyrant, commenced at Rome about the middle of November, in the year of our Lord 64. . . . This dreadful persecution ceased but with the death of Nero. The empire, it is well known, was not delivered from the tyranny of this monster until the year 68, when he put an end to his own life.[44]

Nero dies on June 8, A.D. 68, forty-two months after initiating the persecution but for a few days.

Nero Caesar fits the bill for the personal manifestation of the beast in

---

[39] Philostratus, *Life of Apollonius* 4:38.

[40] Eusebius, *Ecclesiastical History* 2:25:3.

[41] Sulpicius Severus, *Sacred History* 2:28. See also Tertullian (A.D. 160-220), *On the Mantle 4; Apology* 5; Paulus Orosius (A.D. 385-415), *The Seven Books of History Against the Pagans* 7:7.

[42] Tacitus, *Annals* 15:44.

[43] Suetonius, *Nero* 16.

[44] John L. von Mosheim, *History of Christianity in the First Three Centuries*, 2 vols., (New York: Converse, 1854), 1:138,139.

Revelation. This beast, who wields a sword against the saints, ultimately dies of a sword wound himself: "He who leads into captivity shall go into captivity; he who kills with the sword must be killed with the sword. Here is the patience and the faith of the saints" (Rev. 13:10). History well attests that Nero kills by the sword. For example, tradition teaches that the Apostle Paul dies under Nero by decapitation with a sword.[45] Tertullian credits "Nero's cruel sword" as providing martyr's blood as seed for the church.[46] He urges his Roman readers: "Consult your histories; you will there find that Nero was the first who assailed with the imperial sword the Christian sect."[47]

Nero's own death is by sword, as well. According to Suetonius, he "drove a dagger into his throat, aided by Epaphroditus, his private secretary."[48] He not only kills others by the sword, but himself, as Revelation prophesies.

The Mark of the Beast

In Revelation 13:16-17 we learn of the famous mark of the beast: "And he causes all, both small and great, rich and poor, free and slave, to receive a mark on their right hand or on their foreheads, and that no one may buy or sell except one who has the mark or the name of the beast, or the number of his name."

In antiquity slaves literally receive a mark to demonstrate their loyalty to a master (e.g., Exo. 21:6; Deut. 15:17). Similarly, in John's days soldiers brand themselves to show their allegiance to the emperor.[49] The practice of physical marking is commonplace in ancient times, and is still practiced today in Hindu countries, especially among Vishnu and Siva devotees.[50]

In keeping with the common practice of marking people with seals, Scripture also refers to God's marking his people with a seal. Sometimes it is through a visible sign or action, as with circumcision (Rom. 4:11) and baptism (Matt. 28:19). At other times it is by means of a spiritual seal that God alone knows (2 Tim. 2:19; Eph. 1:13; John 3:33).

---

[45] Eusebius, *Ecclesiastical History* 2:25:5; Tertullian, *The Exclusion of Heretics* 36; the Syriac *The Teaching of the Apostles*.

[46] *Exclusion* 21.

[47] Tertullian, *Apology* 5.

[48] *Nero* 49.

[49] Ulrich Wilckens, "ψαραγμα (*charagma*)" in G. Friedrich, ed., *Theological Dictionary of the New Testament*, 10 vols., (Grand Rapids: Eerdmans, 1974), 9:416-417.

[50] Vishnu devotees "wear a 'V'-shaped mark chalked in white with a vertical red (or yellow) stroke in the middle on their forehead and sometimes on their forearms." Siva devotees have a different mark but it is also on their foreheads. Gift Siromoney, "Hinduism," in J. D. Douglas, ed., *The New 20th-Century Encyclopedia of Religious Knowledge* (Grand Rapids: Baker, 1991), 392.

In Revelation *God's* act of sealing is clearly symbolic, involving a *spiritual* action that does not require a literal, visible seal. The saints are spoken of as "sealed" in Revelation 2:17; 3:12; and 7:3. None of these divine seal-markings is physical, however; and neither is the beast's marking, which appears in the context of the marked saints. Revelation 14:1, which immediately follows Revelation 13:17-18, reads: "Then I looked, and behold, a Lamb standing on Mount Zion, and with Him one hundred and forty-four thousand, having His Father's name written on their foreheads."

The beast's marking of the hand and forehead in Revelation 13:17-18 seems to be a literary device parodying God's divine sealing of his saints.[51] Marking the hand represents the governing of one's labor; marking the forehead pictures the control of one's thoughts. Consequently, in the highly wrought imagery of Revelation, the beast's "mark" suggests he controls his citizens as completely (in a human sense) as God controls his saints. Scripture portrays divine dominion as a binding of the law on the hand and forehead (Deut. 6:8; 11:18). Marking someone in the right hand or forehead, therefore, mimics God's dominion. In Revelation 13 the beast controls (marks) the lives and livelihood of Israel.

The listing of the several types of people "marked" — from rich and great to slave and poor (Rev. 13:16) — simply shows that the Roman emperor's tyrannical dominion is total. In fact, Nero himself humiliates and dominates even the senatorial class of Rome,[52] though his action in Revelation 13 focuses on those in "the Land," i.e. Palestine (Rev. 13:14). In Israel the Roman emperor dominates the Jews even before Nero's time. The emperor disgraces the priesthood by housing and controlling the high priestly vestments[53] and by governing the Temple and priesthood. [54] He humbles the leadership of Israel by installing the Idumean half-breed Herod as king[55] and then later by removing the Herodian dynasty.[56] He builds military towers and digs subterranean corridors to allow Romans control of the Temple.[57] Nero increases this imperial domination of the Jews by politics and war. He appoints over the Land evil procurators (Albinus and Gessius Florus) who abuse, plunder, and taunt Israel;[58] he later commissions General Vespasian to destroy the

---

[51] We should also note that the unholy trinity of Beast, false prophet, and dragon (Rev. 16:13; 20:10) seems to mimic the Holy Trinity (Rev. 1:4-5).

[52] Suetonius, *Lives of the Twelve Caesars*, 12:1.

[53] Josephus, *Antiquities* 15:11:4; 20:1:1.

[54] *Ant.* 20:1:3.

[55] *Ant.* 14:14:4; *Wars* 2:14:4.

[56] *Ant.* 18:5:1.

[57] *Ant.* 15:11:4; 15:11:7.

[58] *Ant.* 18:1:6; 18:11:1.

Land and the Temple.[59] Earlier in Christ's ministry we see the problem of the idolatrous coinage demanded by the Romans for tax purposes (Matt. 22:17-21).

This mixture of spiritual/symbolic (i.e., the mark of the beast) and literal/historical (i.e., the political dominion of the beast) is not unprecedented in Revelation. The literal destruction of the Land (Israel) follows after an angel spiritually marks God's elect (Rev. 7:1ff). After God measures (i.e., marks) his elect worshipers (Rev. 11:1), the Temple is physically destroyed (Rev. 11:2). So in Revelation 13 (as elsewhere) the beast mimics God's actions in his spiritual battle against God.

Double Fulfillment?

There are those, moved by the strong arguments for a preteristic understanding of Revelation, who nevertheless hold there is still a beast in our future. The means by which they attempt this is through "double fulfillment." These interpreters argue that though there is a past fulfillment of the beast, there will nevertheless be another climactic fulfillment in the future. Such an approach to the beast of Revelation is highly unlikely. Let me briefly list the objections against any double-fulfillment of the beast.

First, the beast prophecy is set in a very clear context calling for its *soon* fulfillment (Rev. 1:1, 3; 22:6, 10). John emphasizes the point so frequently, clearly, and vigorously that any fulfillment millennia distant would evacuate its predictive expectation of all meaning and integrity. The interpretive angel of God *commands* John himself to expect the events of Revelation: "And he said to me, 'Do not seal the words of the prophecy of this book, for the time is at hand'" (Rev. 22:10). Unlike Daniel who writes much earlier (Dan. 12:9), John does not seal his prophecy, because fulfillment is "soon" and "at hand."

Second, we really stretch credibility if we argue that all the many details of the beast (and why not of all of Revelation?) are to be fulfilled in incredible detail *again* later. The beast himself plays a large and complicated role in Revelation. A careful reading of Revelation shows a whole complex of inter-related, intricately woven themes, personalities, and events, all of which would have to find exact fulfillment twice.

Third, the beast clearly belongs to the first century Roman era, irrespective of the many time qualifiers scattered throughout Revelation. The sixth head of the beast is presently reigning (Rev. 17:9-10). Early Roman imperial history fits the pattern perfectly. Five emperors die before Nero; Nero is the sixth; the one to follow reigns only briefly. The data fit so remarkably well that there is no necessity for looking elsewhere.

---

[59] *Wars* 3:1:1-2.

Conclusion

John writes Revelation around A.D. 65 or 66, just after the initiation of the Neronic persecution (A.D. 64) and on the eve of the formal engagement of the Jewish War against Rome (A.D. 67). He speaks directly to the original Christian audience regarding the extreme difficulties they are facing; he also explains Jerusalem's approaching removal by God's wrath.

We should understand Revelation preteristically, rather than futuristically. We today need not fear the appearance of the beast in our future or our children's future; he has had his day. Neither is the prophecy capable of double-fulfillment, once in the first century and again toward the end of history.

CHAPTER SIX

BABYLON THE GREAT, MOTHER OF HARLOTS
Revelation 17:1-10

And on her forehead a name was written: MYSTERY, BABYLON THE GREAT, THE MOTHER OF HARLOTS AND OF THE ABOMINATIONS OF THE EARTH. And I saw the woman, drunk with the blood of the saints and with the blood of the martyrs of Jesus. And when I saw her, I marveled with great amazement.

Revelation 17:5-6

Introduction

In the preceding chapter I analyze the data in Revelation regarding the beast. In preparation for that I highlighted several important interpretive issues demonstrating his relevance to the *first century readers* of Revelation. The reader should keep those interpretive foundations in mind as I deal with the identity of the one who sits on the beast, the wicked "Babylon the Great, Mother of Harlots."

By way of introduction to this chapter, I must consider the overarching theme of Revelation. A proper grasp of that theme will not only open up the identity of the harlot, but Revelation's basic message as well. Of course, this synthetic overview requires supplementation by an analytic inquiry into the constituent elements of John's treatment of the harlot that will follow.[1]

The Theme of Revelation

> Behold, He is coming with the clouds, and every eye will see Him, even those who pierced Him; and all the tribes of the earth will mourn over Him. Even so. Amen. (Rev. 1:7)

---

[1] For a more detailed study, see my chapter in Pate, *Four Views on the Book of*

Most commentators recognize this verse as the theme statement by John. But what is its *meaning?* How shall we interpret it, especially considering the *relevance factor* and *temporal delimitation?* Because of a fundamental misunderstanding of some of its imagery, many assume this verse speaks of the Second Advent of Christ still in our future. Though there is a surface plausibility in this understanding, the contextual setting belies such an approach. Let me briefly outline the evidence for a "coming" that is pre-Second Advent.

Christ's Judgment Coming

First, the wider interpretive context of this "coming" includes the Old Testament. This cloud-coming of Christ in judgment is reminiscent of Old Testament cloud-comings of God. In the Old Testament God "comes" upon Israel's enemies in general (Psa. 18:7-15; 104:3), upon Egypt (Isa. 19:1), and upon disobedient Israel in the Old Testament (Joel 2:1, 2). For example, Isaiah 19:1 warns: "The oracle concerning Egypt. Behold, the LORD is riding on a swift cloud, and is about to come to Egypt; the idols of Egypt will tremble at His presence, and the heart of the Egyptians will melt within them." Thus in terms of the wider biblical context the general notion of a divine "coming" other than the consummational Second Coming is biblically plausible.

Second, focusing on the context more narrowly, we should note that Christ's own teaching about his "coming" also allows for such a pre-Second Advent coming. Christ expressly informs the Jewish leaders in process of condemning him to death that they themselves will witness his judgment coming: "The high priest answered and said unto him, I adjure thee by the living God, that thou tell us whether thou be the Christ, the Son of God. Jesus saith unto him, Thou hast said: nevertheless I say *unto you, Hereafter shall ye see* the Son of man sitting on the right hand of power, and coming in the clouds of heaven" (Matt. 26:63-64, emphases mine).

This judgment coming, which I analyze in Chapter 2 (dealing with Matthew 24), will occur in his generation (Matt. 24:30, 34). This is the coming of the King/kingdom that some of his followers will witness in their lifetimes: "I tell you the truth, some who are standing here will not taste death before they see the kingdom of God come with power" (Mark 9:1). These verses fit nicely with the time-setting of Revelation 1:7: remember that just a few verses before this verse, John writes:

> The Revelation of Jesus Christ, which God gave Him to show to
> His bond-servants, the things which must shortly take place; and

---

Revelation. For a college level course, see my tape set: "The Divorce of Israel." Available from Covenant Media Foundation: 1-800/553-3938.

He sent and communicated it by His angel to His bond-servant John, who bore witness to the word of God and to the testimony of Jesus Christ, even to all that he saw. Blessed is he who reads and those who hear the words of the prophecy, and heed the things which are written in it; for the time is near. (Revelation 1:1-3)

Third, the specific framework of the coming mentioned in Revelation focuses upon first century Israel. Revelation 1:7 warns that he is coming upon "those who pierced Him." Consequently, "all the tribes of the earth [τῆς γῆς, *tes ges*, literally, "the land"[2]]" will "mourn." These contextual indicators point to first century Israel's history.

The phrase "the tribes of the land" is a familiar designation for Israel.[3] In fact, in Revelation 7 those sealed in the "earth" (or "land") are from the twelve tribes of Israel (Rev. 7:1, 4-8).

Furthermore, the New Testament emphatically points out the responsibility of first century Israel for crucifying Christ[4] — as do the early Church Fathers.[5] History's most horrendous crime, the crucifixion of Christ, is charged to the first century Jews by the Apostles. For instance: "The God of our fathers raised up Jesus, whom you had put to death by hanging Him on a cross" (Acts 5:31). And that crime is quite relevant to the judgments of Revelation that are coming soon (Rev. 1:1, 3; 22:6, 10), and by the mediation of the slain Lamb (Rev. 5:6, 12; 6:16; 13:8; 14:10).

Drawing this information together and adding to it the historical facts of the era, we learn that the Jews, who "pierced Christ" (Rev. 1:7), suffer the devastation of the Jewish War with Rome from A.D. 67 to 70, resulting in the destruction of hundreds of thousands of the Jews in Judea and the enslavement of thousands more. As I note in Chapter 3, the Jewish historian Flavius Josephus writes as an eye-witness to the tragic events, reporting that 1,100,000 Jews perish in the siege of Jerusalem (*Wars* 6:9:3). This also results in the devastation of Jerusalem, the destruction of the Temple, and the cessation of the sacrificial system.

So then, we may easily explain the expectation of a judgment-coming of Christ in the first century in terms of the biblical and historical record. Thus the point remains: John clearly expects the fast approaching fulfillment of the

---

[2] See: Alfred Marshall, *Interlinear Greek-English New Testament* (Grand Rapids: Zondervan, 1959), 957.

[3] See mention of Israel's "tribes" in context of mention of "the land": Num. 26:55; 33:54; 34:13; Josh. 11:23; 13:7; 14:1; 14:4; Eze. 45:8; 47:13; 47:21; 48:29.

[4] John 19:6, 15; Acts 2:22-23, 36; 3:13-15; 5:30; 7:52; 1 Thess. 2:14-15.

[5] See my *The Beast of Revelation* (2d. ed.: Tyler, Tex.: Institute for Christian Economics, 1995), 92.

judgments of Revelation, including the fulfillment of Revelation's theme as stated in 1:7.

God's Divorce of Israel

Now I would like to paint the thematic idea in a little more graphic detail. Not only is Israel's destruction by the judgment-coming of Christ the focus of Revelation, but it is set forth in an interesting fashion.

We should remember that in the Old Testament Israel is the wife of Jehovah God. "For your Maker is your husband—the LORD Almighty is his name—the Holy One of Israel is your Redeemer; he is called the God of all the earth" (Isa. 54:5). The marriage idea in Scripture involves a covenantal relation (e.g., Prov. 2:17; Mal. 2:14),[6] as does the "marriage" of God to Israel (e.g., Eze. 16:8, 60). Oftentimes the prophets mention the marital relation between God and Israel.[7]

But Israel chases after foreign gods, thereby committing spiritual adultery through "harlotry": "See how the faithful city has become a harlot! She once was full of justice; righteousness used to dwell in her—but now murderers!" (Isa. 1:21). "Behind your doors and your doorposts you have put your pagan symbols. Forsaking me, you uncovered your bed, you climbed into it and opened it wide; you made a covenant with those whose beds you love, and you looked on their nakedness" (Isa. 57:8).[8] The prophets continually labor to call her back to covenant faithfulness (Isa. 6:8-12; cf. Matt. 23:29-31). Unfortunately for Israel, the prophets's labors are futile in that she finally crucifies her Messiah, Christ the Lord who is God's only begotten Son.

Revelation portrays God's judicial divorce decree against Israel for spiritual adultery. As the actual drama of Revelation opens, we discover God sitting on his judicial throne: "Immediately I was in the Spirit; and behold, a throne set in heaven, and One sat on the throne" (Rev. 4:2). Revelation mentions God's throne in fourteen of its twenty-two chapters. In fact, of the sixty-two appearances of the word "throne" in the New Testament, forty-six of these are in Revelation. The judicial element in Revelation is quite strong; one of the first pleas we hear in Revelation is for vindication by the martyred saints: "And they cried with a loud voice, saying, 'How long, O Lord, holy and true, until You judge and avenge our blood on those who dwell on the earth?'" (Rev. 6:10).

---

[6] Ray R. Sutton, *Second Chance: Biblical Principles of Divorce and Remarriage* (Ft. Worth, Tex: Dominion Press, 1988).

[7] See also: Jer. 2:2, 32; 31:32; Eze. 16.

[8] See also: Deut. 31:16; Jdgs. 2:17; 8:27, 33; 1 Chron. 5:25; 2 Chron. 21:13; Psa. 73:27; 106:39; Isa. 57:8; Jer. 2:2, 20; 3:1-20; 4:30; 11:15; 13:27; Eze. 6:9; 16:1ff; 23:30; Hos. 2:5; 3:3; 4:12, 15; 9:1.

In Revelation 5 the preparation for the judgment scenes begins in earnest. In his hand God holds a seven sealed scroll: "And I saw in the right hand of Him who sat on the throne a scroll written inside and on the back, sealed with seven seals" (Rev. 5:1). This scroll seems to represent his divorce decree against Israel.

In Deuteronomy 24 God's Law requires the presenting of a "writing of divorcement" in cases of divorce (cp. Matt. 19:7; Mark 10:4). Here in Revelation God publicly presents Israel's divorce papers, patterned on the Old Testament threatening of such. In Isaiah 50:1 we read: "Thus says the LORD: 'Where is the certificate of your mother's divorce, whom I have put away? Or which of My creditors is it to whom I have sold you? For your iniquities you have sold yourselves, and for your transgressions your mother has been put away.'" Jeremiah records a similar statement: "Then I saw that for all the causes for which backsliding Israel had committed adultery, I had put her away and given her a certificate of divorce; yet her treacherous sister Judah did not fear, but went and played the harlot also" (Jer. 3:8).

The description of Revelation's scroll reminds us of Ezekiel 2:1-3:7, where Ezekiel receives a scroll that, like Revelation's, has writing on both front and back: "Now when I looked, there was a hand stretched out to me; and behold, a scroll of a book was in it. Then He spread it before me; and there was writing on the inside and on the outside, and written on it were lamentations and mourning and woe" (Eze. 2:9-10). Ezekiel's scroll concerns lamentation and woe upon Israel: "'Moreover He said to me, 'Son of man, eat what you find; eat this scroll, and go, speak to the house of Israel. . . . But the house of Israel will not listen to you, because they will not listen to Me; for all the house of Israel are impudent and hard-hearted'" (Eze. 3:1, 7). This is much like the events set in motion by the opening of the seven sealed scroll of Revelation (e.g., Rev. 8:13; 9:12; 11:14; cf. Rev. 8:1-2).

The seven seals on Revelation's scroll also reflect the seven-fold judgment God threatens upon Israel in Leviticus 26:14-33. God warns that these covenantal curses will come if Israel should forsake her covenant God: "then I also will walk contrary to you, and I will punish you yet *seven* times for your sins. And I will bring a sword against you that will execute the vengeance of My covenant; when you are gathered together within your cities I will send pestilence among you; and you shall be delivered into the hand of the enemy" (Lev. 26:24-25). The seven-fold Levitical judgments have a strong influence on the judgment imagery of Revelation. When these seven seals open, the preliminary judgments begin. For the most part Revelation 6 through 19 amplify the covenantal judgments upon Israel.

The punishment in God's Law for adultery is death by stoning (Deut. 22:22-24). So in Revelation John witnesses enormous hailstones raining down on Jerusalem: "From the sky huge hailstones of about a hundred pounds [ταλαντιαία; *talantiaia*] each fell upon men" (Rev. 16:21). Josephus records the historical fulfillment for us:

> The engines [i.e., catapults], that all the legions had ready prepared for them, were admirably contrived; but still more extraordinary ones belonged to the tenth legion: those that threw darts and those that threw stones, were more forcible and larger than the rest, by which they not only repelled the excursions of the Jews, but drove those away that were upon the walls also. Now, the stones that were cast, were of the weight of a talent [ταλαντιαῖοι, talantiaioi], and were carried two furlongs and further. The blow they gave was no way to be sustained, not only by those that stood first in the way, but by those that were beyond them for a great space.[9]

God capitally punishes Israel for covenantal adultery. But there is more.

Israel is not only Jehovah's wife in the Old Testament, but as such she is a priestly nation, appointed to serve him before the nations: "You shall be to Me a kingdom of priests and a holy nation" (Exo. 19:6; cp. Isa. 61:6). Thus another Old Testament Law comes to bear: "The daughter of any priest, if she profane herself by playing the harlot, she profanes her father, she shall be burned with fire" (Lev. 21:9).[10] Consequently, Revelation records the priestly nation's conflagration: "The beast and the ten horns you saw will hate the prostitute. They will bring her to ruin and leave her naked; they will eat her flesh and burn her with fire" (Rev. 17:16).

After recording the legal condemnation and the judicial execution of Israel as a harlotrous priest-wife, John turns to view the new bride (Rev. 21-22): "Then I, John, saw the holy city, New Jerusalem, coming down out of heaven from God, prepared as a bride adorned for her husband" (Rev. 21:2). This occurs after the "Marriage Supper of the Lamb" (Rev. 19:9-17). This city is a *New* Jerusalem. According to Galatians 4:24-30 and Hebrews 12:22-23, this "New Jerusalem" is the Church, whose source is Heaven.

Thus, the theme of Revelation is God's executing his divorce decree against Israel and subsequently capitally punishing her for spiritual adultery. Following this the Lord presents his new bride, the Church.

First Century Jerusalem as the Babylonian Harlot

In Revelation 17:3ff John views a horrible sight. Sitting upon the beast is a wicked harlot:

---

[9] *Wars* 5:6:3.

[10] I will say more below in regard to Israel's priestly status

I saw a woman sit upon a scarlet colored beast, full of names of blasphemy, having seven heads and ten horns. And the woman was arrayed in purple and scarlet color, and decked with gold and precious stones and pearls, having a golden cup in her hand full of abominations and filthiness of her fornication: And upon her forehead [was] a name written, MYSTERY, BABYLON THE GREAT, THE MOTHER OF HARLOTS AND ABOMINATIONS OF THE EARTH. And I saw the woman drunken with the blood of the saints, and with the blood of the martyrs of Jesus: and when I saw her, I wondered with great admiration.

The woman's sitting on the seven headed beast leads some to imply that she represents the city of Rome. There are two primary reasons for this assumption: (1) She is sitting upon the seven hills (Rev. 17:9), and (2) she is called "Babylon." But the name "Babylon" does not historically belong either to Rome or to Jerusalem, and thus cannot be proof that the city is Rome rather than Jerusalem. And though the sitting on the seven hills seems to suggest the city of Rome, there are ample reasons why this identity is mistaken. I am convinced beyond any doubt that this harlot is Jerusalem. As Ford notes of John, "the author has blended the prophetic theme of 'harlot' (cf. Hosea, Isaiah, Jeremiah, Ezekiel) with the Levitical text."[11] I believe she is correct and will attempt to demonstrate why below.

In this section I will provide specific exegetical evidence from Revelation identifying the harlot as first century Jerusalem. This interpretation is a minority viewpoint in evangelical circles, but I do believe it is valid. Unfortunately, due to space limitations I can only summarize the evidence. It would take a commentary on Revelation to answer all the questions that might arise.[12]

The Time-Frame for Babylon's Destruction

By the very nature of the case, the time delimitations so emphasized in Revelation strongly suggest Jerusalem as the evil Babylonian harlot. As I indicate in the preceding chapter, John forcefully emphasizes the nearness of the events. They "must shortly come to pass" (e.g., Rev. 1:1; 22:6) for "the time is at hand" (e.g., Rev. 1:3; 22:10).

---

[11] J. Massyngberde Ford, *Revelation* (*The Anchor Bible*) (Garden City, N.Y.: Doubleday, 1975), 283. Her treatment of the Harlot in Revelation is quite impressive. See especially ch. 14.

[12] See my forthcoming: *Revelation: A Tale of Two Cities* (Atlanta: American Vision, 2000). For some excellent treatments of Revelation from this general perspective see: Chilton, *The Days of Vengeance* and Cornelius Vanderwaal, *Search the Scriptures*, 10 vols., (St. Catherines, Ont.: Paideia, 1978), 10:79-111.

It does not seem likely that the harlot's utter judgment (which covers at least chapters 14-18) would speak of imperial Rome, because Rome does not fall until A.D. 410. This is well over 300 years after John writes and does not easily fit the time constraints. In addition, the Rome John presents in Revelation has seven heads representing seven kings (as noted in the preceding chapter). The seven kings are the first seven emperors of Rome — emperors of the first century only. Rome beyond this era is not in view.

Still less likely is any identity of the harlot that makes her future to our own time, for then the events would stretch two thousand (or more!) years into John's future. But Jerusalem's destruction, a most relevant, remarkable, and well-prophesied event, occurs in the first century while the Jewish rebels who crucify Christ are still living.

The Defining Sin of Babylon

The wicked Babylonian harlot is defined by an event that points only to Jerusalem. John frequently designates her as "the great city" (ἡ μεγάλη πόλις, *he megale polis*): "And a strong angel took up a stone like a great millstone and threw it into the sea, saying, Thus will Babylon, the great city, be thrown down with violence, and will not be found any longer" (Rev. 18:21).[13]

In an important interpretive statement, the first occurrence of the phrase "the great city" provides a geographical and historical clue to her identity. Revelation 11:8 speaks of the death of two prophets during the era Revelation covers: "And their dead bodies shall lie in the street of *the great city* (πόλεως τῆς μεγάλης, *poleos tes megales*) which spiritually is called Sodom and Egypt, where also our Lord was crucified" (emphasis mine). The city is described *spiritually* as "Sodom and Egypt" and *historically* as the place "where also our Lord was crucified." This is clearly a reference to Jerusalem for that is the historical site of the crucifixion of Christ (Luke 13:33; Matt. 23:34-37). In addition, just six verses before this statement and in the same context (Rev. 11:1-2), John mentions the Temple in the holy city. This must be the Temple of God in Jerusalem. This affords further confirmation of the identity of this "great city."

Some commentators object to identifying Jerusalem as "the great city" in that Rome was historically greater. But we must understand that John the Apostle, a Christian Jew, calls Jerusalem "the great city" because of her unparalleled *covenantal* significance in *redemptive history*. "Jerusalem" appears in Scripture 623 times. She is called by many titles indicating her greatness: "the city of the great king" (Psa. 48:2; Matt. 5:35), "the city of God" (Psa. 46:4; 48:1; 87:3), "the joy of the whole earth" (Psa. 48:2; Lam. 2:15), and other

---

[13] Cf. Rev. 14:18;16:19; 17:18; 18:10, 16, 18, 19.

laudable names. She is even called "the great city" in a couple of prophecies regarding her Old Testament destruction by *Babylon*: "People from many nations will pass by this city and will ask one another, 'Why has the LORD done such a thing to this *great city*?'" (Jer. 22:8). "How deserted lies the city, once so full of people! How like a widow is she, who once was *great among the nations*! She who was queen among the provinces has now become a slave" (Lam. 1:1).

Even non-biblical authors of both pagan and Jewish provenance call Israel a great city. The Roman lawyer Appian designates Jerusalem as a great city.[14] Roman historian Tacitus calls her a "famous city," while Roman naturalist Pliny deems her "by far the most famous city of the ancient Orient."[15] In the Sibylline Oracles, Josephus, and the Jewish Talmud we discover the same tendency.[16] Josephus speaks of Jerusalem's collapse: "And where is now that *great city* (ἡ μεγάλη πόλις, *he megale polis*) the metropolis of the Jewish nation, which was fortified by so many walls round about, which had so many fortresses and large towers to defend it, which could hardly contain the instruments prepared for the war, and which had so many ten thousands of men to fight for it?" (*Wars* 7:8:7). One of the Dead Scrolls — from the first century — labels her as "the princess of all nations" (4QLam).

Furthermore, in the flow of Revelation's drama, the "great city" is replaced by another great city at the end of the book: the holy *Jerusalem* coming down out of heaven: "And he carried me away in the Spirit to a great and high mountain, and showed me the holy city, Jerusalem, coming down out of heaven from God" (Rev. 21:10). The paralleling and contrasting of Jerusalems fit well with the flow of Revelation and provide further confirmation for our identity of the harlot as Jerusalem.

Jerusalem as a Pagan Enemy

If my analysis is correct, John calls Jerusalem by the pagan name of "Babylon" (Rev. 14:8; 16:19; 17:5; 18:2, 10, 21). Earlier he attributes pagan names to her that are parallel with the designation "Babylon." In Revelation 11:8 he calls her "spiritually Sodom and Egypt." Isaiah does the same when he calls Jerusalem "Sodom" and "Gomorrah" (Isa. 1:1, 10). In a text emphasizing the unfaithfulness of Jerusalem to God, Ezekiel alludes to her as Sodomlike by calling her "Sodom's sister" (Eze. 16:46, 48, 53, 55-56) and the offspring of the Amorites and Hittites (Eze. 16:45).

---

[14] *The Syrian Wars* 50.

[15] Tacitus, *Histories* 5:2; Pliny, *Natural History* 5:14:70.

[16] Sibylline Oracles 5:150-154, 225-227, 408-413; Josephus *Wars* 7:8:7; *Against Apion* 1:197. See also Talmudic references in Alfred Edersheim, *Sketches of Jewish Social Life* (Grand Rapids: Eerdmans, rep. 1975 [n.d]), 82.

The idea of such name-calling is that Jerusalem does not conduct herself as the wife of God; rather, she acts as one of his enemies — like Sodom, Egypt, and Babylon. The Jewish historian Josephus describes those who dwell in Jerusalem during the Jewish War, comparing their destruction to Sodom's:

> I suppose that had the Romans made any longer delay in coming against these villains, the city would either have been swallowed up by the ground opening upon them, or been overflowed by water, or else been destroyed by such thunder as the country of Sodom perished by, for it had brought forth a generation of men much more atheistical than were those that suffered such punishments; for by their madness it was that all the people came to be destroyed (*Wars* 6:13:6).

The fact that the harlot sits on the seven-headed beast (obviously representative of Rome) does not indicate *identity with* Rome, but rather *alliance with* Rome against Christianity. By calling upon Roman authority, the Jews demand Christ's crucifixion and prompt the persecution of Christians (cp. John 19:6-12; Acts 17:7; 21:10-11; 25:2-8; 28:17; 1 Thess. 2:14-16).

The Autopsy of the Harlot

Filling the harlot is the blood of the saints, according to Revelation 16:6; 17:6; and 18:21, 24. For instance, Revelation 18:24 says: "In her was found the blood of prophets and of the saints, and of all who have been killed on the earth [*sc.* the Land]." Of course, with the eruption of the Neronic persecution Rome is awash with the blood of the saints. But Rome has only recently enrolled in the persecuting ranks of God's enemies.[17] For decades before the Roman persecution Acts portrays *Jerusalem* as the persecutor and Rome as the protector of Christianity. Besides, Rome is not guilty of killing any of the Old Testament prophets, as is Jerusalem.[18]

In the context of the Olivet Discourse, Jesus reproaches Jerusalem and specifically condemns her leaders:

> And you say, "If we had lived in the days of our forefathers, we would not have taken part with them in shedding the blood of the prophets." So you testify against yourselves that you are the descendants of those who murdered the prophets. Fill up, then, the mea-

---

[17] See: Gentry, *Before Jerusalem Fell: The Dating of the Book of Revelation* (3d. ed.: Atlanta.: American Vision, 1999), ch. 17.

[18] Jer. 2:30; Matt. 5:12; 21:33-38; 23:31-37; Acts 7:52; 1 Thess. 2:15.

sure of the sin of your forefathers! You snakes! You brood of vipers! How will you escape being condemned to hell? Therefore I am sending you prophets and wise men and teachers. Some of them you will kill and crucify; others you will flog in your synagogues and pursue from town to town. And so upon you will come *all the righteous blood that has been shed on earth* (τῆς γῆς, *tes ges*, literally "the land"), from the blood of righteous Abel to the blood of Zechariah son of Berekiah, whom you murdered between the temple and the altar. (Matt. 23:30-35)

This statement is very close to the language of Revelation. At the autopsy of the harlot we discover that "in her was found the blood of prophets and of the saints, and of all who have been killed on the earth" (Rev. 18:24).

Matthew 23:35a
that upon you may fall the guilt of all the righteous blood shed on earth.

Revelation 18:24
In her was found the blood of prophets and of saints and of all who have been slain on the earth.

Interestingly, Christ's oracle against Jerusalem calls down woes upon her (Matthew 23:13-16, 23, 25, 27, 29), woes such as those in John's prophecy (Rev. 8:11; 9:12; 11:14).

Before his stoning, Stephen rebukes Jerusalem: "Which of the prophets have not your fathers persecuted? And they have slain them who showed before of the coming of the Just One, of whom ye have been now the betrayers and murderers" (Acts 7:51-52). Throughout Revelation it is the *slain Lamb* who acts in judgment upon his slayers, the Jews. "Then I saw a Lamb, looking as if it had been slain, standing in the center of the throne, encircled by the four living creatures and the elders. He had seven horns and seven eyes, which are the seven spirits of God sent out into all the earth" (Rev. 5:6; cp. 5:12; 13:8). Revelation mentions this Lamb twenty-seven times.[19]

In fact, Jerusalem literally calls down her own judgment for slaying this Lamb of God: "All the people answered, 'Let his blood be on us and on our children!'" (Matt. 27:25). For this reason Jesus warns her daughters in the first century about her fast approaching judgment:

---

[19] See: Rev. 5:6, 8, 12-13; 6:1, 16; 7:9-10, 14, 17; 12:11; 13:8, 11; 14:1, 4, 10; 15:3; 17:14; 19:7, 9; 21:14, 22-23; 22:1, 3.

But Jesus turning to them said, "Daughters of Jerusalem, stop weeping for Me, but weep for yourselves and for your children. For behold, the days are coming when they will say, 'Blessed are the barren, and the wombs that never bore, and the breasts that never nursed.' Then they will begin to say to the mountains, 'Fall on us,'"and to the hills, 'Cover us.' For if they do these things in the green tree, what will happen in the dry?" (Luke 23:28-31).

This lament-warning sounds eerily like Revelation 6:16-17: "And they said to the mountains and to the rocks, 'Fall on us and hide us from the presence of Him who sits on the throne, and from the wrath of the Lamb; for the great day of their wrath has come; and who is able to stand?'" And are not the tongues spoken in Acts 2 harbingers of the coming "great and glorious day of the Lord" (Acts 2:20) warning Jerusalemites to "be saved from this perverse generation" (Acts 2:40)?[20] Did not Jewish converts to Christ in Jerusalem sell their property in Jerusalem (Acts 2:45) because it will soon by of zero worth?

The Attire of the Harlot
The harlot's attire is also helpful for confirming her identity. "The woman was dressed in purple and scarlet, and was glittering with gold, precious stones and pearls. She held a golden cup in her hand, filled with abominable things and the filth of her adulteries. This title was written on her forehead: Mystery Babylon the Great the Mother of Prostitutes and of the Abominations of the Earth" (Rev. 17:4-5). "Alas, alas, that great city that was clothed in fine linen, purple, and scarlet, and adorned with gold and precious stones and pearls!" (Rev. 18:16).

As I indicate above, Israel is a priestly nation (Exo. 19:6; Isa. 61:6) and Jerusalem is her capital, wherein stands the only Temple of God (Psa. 68:29; Mark 11:15; Luke 4:9). The colors associated with the priestly worship at the Temple (and before that the Tabernacle) describe the attire of the harlot. She is arrayed in the Jewish priestly colors of scarlet, purple, and gold, and with fine line (Exo. 28:5-6, 8, 11, 13-15, 20, 22-24, 26-27, 33, 36). Edersheim observes: "To these the high-priest added other four distinctive articles of dress, called 'golden vestments,' because, unlike the robes of the ordinary

---

[20] O. Palmer Robertson, *The Final Word: A Biblical Response to the Case for Tongues and Prophecy Today* (Edinburgh: Banner of Truth, 1993), 41-49. Kenneth L. Gentry, Jr., "A Theological Analysis of Tongues" audio-cassette tape set #9 (P.O. Box 388, Placentia, California 92871).

priests, gold, the symbol of splendour, appeared in them." [21]

Josephus even mentions a specially prominent "Babylonian curtain" hanging in the Temple:

> but then this house [i.e., the Temple], as it was divided into two parts, the inner part was lower than the appearance of the outer, and had golden doors of fifty-five cubs altitude, and sixteen in breadth; but before these doors there was a veil of equal largeness with the doors. It was a Babylonian curtain, embroidered with blue, and fine linen, and scarlet, and purple, and of a contexture that was truly wonderful. (Wars 5:5:4)

Josephus mentions all of this while carefully explaining and emphasizing the color decor of the Temple. He also highlights the tremendous amount of gold plating on the Temple:

> Now the outward face of the temple in its front wanted nothing that was likely to surprise either men's minds or their eyes: for it was covered all over with plates of gold of great weight, and, at the first rising of the sun, reflected back a very fiery splendour, and made those who forced themselves to look upon it to turn their eyes away, just as they would have done at the sun's own rays (*Wars* 5:5:6).

Even more remarkable, perhaps, is the harlot's crown. She wears a blasphemous tiara on her forehead that serves as a negative image of the holy tiara which the Jewish high priest wore: "This title was written on her forehead: Mystery Babylon the Great the Mother of Prostitutes and of the Abominations of the Earth" (Rev. 17:5). God's Law describes the high priest's tiara: "Make a plate of pure gold and engrave on it as on a seal: Holy to the Lord" (Exo. 28:36). In essence, John is denouncing Jerusalem as does Isaiah before him: "See how the faithful city has become a harlot! She once was full of justice; righteousness used to dwell in her—but now murderers!" (Isa. 1:21).

In addition, this wicked harlot holds a gold cup in her hand, as does the high priest on the Day of Atonement, according to the Jewish Talmud.[22] Interestingly, the Temple's main door has on it golden vines with great clusters of grapes (from which wine is derived). The golden grape clusters on the

---

[21] Alfred Edersheim, *The Temple: Its Ministry and Services* (Grand Rapids: Eerdmans, rep. 1958 [n.d.]), 96-97.

[22] Golden bowls were used elsewhere in the Levitical services. See: Exo. 25:29; 37:16, 17.

vine are very prominent, being the size of a man (Josephus, *Wars* 5:5:4). These suggest the golden cup filled with blood.

The Negative Image

In Revelation John paints an obvious literary contrast between the evil harlot and the chaste bride. This strongly suggests the harlot's identity as Jerusalem. The contrast between the harlot in the wilderness below (Rev. 17:3) and the New Jerusalem from heaven above (Rev. 21:2) is quite conspicuous.

A careful analysis of Revelation leads to the conclusion that John is comparing *two Jerusalems*, much like in Galatians and Hebrews. In Galatians we read of Paul's comparison: "Now Hagar stands for Mount Sinai in Arabia and corresponds to the present city of Jerusalem, because she is in slavery with her children. But the Jerusalem that is above is free, and she is our mother" (Gal. 4:25-26). The writer of Hebrews addresses Jewish converts to Christianity and deals with their conversion from Judaism to Christianity: "You have not come to a mountain that can be touched and that is burning with fire; to darkness, gloom and storm. . . . You have come to Mount Zion, to the heavenly Jerusalem, the city of the living God" (Heb. 12:18, 22b).

Let us now survey some of the evidence for this contrast, which seems intentional.

The Appearing of the Women. The *way* John comes to see each of these women is clearly related. Both even occur under the guidance of (apparently) the same angel:

> And there came one of the seven angels which had the seven vials, and talked with me, saying unto me, Come hither; I will shew unto thee the judgment of the great whore that sits upon many waters. (Rev. 17:1).

> And there came unto me one of the seven angels which had the seven vials full of the seven last plagues, and talked with me, saying, Come hither, I will shew thee the bride, the Lamb's wife. (Rev. 21:9)

But for a few minor details the introductory language here is identical. In this intricately crafted work of art the contrast seems quite intentional, and for the purpose of comparison. There is some important relationship between these two women. John is presenting a positive and a negative image — the harlot being the negative and the Bride the positive. This fits well with the contrasts between the "Jerusalem that now is" (i.e., first century earthly Jerusalem) and "the Jerusalem which is above" (i.e., the New Covenant Church).

The Character of the Women. Not only is John transported to see these women in an identical *manner*, but the two women are immediately contrasted as to *character*.

> Come here, I will shew unto thee the judgment of *the great whore* that sits upon many waters with whom the kings of the earth committed fornication, and the inhabitants of the earth were made drunk with the wine of her fornication. (Rev. 17:1-2)

> Come hither, I will shew thee the *bride, the Lamb's wife*. And he carried me away in the Spirit to a great and high mountain, and showed me the great city, the holy Jerusalem, descending out of heaven from God, having the glory of God. And her light was like a most precious stone, like a jasper stone, clear as crystal. (Rev. 21:9-11)

In both Christ's and the apostles's ministries, Israel appears as the great enemy of God who resists the calling of Messiah: "O Jerusalem, Jerusalem, you who kill the prophets and stone those sent to you, how often I have longed to gather your children together, as a hen gathers her chicks under her wings, but you were not willing" (Matt. 23:37). The Jews "always heaps up their sins to the limit" and upon them "the wrath of God has come at last" (1 Thess. 2:16b; cp. Matt. 23:32).

In contrast, the New Covenant Church that replaces Jerusalem is a chaste bride: "I promised you to one husband, to Christ, so that I might present you as a pure virgin to him" (2 Cor. 11:2b). "Christ loved the church and gave himself up for her to make her holy, cleansing her by the washing with water through the word, and to present her to himself as a radiant church, without stain or wrinkle or any other blemish, but holy and blameless" (Eph. 5:25b-27). She replaces Israel as God's covenantal institution: "I say to you that many will come from the east and the west, and will take their places at the feast with Abraham, Isaac and Jacob in the kingdom of heaven. But the subjects of the kingdom will be thrown outside, into the darkness, where there will be weeping and gnashing of teeth" (Matt. 8:11-12; cp. 23:33-45).

The Environment of the Women. The angel carries John to contrasting environments where he sees the two women. Their environments are reflective of their character and indicative of their spiritual status and destiny.

> So he carried me away in the spirit into *the wilderness* and I saw a woman sit upon a scarlet colored beast. (Rev. 17:3)

> And he carried me away in the spirit to *a great and high mountain*, and

shewed me that great city, the holy Jerusalem, descending out of heaven from God. (Rev. 21:10)

The wilderness theme of Scripture portrays God's judgment, for God originally saves Israel from "the howling waste of a wilderness" (Deut. 32:10).[23] Divine judgments befall Israel as a wilderness experience (Isa. 64:10; Jer. 4:11). When God marries Israel he takes her from the wilderness to be his wife: "Go and cry in the hearing of Jerusalem, saying, 'Thus says the LORD: "I remember you, the kindness of your youth, the love of your betrothal, when you went after Me in the wilderness, in a land that was not sown"'" (Jer. 2:2). In Revelation, Jerusalem the harlot returns to the wilderness under the wrath of the Lamb.

In contrast, by his grace God elevates the New Jerusalem, as the Church of Jesus Christ, to a great, high mountain. The Old Testament associates the strength (Psa. 30:7; 65:6; Isa. 40:9), steadfastness (Psa. 90:2; Prov. 8:25), and protection (Psa. 125:2) that mountains afford men with the grace and blessing of God. Thus, originally Jerusalem is "the city of our God, his holy mountain" (Psa. 48:1). Now the prophetic *New* Jerusalem will be high and lifted up, according to Revelation (see also: Isa. 2:2-4; 11:9-10; 25:6-7; 65:25).

We could bring forward other contrasts between the harlot Babylon and the New Jerusalem, such as their divergent dress (Rev. 17:4; 21:2, 11ff), their differing relationships with kings (Rev. 17:2; 21:24), and so forth. But these are sufficient to demonstrate John's intentional comparison and contrast of the two cities. One is the place (Jerusalem) where Christ is crucified (Rev. 11:8), the other is called the "*New* Jerusalem" (Rev. 21:2). Surely the harlot is first century Jerusalem, the capital of Israel.

Conclusion

Revelation is one of the most misunderstood books of Scripture. Because of a fundamental misapprehension of its overarching message too many interpreters misapply its woeful judgment scenes. Too many Christians today fear the soon appearing of the horrid Babylonian harlot. They fear she will join forces with the beast for a while to wreak havoc upon the earth.

This widespread, culturally debilitating misinterpretation not withstanding, ample evidence exists that the harlot and her awful mission are in our distant past. The harlot, Babylon the Great, is first century Jerusalem. The chaos, horror, and despair she wreaks upon God's people are long past.

---

[23] David Chilton, *Paradise Restored: A Biblical Theology of Dominion* (Tyler, Tex.: Institute for Christian Economics, 1985), ch. 6.

CONCLUSION

But Jesus immediately said to them: "Take courage! It is I. Don't be afraid."

Matthew 14:27

A Reflection on Eschatological Evil

The design of this book is to analyze the leading prophecies of eschatological evil, prophecies that collectively warn of "perilous times." In the preceding chapters we analyze some of the classic passages speaking of such times. Though a great number of Christians are convinced of the imminent outbreak of apocalyptic events, a careful study of the Scriptures shows they are misconstruing their foundational passages. And if the very *reasons* for the expectation of such prophetic events are fallacious, then the fears arising from them should quickly evaporate.

In the preceding pages I provide studies of the key prophecies of Scripture employed by modern prophecy buffs. In each case we find that these popular prophecies are fulfilled in the first century — almost two thousand years ago.

The attempt to make Daniel's seventy weeks fit into our future involves the interpreter in one of the most strained approaches to Scripture in all of evangelical theology. That the prophecy must unfold up to the very moment of the crucifixion of Christ only to skip it altogether is odd enough. But then the time element that forms the very structure of the prophecy must be radically altered to allow for an unexpected gap in its chronology, a gap already four times longer than the whole time-frame itself. Rather than such an interpretive approach, I show that the prophecy finds its focus on and terminus in the greatest events of all redemptive history: the ministry and death of the Messiah, Jesus Christ.

Following the Daniel study, we consider Christ's great prophecy in Matthew in which he warns of "wars and rumors of wars." In the very course of the prophecy, Christ's own words confine these wars and related events to his own generation then living (Matt. 24:34). That generation will witness the

151

destruction of the Temple (Matt. 24:1-2). Though Christ's apocalyptic language is admittedly difficult in places, I note that the internal time limitations tie the "great tribulation" to the first century and that we must interpret the language according to the canons the Old Testament prophets establish. We may easily apply the apocalyptic imagery to the devastating events surrounding the destruction of Jerusalem and the Temple in A.D. 70.

As we continue our study of apocalyptic prophecy, I analyze the infamous 2 Thessalonians prophecy of the "man of lawlessness." As with the prophecies of Daniel and Christ, we see that our fears of impending catastrophic judgment are misplaced. Paul writes to the Thessalonians of an evil figure relevant to them: Nero Caesar. He speaks of the present restraining of the lawless one in the mid-first century; and of the temple of God that is destroyed in A.D. 70. In order to project this eschatological personage into our future, the interpreter must propose a restraining that is in effect for two thousand year and an unexplained re-building of the temple. And this despite the impossibility of the original audience understanding it.

And what study of eschatological evil could omit an inquiry into John's famous Revelation? Yet here again we see that the first century is the scene of the prophetic chaos. In the very opening of his great work, John informs us that these things are to "shortly come to pass" because the "time is at hand" (Rev. 1:1, 3). Taking account of the highly wrought symbolism John employs, the beast imagery fits the notorious Nero Caesar like paint fits to the wall. This dastardly beast is the first and most vicious imperial persecutor of the fledgling new covenant church, a political figure of immense proportions and most relevant to John's original audience. And he portrays the apostate Judaism that crucifies Christ and persecutes his Church as a faithless wife — indeed, as an adulterous harlot. Both of these evil characters and their associated judgments have an undeniable first century relevance. The relevance is so remarkable that even some dispensationalists are admitting a first century fulfillment (though they expect these events to occur again at the end of history).[1]

Simply put: our study in eschatological evil proves that the perilous times of Scripture are in the first century.

I indicate in the Introduction to his book, however, that a *positive* reason for studying such negative conceptions exists: the prophetically determined chaos of Scripture is in our past, and because of this *our future is ultimately bright with hope.*

In this Conclusion I will briefly outline the eschatological hope that lies

---

[1] C. Marvin Pate and Calvin B. Haines, Jr., *Doomsday Delusions: What's Wrong with Predictions About the End of the World* (Downers Grove, Ill.: InterVarsity, 1995), 27.

before us as Christians. Hopefully the study has whetted your appetite so that you will seek out the true nature of the future. The case for future-oriented optimism is contained in the system of eschatology known as "postmillennialism," which teaches that Christ will return after ("post") an era of millennial glory. I set forth the full case for postmillennialism in my 600 page book: *He Shall Have Dominion: A Postmillennial Eschatology*.[2] I defend it from other viewpoints in *Three Views of the End of the Millennium and Beyond* and *Always Reforming: A Dialogue of Differences within the Reformed Faith*.[3] But let me briefly survey some of the data that leads to a postmillennial hope.

The Anticipation of Gospel Glory

Rooted in the Old Testament and coming to fruition in the New Testament, is the expectation of the victorious spread of righteousness, a view which we may designate Gospel Glory. Indeed, at the very creation of man, God so designs and commissions him as to expect the worldwide operation of righteous cultural endeavor. A vital aspect of the image of God in man is his drive to dominion, a drive that must be governed by godly principles in order to fulfill its true intent:

> Let us make man in our image, in our likeness, and let them rule over the fish of the sea and the birds of the air, over the livestock, over all the earth, and over all the creatures that move along the ground. So God created man in his own image, in the image of God he created him; male and female he created them" (Gen. 1:26-27).[4]

The fall of Adam shortly after creation brings chaos into the created order, to be sure. Consequently, the first prophetic promise in Scripture expects a long struggle between Christ and Satan. Yet it promises that Christ will

---

[2] Kenneth L. Gentry, Jr., *He Shall Have Dominion: A Postmillennial Eschatology* (2d. ed.: Tyler, Tex.: Institute for Christian Economics, 1997). A college course I teach on postmillennialism is available on audio cassette: Set #5, "Postmillennial Eschatology." Gentry, P.O. Box 388, Placentia, CA 92871.

[3] Darrell L. Bock, ed., *Three Views of the End of the Millennium and Beyond* (Grand Rapids: Zondervan, 1998) and David G. Hagopian, ed., *Always Reforming: A Dialogue of Differences within the Reformed Faith* (Phillipsburg, N.J.: Presbyterian and Reformed, 1999).

[4] Kenneth L. Gentry, Jr., *The Greatness of the Great Commission: The Christian Enterprise in a Fallen World* (2d ed.: Tyler, Tex.: Institute for Christian Economics, 1993), ch. 1. A four tape study of the "Dominion Mandate" is available from the author (set # 13). See address in footnote above.

ultimately win the victory in history: "And I will put enmity between you and the woman, and between your offspring and hers; he will crush your head, and you will strike his heel" (Gen. 3:15).

In developing this victory hope for God's seed, the Abrahamic Covenant promises the spread of salvation to "all the families of the earth" (Gen. 12:1-4). According to the New Testament apostolic interpretation, the Gospel is the tool for the spread of the Abrahamic blessings: "The Scripture foresaw that God would justify the Gentiles by faith, and announced the gospel in advance to Abraham: 'All nations will be blessed through you. . . .' If you belong to Christ, then you are Abraham's seed, and heirs according to the promise" (Gal. 3:8, 29).

The Old Testament revelation traces the development of the promise of God through the Patriarchal and Mosaic periods. The great hope of God's promise will ultimately come to pass in the appearance of the Messiah, who will cause God's glory and righteousness to cover the earth: "The scepter will not depart from Judah, nor the ruler's staff from between his feet, until he comes to whom it belongs and the obedience of the nations is his" (Gen. 49:10; cf. 22:17; Num. 24:17-19).

The prophets of the Old Testament continue the hope of Gospel Glory when they command kings and judges to bow to Christ, and promise that the ends of the earth will turn to God in salvation (Pss. 2; 22; 72; Isa. 9:1-7; 11:1-10; Mic. 4:1-3). One of the clearest such prophecies is contained in Isaiah 2:2-4:

> In the last days the mountain of the LORD's temple will be established as chief among the mountains; it will be raised above the hills, and all nations will stream to it. Many peoples will come and say, 'Come, let us go up to the mountain of the LORD, to the house of the God of Jacob. He will teach us his ways, so that we may walk in his paths.' The law will go out from Zion, the word of the LORD from Jerusalem. He will judge between the nations and will settle disputes for many peoples. They will beat their swords into plowshares and their spears into pruning hooks. Nation will not take up sword against nation, nor will they train for war anymore.

Contrary to so much of the contemporary Christian Zionistic movement,[5] the Gospel Glory era will be apart from Jewish exaltation and the re-institution of Old Testament ceremonial distinctives. All saved people will be on an

---

[5] See: Ken Sidey, "For the Love of Zion," *Christianity Today* 36:3 (March 9, 1992) 46-50.

equal footing with God. Isaiah 19:24-25 reads: "In that day Israel will be the third, along with Egypt and Assyria, a blessing on the earth. The LORD Almighty will bless them, saying, 'Blessed be Egypt my people, Assyria my handiwork, and Israel my inheritance'" (cf. Jer. 3:16-17; 31:31-34; 48:47; 49:6, 39). Jew and Gentile alike will rejoice in glorious harmony in the abundant salvation of the triune God, as the New Testament demands (Rom. 10:12; Gal. 3:28; 6:15; Col. 3:11).

The prophets foresee the beginning of Gospel Glory in the ascension of Christ to the right hand of God. "In my vision at night I looked, and there before me was one like a son of man, coming with the clouds of heaven. He approached the Ancient of Days and was led into his presence. He was given authority, glory and sovereign power; all peoples, nations and men of every language worshiped him. His dominion is an everlasting dominion that will not pass away, and his kingdom is one that will never be destroyed" (Dan. 7:13-14). The New Testament record of Christ's birth reflects on the Old Testament Gospel Glory Theme, showing that Christ's first coming begins the fruition of the promises (Luke 1:67-75).

The Nature of Gospel Glory

The kingdom of Christ, which relates so closely to the gospel, is not a future, Armageddon-introduced, political kingdom. Such a conception is the error of the first century Jews. They want a political kingdom to overthrow Rome: "Jesus, knowing that they intended to come and make him king by force, withdrew again to a mountain by himself" (John 6:15; cp. Luke 17:20). When Christ refuses to offer them such, they reject him. Even his disciples are disappointed, partly due to this carnal conception of God's glorious deliverance: "We were hoping that it was He who was going to redeem Israel. Indeed, besides all this, today is the third day since these things happened" (Luke 24:21).

The fundamental power of the kingdom is the "gospel of the kingdom" (Matt. 4:23; 9:35), hence our speaking of Gospel Glory. "Now after John was put in prison, Jesus came to Galilee, preaching the gospel of the kingdom of God, and saying, 'The time is fulfilled, and the kingdom of God is at hand. Repent, and believe in the gospel'" (Mark 1:14-15). The basic function of the kingdom is the promotion of God's truth: "You are right in saying I am a king. In fact, for this reason I was born, and for this I came into the world, to testify to the truth. Everyone on the side of truth listens to me" (John 18:37).

The kingdom of Christ, then, is essentially a spiritual kingdom (Rom. 14:17) that operates from within the heart: "Now when He was asked by the Pharisees when the kingdom of God would come, He answered them and said, 'The kingdom of God does not come with observation; nor will they say, "See here!" or "See there!" For indeed, the kingdom of God is within you'" (Luke 17:20-21). Men enter the kingdom of Christ by means of the new birth (John 3:3), so that his newborn followers may rest in the comfort that "He has rescued us from the dominion of darkness and brought us into the kingdom of the Son he loves" (Col. 1:13). Christ rules his kingdom from heaven (John 18:36; Eph. 1:19-23) by his spiritual presence through the indwelling of the Holy Spirit (John 7:39; Rom. 8:9; 1 Cor. 3:16).

Israel as a *geo-political entity* has been set aside once-for-all as the specially favored nation of God (Matt. 8:11-12; 21:43). This is because of her prominent role in crucifying Christ (Acts 2:22-23, 36; 3:13-15; 5:30; 7:52; 1 Thess. 2:14-15). Christ's kingdom includes people of all races on an equal basis (Isa. 19:19-25; Zech. 9:7; Eph. 2:12-17), including the eventual inclusion of a great majority of the Jewish race through the loving and gracious overtures of the Spirit empowered Church of Jesus Christ (Rom. 11:11-25).

The New Covenant Church is the fruition of the purpose of Israel of old. Thus, she is called "the Israel of God" (Gal. 6:16), "the circumcision" (Phil. 3:3), "the seed of Abraham" (Gal. 3:7, 29), the "Jerusalem above" (Gal. 4:24-29), the "temple of God" (Eph. 2:21), "a royal priesthood" and a "peculiar people" (1 Pet. 2:9-10; Tit. 2:14), "the dispersion" (1 Pet. 1:1). Non-Christian Jews are considered to falsely call themselves "Jews" (Rev. 2:10; 3:10).

Consequently, the New Testament applies Jewish promises to the Church. For instance, the New Covenant promised with Israel and Judah (Jer. 31:31-34) becomes the New Covenant for the New Testament Church (Matt. 26:28). The rebuilding of the Temple (in Ezekiel) becomes the building of the new covenant phase Church (Eph. 2:19-21; 1 Pet. 2:5-9). The tabernacle of David also finds fulfillment in the new covenant Church (Acts 15:13-18). Promise of long life in "the land" (Exo. 20:12) transforms into hope for long life in "the earth" (Eph. 6:3). On and on we could go.

The Coming of Gospel Glory

The prophesied kingdom of Christ comes near in the early ministry of Christ because the "time was fulfilled" (Mark 1:14-15). In fact, John the Baptist is a marker separating the fading Old Testament era from the dawning kingdom era (Matt. 11:11-14; Mark 1:14-15).

Christ's power over demons is evidence the kingdom comes in his earthly ministry: "If I drive out demons by the Spirit of God, then the kingdom of God has come upon you" (Matt. 12:28; Luke 11:20). Thus, the kingdom is not to await some future, visible coming (Luke 17:20-21).

Christ claims to be king while on earth (John 12:12-15; 18:36-37) and is enthroned as king following his resurrection and ascension (Acts 2:30ff). From then on we hear of his being in a royal position at the right hand of Almighty God (Rom. 8:34; Eph. 1:20; 1 Pet. 3:22). Because of this, first century Christians proclaim him as king, as their enemies well-knew: "They are all defying Caesar's decrees, saying that there is another king, one called Jesus" (Acts 17:7b; cp. Acts 3:15; Rev. 1:5). He is enthroned with regal dignity, authority, and power (Eph. 1:22; Phil. 2:9).

Beginning with the first century people are translated into the kingdom of Christ at their conversions (Col. 1:12, 13; 4:10; 1 Thess. 2:12). Christianity is Christ's kingdom (Rev. 1:6; 9) and Christians are now mystically seated with him in rulership positions: "And God raised us up with Christ and seated us with him in the heavenly realms in Christ Jesus" (Eph. 2:6; cp. Eph. 1:3; 1 Cor. 3:21-22).

The Means of Gospel Glory

How shall this postmillennial hope come to pass? Evangelism is the essential pre-condition to the postmillennial hope of Gospel Glory. Apart from Christ we can do nothing (John 15:5); in Christ we can do all things (Phil. 4:13, 19; Matt. 17:20). Thus, in that he possesses "all authority in heaven and on earth" (Matt. 28:18) Christ's Great Commission expects his people to win massive numbers of converts. These are to be baptized in his name and instructed in "all things" he taught (Matt. 28:19).[6] Due to the glorious presence of Christ with us the Great Commission expects the conversion of *all* nations (Matt. 28:19), as do the prophets (Isa. 2:1-4; Mic. 4:1-4). Christ is presently ruling and reigning from heaven (1 Cor. 15:25a; Eph. 1:19-23; Rev. 1:5). He will not return in his Second Advent until "the end" of history (Matt. 25:31; 1 Cor. 15:24) when he turns his rule over to the Father (1 Cor. 15:28).

Our Christian witness involves scattering the darkness and exposing evil (Matt. 5:13-14; Eph. 5:11). We are to be calling men to repentance from *all* unrighteousness in *every* realm (Luke 24:47; 3:8), so that "every thought" is "taken captive" to God and Christ (Eccl. 12:13; 2 Cor. 10:5). Christians are to live and act in every area of life — personal, social, political — with body, soul, mind, and strength (Mark 12:37) to the glory of God (1 Cor. 10:31; Col. 3:17). We do this because we must give an account of every word and deed (Eccl. 12:14; Matt. 12:36; 2 Cor. 5:10).

God's redemption provided in Christ is designed to bring the *world* as a system to salvation (John 1:29; 3:17; 1 John 2:2) as redemption flows to all men toward the end of history (John 12:31; 1 Tim. 2:6). The falling away of the Jews in their first century apostasy allows for mass conversions among the

---

[6] Gentry, *The Greatness of the Great Commission.* Gary North, *Millennialism and Social Theory* (Tyler, Tex.: Institute for Christian Economics, 1990).

Gentiles throughout history (Rom. 11:12; Acts 13:46-47). Eventually, though, God will convert the vast majority of Jews and Gentiles to himself by the "reconciliation of the world" (Rom. 11:15; 2 Cor. 5:19). Consequently, biblical prophecy expects a time when the majority of the world's population will be converted to Christ by means of the Gospel. Thus, as Christians we cannot omit cultural endeavors as we seek the redemption of all of life to God's glory.[7]

God normally works in history in a gradualistic manner, as we see in the gradual, ages-long unfolding of his plan of redemption (from Adam until Christ) and the revelation of himself in Scripture (from Genesis to Revelation). The kingdom comes gradualistically, as well, growing and ebbing ever stronger over the long run:

> He presented another parable to them, saying, "The kingdom of heaven is like a mustard seed, which a man took and sowed in his field; and this is smaller than all other seeds; but when it is full grown, it is larger than the garden plants, and becomes a tree, so that the birds of the air come and nest in its branches." He spoke another parable to them, "The kingdom of heaven is like leaven, which a woman took, and hid in three pecks of meal, until it was all leavened." (Matthew 13:31-33)

See also: Daniel 2:35ff; Ezekiel 17:22-24; 47:1-9; and Mark 4:26-29. *Before* Christ's Second Advent he will conquer his enemies (1 Cor. 15:24); the last enemy, death, will be conquered at his Return, when we are resurrected (1 Cor. 15:26).

The Means of Gospel Glory

To doubt the possibility of world redemption and Gospel Glory is to denigrate the gifts God has given the Church. Christ's gifts to the Church well equip her for the task of winning the world to him: the Church has the very presence of the resurrected Christ (Matt. 28:20; Col. 1:27) and the outpoured Holy Spirit (Acts 2:16ff; 1 Cor. 3:16). God the Father delights in the salvation of sinners (Eze. 18:23; Luke 15:10). The Gospel is nothing less than "the power of God unto salvation" (Rom. 1:16; 1 Cor. 1:18, 24).

In addition, Satan's binding is effected in principle in the ministry of Christ (Matt. 12:28-29; Luke 11:22-22), casting him down from his dominance (John

---

[7] Gary North, *Dominion Covenant: Genesis* (Tyler, Tex. Institute for Christian Economics, 1982). Greg L. Bahnsen and Kenneth L. Gentry, Jr., *House Divided: The Breakup of Dispensational Theology* (2d. ed.: Tyler, Tex.: Institute for Christian Economics, 1997).

12:31; Luke 17:10) on the basis of Christ's redemptive labor (Col. 3:15; Heb. 2:14). Because of this Christians may resist the devil and cause him to flee (Jms. 4:7; 2 Thess. 3:3; 1 John 5:18). We may even crush him beneath our feet (Rom. 16:20) because "greater is he that is in you, than he that is in the world" (1 John 4:4).

This, in brief, is the postmillennial hope which reflects the case for Gospel Glory and imparts hope, even in periods of chaos. We must understand that the Bible warns us that there will be "perilous times" (2 Tim. 3:1). What it does *not* teach is that *all* history will be one uninterrupted time of peril. After all, "the earth is the Lord's and the fulness thereof," as Scripture often proclaims.[8]

---

[8] Exo. 9:29; 19:5; Lev. 25:23; Deut. 10:14; 1 Sam. 2:8; 2 Chron. 29:11, 14; Job 41:11; Psa. 24:1; 50:12; 89:11; Psa. 115:16; 1 Cor. 10:26, 28.

RESOURCES

Select Bibliography of Postmillennial or Preterist Books

Alexander, J. A. *Commentary on the Prophecies of Isaiah*. Grand Rapids: Zondervan, rep. 1977 (1878).

Bock, Darrell L. , ed. *Three Views of the End of History and Beyond*. Grand Rapids: Zondervan (1999).

Boettner, Loraine, *The Millennium*. 2d ed. Phillipsburg, N.J.: Presbyterian and Reformed, 1984.

Brown, David. *Christ's Second Coming: Will It Be Premillennial?* Edmonton, AB: Still Waters Revival, rep. 1990 (1882).

Chilton, David. *Paradise Restored: An Eschatology of Dominion*. Ft. Worth: Dominion, 1985.

Chilton, David. The Great Tribulation. Ft. Worth: Dominion, 1987.

Davis, John Jefferson. *Christ's Victorious Kingdom*. Moscow, Ida.: Canon, 1995.

DeMar, Gary, *Last Days Madness: Obsession of the Modern Church* (3d. ed.: Atlanta: American Vision, 1997).

Gentry, Kenneth L., Jr., *The Beast of Revelation*. 2d ed.: Tyler, Tex.: Institute for Christian Economics, 1995.

_____. *Before Jerusalem Fell: Dating the Book of Revelation*. 3d ed.: Atlanta: American Vision, 1999.

_____, Gary DeMar, and Ralph Barker. *DeMystifying Revelation* (video cassette interview of Gentry). Atlanta: American Vision, 1997.

_____. *God's Law in the Modern World: The Continuing Relevance of Old Testament Law*. Tyler, Tex.: Institute for Christian Economics, 1997.

_____. *The Greatness of the Great Commission: The Christian Enterprise in a Fallen World*. 2d. ed. Tyler, Tex.: Institute for Christian Economics, 1993.

_____. *He Shall Have Dominion: A Postmillennial Eschatology*. 2d. ed. Tyler, Tex.: Institute for Christian Economics, 1997.

_____. *Revelation: A Tale of Two Cities*, Atlanta: American Vision, 2000.

Hagopian, David G., ed. *Always Reforming: A Dialogue of Differences within the Reformed Faith*. Phillipsburg, N.J.: Presbyterian and Reformed, 1999.

Henry, Matthew. *Commentary on the Whole Bible*. (Old Tappan, N.J.: Revell, n.d.).

Ice, Thomas D. and Kenneth L. Gentry, Jr. *The Great Tribulation: Past or Future?* Grand Rapids: Kregel, 1999.

Kik, J. Marcellus. *The Eschatology of Victory*. Phillipsburg, N.J.: Presbyterian and Reformed, 1971.

Lightfoot, John. *A Commentary on the New Testament from the Talmud and Hebraica.* 4 vols. (Peabody, Mass.: Hendrickson, rep. 1989 [1674].

Matthison, Keith A. *Postmillennialism.* Phillipsburg, NJ.: 1999.

McLeod, Alexander. *Governor of the Nations of the Earth* (Elmwood Park, N.J.: Reformed Presbyterian, 1992 [1803]),

Murray, Iain. *The Puritan Hope: Revival and the Interpretation of Prophecy.* Edinburgh: Banner of Truth, 1971.

Murray, John. *Epistle to the Romans. New International Commentary on the New Testament.* 2 vols. Grand Rapids: Eerdmans, 1965.

North, Gary. *The Dominion Covenant: Genesis.* Tyler, Tex.: Institute for Christian Economics, 1982.

_____. *Millennialism and Social Theory.* Tyler, Tex.: Institute for Christian Economics, 1990.

Pate, C. Marvin, ed. *Four Views on the Book of Revelation.* Grand Rapids: Zondervan, 1998.

Rushdoony, Rousas J. *God's Plan for Victory: The Meaning of Postmillennialism.* Vallecito, Calif.: Ross House, 1977.

Sandlin, Andrew. *A Postmillennial Primer.* Vallecito, Calif.: Chalcedon, 1997.

Sproul, R. C. *The Last Days According to Jesus.* Grand Rapids: Baker, 1998.

Symington, William. *Messiah the Prince.* Edmonton: AB: Still Waters Revival, rep. 1990 [1884].

Terry, Milton S. *Biblical Apocalyptics: A Study of the Most Notable Revelations of God and of Christ.* Grand Rapids: Baker, rep. 1989 [1898].

Warfield, Benjamin B. *Biblical and Theological Studies.* Phillipsburg, N.J.: Presbyterian and Reformed, 1952.

Audio and Audio-Visual Resources

Covenant Media Foundation, 4425 Jefferson Ave., Suite 108, Texarkana, AR 71854; 800/553-3938; Online Catalog: www.cmfnow.com.

Foundations for Biblical Studies, 234 N. Titmus Dr., Mastic, NY 11950

Gentry, Kenneth L., Jr., P. O. Box 388, Placentia, CA 92871 (tapes and books)

Southern California Center for Christian Studies, P.O. Box 328, Placentia, CA 92871

Postmillennial Periodicals

Christianity & Society, P.O. Box 20514, Seattle, WA 98102 or P.O. Box 2, Taunton, Somerset TAI 2WZ England

Contra Mundum, P.O. Box 32652, Fridley, MN 55432-0652

The Counsel of Chalcedon, P.O. Box 888022, Dunwoody, GA 30356-0022

Credena/Agenda, P.O. Box 8741, Moscow, ID 83843-1241

The Journal of Christian Reconstruction, P.O. Box 158, Vallecito, CA 95251

ABOUT THE AUTHOR

Kenneth L. Gentry, Jr., is an ordained minister in the Orthodox Presbyterian Church, a conservative, reformed denomination. He is pastor of the Grace Orthodox Presbyterian Church, 271 S. Avocado St. in Costa Mesa, California. He and his wife, Melissa, have three children, Amanda, Paul, and Stephen.

He is a graduate of Tennessee Temple University (B.A., cum laude), Reformed Theological Seminary (M. Div.), Whitefield Theological Seminary (Th. M.; Th. D., summa cum laude). He also attended Grace Theological Seminary for two years, while a dispensationalist. When a student at Reformed Theological Seminary he studied under noted Christian apologist and theologian, the Rev. Greg L. Bahnsen, Ph.D. There he became close friends with Dr. Bahnsen, leading eventually to several joint ministerial projects. He and Dr. Bahnsen co-authored *House Divided: The Break-up of Dispensational Theology*, a critique of dispensational theology. They also spoke jointly at several theological conferences in the South.

Dr. Gentry is a member of the Evangelical Theological Society and is a Contributing Editor to *The Counsel of Chalcedon* magazine. He has published articles in numerous periodicals including *Christianity Today*, *Tabletalk*, *Christianity & Society*, *The Banner of Truth*, *The Presbyterian Journal*, *The Fundamentalist Journal*, *The Freeman*, *The Journal of Christian Reconstruction*, and *Antithesis*.

He also serves as Faculty member of the Bahnsen Theological Seminary (P.O. Box 328, Placentia, CA 92871), established in honor of the late Dr. Bahnsen. Bahnsen Seminary offers a seminary degree by directed study under tutorial oversight.

He has written several books on eschatology, including *The Beast of Revelation*, *Before Jerusalem Fell: Dating the Book of Revelation*, *He Shall Have Dominion: A Postmillennial Eschatology*, and *The Greatness of the Great Commission: The Christian Enterprise in a Fallen World*. He is a contributor to four eschatological debate books: C. Marvin Pate, ed., *Four Views of the Book of Revelation* (Zondervan); Darrell L. Bock, ed., *Three Views of the End of History* (Zondervan); Thomas D. Ice, ed., *The Great Tribulation: Past or Future?* (Kregel); and David Hagopian, ed., *Always Reforming: A Dialog of Differences within the Reformed Tradition*. He is currently completing a commentary on Revelation entitled: *Revelation: A Tale of Two Cities*.

Dr. Gentry frequently conducts seminars, lectures, radio interviews, and debates on eschatological themes. He is also the founder and director of a correspondence course for Christian writers: *Righteous Writing*. This course provides instruction on reading techniques, research method, improving writing style, securing a publisher, and techniques of book promotion. For more information on various ministries by Dr. Gentry, he may be contacted by e-mail at: klg666@cs.com. Or you may write him at the following address:

Kenneth Gentry
P.O. Box 388
Placentia, CA 92871

SCRIPTURE INDEX
(verses quoted or explained)

SUBJECT INDEX

Abomination, 146
  of desolation, 25, 45,
  57-62

Abortion, 6

Adam, 153

Adultery, 75, 139, 152

AIDS, 6

Amillennialism, 7n, 65,
97

Angel(s), 87, 101, 124

Antichrist, 5, 6, 31-32,
46, 115

Apocalyptic, 1
  imagery, 40, 58n

Apostasy (See also: Jews
C rejection of Christ),
97, 103-104, 152

Apollo, 107, 113n

Armageddon, 2, 4, 9, 115

Artaxerxes I, 16-17

Augustus Caesar, 48, 107

Babylon, 14, 77, 141

Babylonian captivity, 14,
22, 68

Beast of Revelation, 8,
115-134, 140
  mark, 131-133
  Nero as, 126-131
  number 127-128

Birds, 75

Blindness, 99

Blood, 61, 77, 101, 129,
144-145

Burial, 74

Caius Caesar (Caligula),
107, 108, 121

Caligula (See: Caius).

Calendar
  prophetic, 4, 12, 58

Cannibalism, 49

Christ (See also: Messiah)
  baptism, 18, 21-22,
  28
  birth, 9, 23, 36
  crucifixion, 17, 20,
  22-23, 27, 28, 36,
  142, 151
  death (see: Christ C
  crucifixion).
  imminence, 1, 4
  judgment coming,
  71-73, 81, 83, 100-
  102, 112-113, 136-
  138
  ministry length, 17n,
  24-25, 25n, 28
  redemption, 14, 22

Second Coming, ix, 4, 9,
27-28, 29, 43, 64, 69, 71,
92, 100, 112

Church
  age, 42, 62, 118
  continuation of
  Israel, 88, 156
  conquering, 119
  gap theory, 13, 27-
  33

Church fathers, 5

Civilization, 7

Claudius Caesar, 98, 105-
106, 112, 121

Clouds, 83, 136-137

Comet, 113

Covenant, 13-14
  Abrahamic, 154
  confirmation, 23-24,
  32
  curse, 13, 23, 49, 66,
  75, 101, 139
  Daniel, 31-33, 96
  old order, 51

Cyprian, 5

Cyrus, 16

Date-setting, 4, 45n

Day of the Lord, 100,
102, 146